LIFE
BEFORE
DEATH

LIFE
BEFORE
DEATH

A
Spiritual
Journey
of
Mind
and
Body

Lawrence Meredith

Humanics Publishing Group
Atlanta, Georgia

CONTENTS

To My Three Sons:

Larry

Steve

Mark

They won't let me stop climbing

ACKNOWLEDGMENTS

This book is indebted to a great many people, most of whom are given meticulous credit in both the text and the notes. But there are those who must have special thanks for their contribution, some of whom had no idea they were contributing. I am grateful to my students at the University of the Pacific, particularly in the Religion of the Body course, who accepted my invitation to dance and allowed imagination its full outrage. A special word of thanks to Pete and Glena Carroll, who graced the very first Body class and still—in the unforgiving world of professional sports—attempt to treat opponents as partners. And an embrace for Michael Croslin, the young physician, who opened the work of William Calvin and Jonathan Miller to me.

Many of my faculty colleagues at the University of the Pacific knew it was not just a mining operation. Gilbert Schedler has been a source of insight, energy, and sheer fun for thirty years—and, as Chair of the Religious Studies Department, provided me more support and spacious time than any teacher should have. John Smith, a fellow traveler in the mind of Kazantzakis, allows me to relax into revelation, and Herbert Reinelt convinces me—almost—that ontology is not senseless. I thank Kenneth Beauchamp as a psychologist who understands religion better than anyone I know that claims not to understand it at all, Douglas Matheson as my technician of sacred cyberspace, and William Dehning, whose neurons fire in harmonic convergence of music, sport, and ectomorphic id. Glen Albaugh, who metamorphosed from testosterone coach to cosmic sport guru, introduced me to Michael Murphy and reinforced my reading of George Leonard—two of the most accessible guides to Body Religion in the country. A salute to the literate Sy Kahn. I lived in Sy's house for one year and wandered with respectful delight in his brain for twenty-five. A ritual and genuine bow to Dean Robert Benedetti and Provost Philip Gilbertson for granting me professional leave to craft the final revelations shimmering in the brain of Demas.

Don and Susan Meredith have been both America's guests and insouciant hosts to adventurers in existential space. Don's thoughts are both funny and deep—and he has made a life out of being serious about not being serious. I have known and admired Cedric Dempsey, now president of the NCAA, my entire teaching career. He and his wife June do me the high—and sometimes inexplicable—honor of valuing and shaping my opinions. A deep bow to Otis and Marie Shao who taught me what family loyalty means, and who made possible our life-changing experience in Japan. Earle Labor, the great Jack London scholar at Centenary College, and Cecil Williams, the shaman of San

Francisco at Glide Memorial Church, have given a lifetime of professional support and personal friendship.

Maya Angelou, who makes present the sensuousness of words, stands tall in my pantheon of body/mind; and her mother, our long-time neighbor Vivian Baxter, embodied the very essence of sinuous human dignity and earthy spirituality. Janice Mirikitani, poet laureate of intelligent compassion, breaks silences and mends lives. Judith Jackson is an alchemist of well-being and an exquisite auditor of the body—as well as my first cousin.

And what shall I say about my soul-friend, Weldon Crowley, a weird and wondrous historian at Southwestern University, who in 1990 actually embedded in an honorary degree citation the promise of this forthcoming book. Such an infinite gestation should have produced some elephantine ideas, and his mischievous midwifery is not to be blamed for these long-comings.

My thanks to the Fulbright Association for Austria and Indonesia. In Austria at Universität Graz, I was constrained to offer Body Religion swaddled in American culture, daily interrogated by wise men and women: Walter Grünzweig, Walter Hölbling, Elizabeth Kraus, Grete Walter-Klingenstein, Jürgen Peper, Karl Doerry, and transcendent Amerikanistic students. They taught me more than they will ever know about incarnating ideas and embracing the moment.

In Java I was confronted with the genius of tolerance and multiple truth, and I am forever in the debt of Djuhertati Imam Muhni, the director of American Studies at Gadjah Mada University, whose educated geniality opened the world of Islam and cross-cultural understanding. Without David Adams of CIEE, who guided my application from Washington to Yogyakarta, and Pamela Smith and Nelly Polhaupessy of AMINEF (American-Indonesian Educational Foundation) in Jakarta, the year of living strangely would not have been possible.

I am deeply grateful for—and somewhat astonished by—the careful reading and corrections given the text by Judy Roland of Monmouthshire, Wales; the literate encouragement of Cindy Rinehart in Boulder, Colorado; the thoughtful support of Charles Schulz of Number One Snoopy Lane; the secretarial supererogation of Barbara Garcia; the educational sapience of Eugene Rice, who from the nation's capital notes my audit of bankrupt religion; the editorial excellence of John Morearty; and the sophisticated panegyric of J. Wesley Brown, who, energized by the Santa Barbara sun and a long friendship, sensed more than anyone the full body of the work.

I am indebted to Gary Wilson and Christopher Walker at Humanics for giving birth to my embryonic manuscript. And my applause for the magic of Sondra London, who kept the delivery from being stillborn. As Zorba would say, "May flowers rain on thee and apples fall in thy lap." Coins even.

My family is the most important genesis of this journey. My sons, Larry, Steve, and Mark, will recognize their experiences and contributions in the pages that follow. "Toyland, toyland...." No father has had more fun with his children, or been prouder of them as human beings. This book is dedicated to them.

Finally and firstly, I thank my wife, Pat. She has not only listened to all this for years and shared the odyssey, but read the manuscript with microscopic discipline and middleclassic critical standards. God may be the center of the universe, but she is center of my world. If you need an insulin shot to read that, so be it.

As the Indonesians say, *"Mohon ma'af, lahir dan batin."* Free translation: whatever mistakes have been made, indiscretions pursued, irrationalities embraced, irreverences applauded, insights co-opted, histories exploited, expressions mangled, friendships mystified, privacies invaded, motives misjudged, scholarship misdirected, contributions ignored, narcissisms fertilized, and opportunities unrecognized—please forgive me.

FOREWORD

THE TEST OF A BOOK (TO A WRITER) IS IF IT MAKES A SPACE IN WHICH, QUITE
NATURALLY, YOU CAN SAY WHAT YOU WANT TO SAY.
                                    VIRGINIA WOOLF

ONE DOES NOT ONLY WISH TO BE UNDERSTOOD WHEN ONE WRITES; ONE WISHES
JUST AS SURELY NOT TO BE UNDERSTOOD. IT IS NOT BY ANY MEANS NECESSARI-
LY AN OBJECTION TO A BOOK, WHEN ANYONE FINDS IT IMPOSSIBLE TO UNDER-
STAND; PERHAPS THAT WAS PART OF THE AUTHOR'S INTENTION—HE DID NOT
WANT TO BE UNDERSTOOD BY JUST "ANYBODY."
                                    FRIEDRICH NIETZSCHE

IS THERE ANY BABY IN THE BATH WATER?
                                    NORMAN MILLER

Does the world need another book on religion? I don't think so, and even
if it did, I am not capable of writing what it needs. So why am I writing?

Because I am a writer? Sinclair Lewis once defined a writer as one who
writes. But I do not write often, and the stress of structuring my thoughts for
print has released a virus long asleep in its ganglion bed. Red blotches spread
around my chest, sternum to spine, following the nerve line, breaking into
blisters: microscopic craters translating pain into ugliness. The doctor calls it
herpes zoster. The old men call it shingles. I call it incompetence.

It would be more therapeutic if I were building a sanctuary to house an
exorbitant spirit. Zorba saw what the boss was doing, hiding behind all those
books and writing yet another one:

> "You want to build a monastery. That's it! Instead of monks you'd stick
> a few quill drivers like your honored self inside and they'd pass the time
> scribbling day and night. Then, like the saints in the old pictures, printed rib-
> bons would come rolling out of your mouths. I've guessed right, haven't I?"[1]

Perhaps my plastic printer, reams of paper rolling past its ribbons, is a
kind of mechanical saint, and I, a micro-soft abbot with a mystical mouse.

I would rather be in Crete than writing about Kazantzakis. I would rather
be imagining than discoursing on image. The new commandments I found
climbing Sinai in the moonlight, the new Eden I saw from the cauldron of Mt.
Merapi, the new revolutionaries I met in forbidden Beijing, the new politics I

felt in Austria, the new compassion I witnessed in America's city of St. Francis—all seem inaccessible and tantalizing from the exile of this professional leave.

When Federico Fellini died, I remembered his saying that every day one did not make love was a day lost. I always liked that kind of urgency, that capricious denial of the postponed life, as if filmmaking and lovemaking were really one and the same—except that editing was easier in the first than in the second.

David Fanshawe, the British composer, filmmaker and musical explorer ("African Sanctus" and "The Southern Cross"), tells us that he is absolutely driven by the adventure of creativity: "I *will* record this music, I *will* write my oratorio, I *will* visit these remote islands and villages, I *will* enter into these strange rituals." And why? "Brother, when I go into that box, I will have *done* something!"

I mustn't think of this study as a premature box, or a fortress to fend off the world, or a compromise with experience. I am writing to share my conviction that religion is of the body in this world, not some other world in disembodied deprivation, some vaporous spiritual existence. The Hindus teach that there is life before life—and, *mutatis mutandi*, so do the Mormons and the primal scream therapists. The Muslims teach that there is life after death—and so does just about everybody else who is willing to be called religious.

It seems important to me to say directly that both of these views are lethal. Not merely wrong. Spiritual felonies. They deflect attention from the reality we know—which is the present, and diffuse our amazing grace—which is the ecstasy of creative alternative. The view that somehow we occupy a transitory space between life before life and life after death violates the commandment against stealing. It steals our potential for experience, for knowledge. It steals our bodies by pretending we are spirit and it steals our time by pretending it is endless. We have neither "ageless bodies" nor "timeless minds," even though we can bolster our bank accounts by selling immortality. By God, we can't live forever and, for God's sake, we ought to be living right now.

There seems to be no bottom to the nonsense hawked by spiritual entrepreneurs. I used to think that God was infinite. Whether that's a fair description of Deity will remain a question, but I know something that is infinite: our unwillingness to accept the gift of life as defined by death and as experienced in the crucible of flesh.

I am writing to say that even though we don't have much time, we do share all the time there is with a universe still expanding into existential space. The question addressed in these reflections is this: What constitutes life before death?

As you begin this adventure, I invite you to consider the following questions. Only if you answer *all* these questions correctly will you be safe on the journey. You will find the answers scattered throughout this ascent, but they are not always obvious. And you must respond to the questions *before* the answers emerge from the context.

Only when you stand on the summit of the mountain of fire at the end, will you understand what you have risked by accepting this invitation.

> *What is quicker than the wind?*
> *What can cover the earth?*
> *Who are more numerous: the living or the dead?*
> > *Why?*
> *Give me an example of space.*
> *Give me an example of grief.*
> *Give me an example of poison.*
> *Give me an example of defeat.*
> *Which came first: day or night?*
> *What is the cause of the world?*
> *What is your opposite?*
> *What is madness?*
> *What in each of us is inevitable?*
> *What is the greatest wonder?*

I have no illusions about the objectivity of this effort. Insight is context. The ideas presented in this book emerge out of my personal intellectual odyssey over the past twenty-five years. They are located in place and time quite intentionally, because a religion of the body does not have the luxury of abstraction. "Truth," said Sören Kierkegaard, "is relationship."

And surely, as these reflections draw to a close, my flesh will know the truth, my skin radiate unravaged deliverance, and my body tingle only with anticipation of dance on the shores of Crete. My sainted printer will lie dormant, the eye of the computer dark, my journey on display near the margins of belief.

THE PARABLE OF HOMELESS RELIGION

Once upon a time—our own time—anytime, there was a homeless orphan named Religion. "Where can I live?" he cried, and went off searching for a home.

He knocked on the door of Morality. Morality answered, "Yes, you may live here, but you must stay in the attic, for after all, Ethics is Religion." As Religion left, he noticed the name "Immanuel Kant" on the door.

He knocked at the house of Psychology. "Yes," said Psychology, "you may come in, but you must live in the basement along with the primordial drives—Sex, Hunger, and Aggression." As Religion turned to go he saw the name "Sigmund Freud" faintly visible on the mailbox, with a curt sign posted: "No longer at this address."

He went to the house of Natural Science, but when Science recognized Religion, the door was summarily shut—with just the suggestion of a patronizing smile. Then, apparently having a change of heart, Science opened the door and said, "Wait—come in—I do have a room for you at the back of the house, a room I've not had time to clean up yet."

Quite weary now, Religion turned away again, and sought out the house of Art. "Yes, you may be my guest, but only as a model for a painting, a theme for a novel, perhaps even a seductive arrangement of tinted glass." In frustration Religion moved off into the shadows.

Where could he go? He tried Business, but soon learned that in the world of Economics, he was either ignored or used as a front for greed.

He stopped at Politics, and there was lectured by one impatient man in a black gown who told him that Church and State must remain separate, while another spoke of Divine Election among the Righteous Few.

He even tried the arena of Sport, where giant men sometimes kneeled in prayer and flaming tongues called out to God. But the price at the gate was far more than he could pay.

Poor, orphaned, homeless one! At length Religion sought out a last resort. He would go to church. Surely here, among the ecclesiology of the ages, he will at least be allowed rest—if not his rightful place of honor.

He knocked and a priest opened the baroque door. "I am Religion. May I come in?" The priest stared at the weary orphan and spoke in gothic tones, "You impostor. Everyone knows there is no True Religion outside the Church." Religion watched the last light eclipsed by the closing door.

He was alone now and began to weep. He soon fell into a troubled sleep filled with visions of judgment and apocalyptic terror. Then Religion heard a gentle voice: "Come now—it is time for you to awaken. I will take you home."

"But I have no home."

Religion stirred and listened to the Stranger speak:

"Poor, misguided Religion—wandering like an unwanted relation, seeking some special place in the world. Has no one ever told you where your home is? It is everywhere. In every realm of life, wherever there is intellectual odyssey, sensuous joy, or ethical judgment, wherever there is coin or political theater, wherever there is birth, imagination, or death, wherever there is celebration of the mystery and magnificence of our existence—you are at home there. You are the heart of it, the depth of it. You are the experience of reality itself."

Religion looked carefully at this Stranger, and saw that the body had a bluish glow, the eyes neither opened nor closed, the feet sprinkled with sand, the wounded hands holding a slab of stone. And as he looked, the body curved and softened, the eyes inviting, intricate designs tracing the hands and feet. The stone was dropped, shattered, and transformed into earth—a child springing from the soil. Running and touching Religion, the little child held tightly—and laughed.

The Stranger began to dance into the dark of morning. And Religion, alive with light, felt shadows dissolve into visions: priests unlocking great doors, judges painting ceilings of commerce, teachers saluting the greatness before them, men and women shocked by the senses electric, scientists pleased by the numbers elegant, attics opened to the sky, athletes moving on the green of time, rivers running up to the sea....

And he knew in that moment what the Stranger had always known. Religion was home.

INTRODUCTION

THROUGH A GLASS SHARPLY:
HOW LONG IS NOW?

Alice went through a looking glass and achieved a kind of immortality. Her adventures seemed to take place *after* she had passed through the mirror and moved into a different kind of time and space, peopled with Humpty Dumptys, unicorns, and deconstructionist queens.

But the experience of the passage itself is missing from the famous fable. We are never told what it felt like to move through transparency and reflection—or to be surrounded by glass itself. *Wenn Du es nicht fülst, wirst Du es nicht erraten.*[2]

It was in April. I was running late for a special event at the university. A lectureship sponsored by the religious studies department was in full sway, and one of the principal guests was waiting for me to escort her to the lecture hall and introduce her for the morning session. In the same morning, I was also supposed to meet the candidate of choice for the vacant chaplaincy position at UOP, a nationally known educator and minister from Harvard who was president of the American Paul Tillich Society. After bustling about the bedroom and stumbling into dignified regalia, I realized that I had left my wallet in the family room. I rushed down the hall and through the living room— dashing pell-mell, like some deranged burglar, towards the missing wallet.

Now it just so happens that our family room was separated from the living room by thick plated glass, with a sliding door which we used to close when the kids were little to block off noise from TV or social gatherings. In those days, to prevent guests from bumping into the closed door, we had fastened a huge colorful flower decal right to its center, announcing to all rational people that despite the transparency, this was not an open space. But that was years before, and since then we had ripped off the decal and kept that sliding door unslidingly open.

As it also happens, we had a young woman who helped us clean the house every two weeks, and this was her day to do her sauber duty. A native German, Karin cleaned with all teutonic thoroughness. Since the separating glass had had no attention in some time—some years in fact—Karin decided to make it sparkle, and in so doing, of course she had to slide the door shut. She and my wife, Pat, were in the family room chatting away and feeling righteous in all that pristine enclosure.

I am a creature of inertia. The state in which I find myself will continue until acted upon by some outside agent. If there were a way to start the day other than moving, I would certainly do it, but once in motion the day only ends by traumatic attrition. By midnight I am finally wide-awake and ready for cosmic creation.[3] Comatose or manic, it's all the same, rather like some object in outer space—orbiting forever, until pulled into some astral body's gravitational field, and perhaps dissolving in the atmosphere of newness.

The state in which I found myself at this moment was one of motion— fast, even obsessive, motion—toward the family room. That motion was soon to be interrupted, for as I ran into the family room I became aware that I was no longer running at all but suspended between the rooms in the midst of great radiating shards of glass, accompanied by showers of particle light and a crashing sound so intense that it stopped time.

It is very odd to be encased in a glass door. I have heard that listening to music under the influence of pot or LSD has the effect of slowing the notes down so much that one can actually see the sound—rather like watching time flow in Dali's "Persistence of Memory." John Brodie, former quarterback of the San Francisco 49ers, once wrote that sometimes he would see the field action in slow motion—so slow, in fact, that he had almost infinite time to find receivers and throw the ball with imperceptible movement. He called it "experiencing a strange clarity," and later compared it to what Zen masters teach as *satori*, the ineffable moment of enlightenment.[4] As far as I know, no one has ever suggested running into a glass door as a path to spiritual aware- ness, but if Zen is the art of total awareness, then I can report my experience as being excruciatingly aware—of knowing the "now" for the first time.[5]

In January, 1993, at the California Institute for Integrated Studies, I heard the duration of "now" defined by William Irvin Thompson, the cultural philosopher who lives and works "at the edge of history." He and his mathe- matician and physicist and neurosurgeon friends who are working on under- standing the evolution of consciousness have calculated just how long the brain needs to react to stimuli and form a pattern beyond the reaction. "Now," they tell me, lasts one-fifth of one-quarter of a second. At last. No more vague exclamations when someone tells us to do it "now." One-fifth of one- quarter of a second. The goddess Nike will be pleased.

So "consciousness" is the act of cross-referencing within our perceptual system: the reptilian brain reacts, the limbic brain discriminates, and the cor- tex imagines. "Consciousness" is the intimate history of our perceptual sys- tem where the temporal ensemble holds off time and becomes a *NOW*, an event distinct from the flow of events we know as sheer reaction divided into patterns called order by the theologians and purpose by the philosophers. As William Calvin puts it in *The River That Flows Uphill*, "consciousness is fun- damentally the brain's ability to simulate the past and the future," thus allow- ing us to make quality judgments in the present.[6] The brain, says Sir Charles

Sherrington, is "an enchanted loom, where millions of flashing shuttles weave a dissolving pattern."[7] We have the magical ability both to recreate reality from the abstraction of sense impression and to simulate reality by recall and fantasy.[8] The cortex allows us to incarnate the Now in language, but only if we realize that the meaning is never fixed in its embodiment. When Robert Jordan in *For Whom the Bell Tolls* discovers a moment of supreme importance out of the flow of his life, he repeats to himself variations on the word "now": now, *ahora, maintenant, heute*. Language, as always, circles the instant by accent and inflection, not by capture and taxidermy. D. H. Lawrence calls this instant "the wild witchcraft."

Evolution flows past the lithosphere of excitation, through the mysteries of the organism in photosynthesis, finally dissolving into thought—which is direct contact with the Now. It is called "waking up" by the new biologists, "enlightenment" by the old Buddhists, "the new birth" by Christians, "the thousand-petaled lotus" by the Hindus, and "the still point" by the mystics.

The techniques of spiritual discipline are designed to get our attention. In fact, the whole purpose of meditation is not to be in touch with a god who transcends human life, but—rather like that "Zen quarterback"—to slow down the perceptual apparatus to the point that it touches the Now. That god is not to be found out there anywhere, but rather in here everywhere.

We do not come into the world, but quite literally out of the world—becoming increasingly aware of our own transformation of survival into pleasure, of reproduction into love, of perception into poetry, of percussion into music, of self into laughter.

The point of this disquisition on "the Now" is clear. Being framed by shattering glass is a spiritual focus at its most dramatic. I ran into instant *satori*—there was no more time, no more past or future. Only that slash of present that severed linear life. And, as all artists know, it is in the shattering of form that meaning is born. A poem is only about what it is. And the *is* is the instant where the expected is demolished. Laughter resides in this same non-space. As Kant reminds us, humor is the sudden transformation of expectedness into nothing. The magical human gift is the ability to create meaning out of the succession of somethings, rather like the persistence of vision that creates a moving picture out of a series of stills—always conscious of the capricious fiction of movement itself.

Of course the present doesn't stay balanced on any still point. In my manic dash to responsibility, in a secondary, secular instant I was back in time and falling to the floor, bleeding all over our new carpet and groaning in shock among the crystal splinters. The fall into time was as evident to me as any moment inside the door of perception, and besides that, I knew I was hurt. The slash of the present had also cut across flesh. Was this a moment of transformation or transfusion?

Pat screamed. She ran to bring compresses for my cuts, and then dashed for the keys to the car for a trip to the emergency room. Karin, having done such a superb job making glass look like air, never lost her persona for even one-fifth of one-quarter of a second. Moving past the exploded door, she gazed quite clinically at her fallen employer, and said like a teutonic Zen master: "You shouldn't have been in such a hurry."

That, as Shakespeare would have agreed, was the unkindest cut of all.

The Space Where God Is

"Now we see through a glass darkly." Not quite. More like: "Now I see through a glass sharply." Actually we don't have to see through anything that's not there, now do we? One learns inside a glass door that meaning is only revealed by shattering that which separates us. This shattering is the space where God is and a religion of the body celebrates that *space.* [9]

The literature investigating these dimensions of the human experience defies distillation, but one book which excites my imagination is the massive compendium, *The Future of the Body*,[10] by Michael Murphy. His conclusion is an invitation:

> The twelve sets of attributes... give rise to extraordinary versions of themselves. Integral practices orient us toward these emergent attributes so that the full spectrum of grace can operate in us. To do this, *they must be sustained by a philosophy that embraces our many parts* [italics mine], by an aspiration for many-sided development, and by surrender to an existence greater than the one with which most of us are presently familiar. They place us on a path toward extraordinary life, which, I believe, includes types of love, joy, and embodiment beyond our present abilities to conceive.[11]

By attributes, Murphy means perception of external events, somatic awareness and self-regulation, communication abilities, vitality, movement abilities, abilities to alter the environment directly, pain and pleasure, cognition, volition, individuation and sense of self, love, bodily structures and processes.[12] The practice is aimed at integration by transformative methods that promote particular kinds of growth and healing, some ancient (Theravada Buddhism's *vipassana* and Zen Buddhist *zazen*) and some modern (psychosynthesis and gestalt therapy). These methods range over "therapeutic, somatic, athletic, and religious disciplines," and defy precise predictive quality, but can be studied according to the capacities they stimulate and the virtues they advance.[13]

This book is my effort *to provide that embracing philosophy* which will sustain the practice as the presence of God in the body of the world. Murphy—and a spate of body movement professionals—take us on philosophical tours in somatic wonderland. But I propose to show the religious nature of that wonderland.

Four billion years of evolution have produced a being that is aware of being aware—a being whose body becomes a metaphor for the world in which it lives, and breathes, and has that being. The living pulse of the universe contracts and expands into conception, incubates an incarnated spirit commanded in infancy to stand, not just to free the hands, but to free the imagination—to allow the humus to become human as the big bang transubstantiates into the big brain, where we can not only find a body, but feel a self.

Yi-Fu Tuan, in his work on the "perspective of experience," expresses this feeling with clarity: "The word 'body' immediately calls to mind an object rather than an animated and animating being." The body is tactile, an "it" out there in space. "In contrast, when we use the terms 'man' and 'world,' we do not merely think of man as an object in the world, occupying a small part of its space, but also of man as inhabiting the world, commanding and creating it."[14] We piously declare that God creates the world, but there is a rich sense in which we participate in the creation of the world. Kant showed this in his *Critique of Pure Reason*: No one ever sees with pure objectivity, ever sees a "thing in itself." What we see is our *idea* of the "thing in itself"[15]—and this idea is correlated with our own bodies:

> ...our geographical knowledge, and even our commonest knowledge of
> the position of places, would be of no aid to us if we could not, by reference
> to the sides of our bodies, assign to regions the things so ordered and the
> whole system of mutually relative positions.[16]

Human beings, then, impose patterns of meaning on space: we insist on the world being in a form which we extrapolate from our own bodies. We become anxious and disoriented when the world we have created does not match the world we are finding. So two quite normal responses are: (1) to deny that the world we are finding is either real or relevant; and (2) to experience the new-found world as painful.

But the space we occupy just now has its definition in Martin Heidegger's *Being and Time*.[17] To have Being, he says, is to exist, and the essence of *Dasein*—Heidegger's operative word—lies in its existence. *Dasein* defies translation, but is generally understood as Being-there, though not in the sense of Being-alongside. Heidegger wants us to understand two crucial points about our Being: (1) that human space is not simply the result of our bodily nature; and (2) that human beings are not "spiritual things" that subsequently have been misplaced "into" a space. *Dasein* itself conveys a sense of Being-in-space, a Being-present-at-hand-together with things that occur. Heidegger calls this kind of Being *existential space*.[18] And in existential space, the fundamental datum is my body.

Directly put, the body is the way we experience the world and project our form onto it. Tables have legs, chairs have arms, the hill has a brow, clocks have faces and hands, the ocean has a breast. Wyoming has its Grand Tetons, and upper New York its finger lakes. Joyce in *Finnegans Wake* uses the metaphor of the body as the earth, the rivers as arteries and blood vessels.[19]

The "lived body," in Merleau-Ponty's famed phrase, is a humanly constructed space.[20] Jonathan Miller, in *The Body in Question*,[21] shows us how we construct the self: drawing a distinction between the "found self" and the "felt self." The found self is the larder—the inventory of parts. The felt self is how we *feel* about the parts—how we feel ourselves to be—the space we create that we call our self. We build up an idea of body over a long period of time, and then invest that idea with the status of "real" body which we might believe is somehow not our actual body.

Jacob Bronowski demonstrates "geometrically" in *The Ascent of Man* [22] how our world changes when we answer the signal to stand. The "standing up" changes our world into new coordinates: vertical/horizontal, right/left, top/bottom, front/back. When we sleep we "lose" our world, and the fear of sleep derives in part from this loss. Sleep is a threat to our orientation as human beings. Getting up in the morning restores that world.

Posture, then, is theological.[23] Our vocabulary becomes geophysical: upright, upstanding, estate, stature, status, statute, institution—all these etymologies point to achievements of order. And the antonyms are equally telling: stumble, collapse, fall, *The* Fall.

"High" and "low" become value-charged words: superior, excel, excellent—*celsus* means high. *Brahman* means "height" in Sanskrit, and devils occupy the "low places" in the New Testament. Jesus goes *up* to Jerusalem, *up* on the cross, *ascends* into heaven.[24] God is always *up*: the gods are up on Mt. Olympus.

"Left" and "right" are similarly charged: it is an arresting intercultural fact that, for most of the world, the right side is considered superior to the left.[25] Sinister is the left-hand path, and the right way—the *correct* way—is the dexterous way. The right hand of the host is the side of prominence. And the ultimate place of honor is at the Right Hand of God.[26]

"Front" and "back" are highly charged: "upfront" means honest and "forthright," while "behind the back" is nasty dealing. It would sound very odd to say that a person went behind his front. The code of the mythic Wild West forbids shooting in the back. Sneaking up is done from the rear—out of the field of vision, out of the light, out of honorable behavior. The front is the future, the rear is the past. The front is light. The back is dark, evil, and demonic. The devil is associated with the anus—and excrement with filth.[27]

But "up" and "down" also work metaphorically for the body. An ass is bad, feet need a special ritual for cleansing. As we move upward we move away from the animal into the face of character and the eyes of the soul. Man, said Aristotle, is a "rational animal." The body below the neck is problematic, while real human, imaginal life goes on in the head—and even in some cultures above the head (as in the yogi's ascension from the anus to the *chakra* of the "thousand-petaled lotus" just above the cranium, safely out of the body at last). The Platonic ideal of dissolving the body into pure idea is repeated by the Gnostics, as well as mystics everywhere. Even Christians abandon their birthright of incarnational theology and are tempted to denigrate the body in favor of something called "spiritual life" or "immortality of the soul."[28]

Standing is powerful: we stand and deliver, and we stand up for our rights. While standing is assertive, lying down is submissive—as in the feline posture, where rolling over signifies submission to the superior male.

Arnold Gesell tells us that when the infant sits up for the first time and smiles, it is a development that goes beyond a DNA-commanded animal change: "It is more than a physical reorientation; it is a new social orientation."[29] The Greeks must have known something about posture too. It's an ancient definition of a humanity itself: "Man is the only animal that walks upright." Once upright, space opens out, and the visual sense takes precedence over the sense of smell.

Our visual genesis begins the human adventure as this *Walking-Upright* becomes *The Fall*. Out of the garden of our animal ancestry, we have fallen upward. From our height we see our naked selves. The selves divide. The man of the body is a miracle of sensation, not a mere conduit of generation. The woman in the body is a mystery of organism, not just a factory for fetuses.[30] Male and female become masculine and feminine and project both genders at once, communicating these identities with every movement—a new language of the body.

This peculiar spirit/body is not exclusively sexual, but sensuous—retaining its reptilian past, but demanding that its nakedness be clothed: with patterns, cities, uniforms, music, perfumes, color, romance, poetry, ledgers, monuments, dance, marriage, paradigms, and stories of the gods.

And none of this civilizing process begins until sport begins:[31] that invented limit that tests excellence,[32] generated only after body survival needs are met. There at last we move beyond dominance and submission, beyond competition and defeat, into communion, where winning is not being number one, but being ourselves—rather like Olympic divers emancipated from contest and silhouetted against the sky.[33]

Here we transform our opponents into our partners.[34] Here we finally begin to know that we are not divided within ourselves into body and mind, and that the brain does not dominate the body, but it processes—and *then* is driven to understand—the full range of body consciousness.

Is this approach to the body "religious"? The world, Luther said, is God's body, and the gospel of John opens with the affirmation that the creative Word that energized all the world was made flesh—and we are invited to behold that flesh, the occasion of glory itself. This creative power is the sole focus of my work.

Every one of us is on a pilgrimage, a search for the grail of meaning. That search may not take us to the baths at Esalen, the trances in Indonesia, the spirit dances of Acoma, or even through a glass door. But we are all required to become healers: shamans of the self exorcising all those demons that would steal away our divine gift, the temple of our bodies. For those who would deny the body divide us against ourselves. Our lives only begin when we run through *some* door of enlightenment, when the body has reached the "still point of the turning world."

The thesis is clear. Following Merleau-Ponty, Jonathan Miller, and Bryan S. Turner,[35] I hold that we not only *have* bodies, but that we *are* bodies. Following William Blake, I hold that the body is that portion of the soul that is discerned by the five senses; that energy is the only life; that energy exudes from the body; and that reason is the outward circumference of that energy. If the world is God's body, then it seems reasonable that God may be defined as pure energy. The soul, then, is defined as the full potential of the body, and consciousness as the focus of energy promoting extraordinary life.

This thesis, the soul of the work, is given a body by the bound book: the five senses are treated as spaces—imaginary dimensions that are physical and metaphysical at the same time.[36] The form of the work is threefold, analogous to the Demeter myth of ancient Eleusinian mysteries: Maiden, Mother, and Crone.[37] Thus, we shall consider birth as potentiality, imagination as creativity, and death as reality.

One will recognize this, then, as the feminine side of the masculine Trinity: the phallic Father, the erotic Son, and the released energy of Spirit. Once again, it is important to see these as dimensions of the present, not as a succession of discrete "beings." In Augustine's view, past and future are all "present" at once in God. "The one becomes two, the two becomes three, and the three becomes the ten thousand things." So reads the *Tao Te Ching*.

In one sense, I see birth as matriarchal, imagination as patriarchal, and death as contextual. Of course I don't mean that only women give birth, or that only men create. That would be just another version of putting women in their place: as quite unfulfilled unless filled with child. We have had quite enough of this in history. One thinks of Pope John Paul II, who, as recently as 1995, reminded the world of the "true" nature of women. "The ministry of femininity manifests and reveals itself in depth through maternity," he told twelve thousand visitors in the Vatican general audience hall. "Woman stands before man as a mother, the bearer of a new human life that is conceived and develops in her and is given birth to the world." The pope summed up the relationship between the sexes with comforting, biblical balance: "He who knows is man, and she who is known is woman, a wife." Places everyone!

Men give birth too, and women's minds transform the world. Both embrace the limits of being. Gestation and transformation are marked off by death, by the context of existential space. The real incarnation is not the mysterious confluence of divine and human, but the sensuous union of male and female. Men like Kazantzakis wanted to think of the earth as female, receiving the seed from the heavens, and such imagery is common enough in literature: God is male and earth is female. So the great cosmic One comes to the frail virgin and impregnates her with all of creation, sustaining and judging while she delivers and nurtures.

Are the feminists right? Must we surrender this imagery? What is there to take its place? How rich will the new information society be with its asexual computer terminals and a superhighway paved with swirling disks of zeros and ones instead of the XX and XY, the phallus boxed up in a hard drive and the vulva revolving in virtual memory? Is this what was meant by the nineties being the decade of women?[38]

I think not. I hold that there is still earthly genius in the Christian embrace. By moving through the various bodily spaces (visual, auditory, olfactory, tactile, and saporific), we can understand the fierce and almost oxymoronic allegiance the Christians felt for the body. And we can participate in healing the mind/body/spirit schism that fractures the very space where God is, and thus diminishes the energy available for extraordinary life.

Whatever else the Christians have done—destroy art they consider blasphemous, destroy people they declare infidels, denigrate intelligence by blocking scientific inquiry, build creedal walls around belief systems, deny brotherhood in the very name of it, relegate sisterhood to the convent and the maternity ward, canonize gullibility, demonize sexual passion—in spite of all this, they have managed to insist that the body is the temple of the Spirit. That God is known through the flesh. That God is birthed, paints pictures, creates healing rituals, embraces compassion, and dies. **God so loved the world** was the way they put it then. **God *is* the world** is the way we must put it now.

PART ONE

BIRTH

CHAPTER ONE

SLOUCHING TOWARDS KYOTO:
THE BODY AS GOD

AND THEY CONVERSED TOGETHER
IN VISIONARY FORMS DRAMATIC WHICH BRIGHT
REDOUNDED FROM THEIR TONGUES IN THUNDEROUS MAJESTY, IN VISIONS
IN NEW EXPANSES, CREATING EXEMPLARS OF MEMORY AND OF INTELLECT
CREATING SPACE, CREATING TIME ACCORDING TO THE WONDERS DIVINE
OF HUMAN IMAGINATION, THROUGHOUT ALL THE THREE REGIONS IMMENSE
OF CHILDHOOD, MANHOOD & OLD AGE.
                    WILLIAM BLAKE

ONE STICKS ONE'S FINGER INTO THE SOIL TO TELL BY THE SMELL IN WHAT LAND
ONE IS: I STICK MY FINGER INTO EXISTENCE—IT SMELLS OF NOTHING. WHERE
AM I? WHO AM I? HOW CAME I HERE? WHAT IS THIS THING CALLED WORLD?
WHAT DOES THE WORLD MEAN? WHO IS IT THAT LURED ME INTO THE THING, AND
NOW LEAVES ME THERE? WHO AM I? HOW CAME I INTO THE WORLD? WHY WAS
I NOT CONSULTED, WHY NOT MADE ACQUAINTED WITH ITS MANNERS AND CUS-
TOMS....? AND, IF I AM TO BE COMPELLED TO TAKE PART IN IT, WHERE IS THE
DIRECTOR? I SHOULD LIKE TO MAKE A REMARK TO HIM.
                    SÖREN KIERKEGAARD

I HAVE BEEN TRYING TO WRITE WHAT HAPPENED BUT IT IS HARD, WISHFUL WORK.
TIME IS BEGINNING TO RUN OUT ON ME, AND THE FORM REMEMBRANCE PUTS ON
THINGS IS MAKING ITS OWN TIME, AND GUIDING MY PEN IN WAYS I DON'T TRUST.
                    E.L. DOCTOROW

A generation ago—a lifetime really—a graduate of our university, a young woman who was desperate to touch life and would not accept the sensual death imposed by institutional demands, created a collage painting, using huge red strokes on and around passionate words written by D. H. Lawrence. Those pulsating words invoked "immediate contact with God" and invited us to "drink life direct from the source" unshielded by lies, crying out for exquisite release of primal vitality.

When she moved on from our community, she left us the collage. She also left her husband and her religious tradition as she searched the world of the self and the other, immersing herself in Polynesian culture, and going on to contact Indian gurus, Chinese Tai Chi masters, Sufi dancers, and Hispanic radicals.

She's a teacher and counselor somewhere now, remarried, and, I hope, happy. The collage still sits on my desk and reminds me every day that human beings don't have to be content with cleaning house while watching the Wheel of Fortune spin.

Reinhold Niebuhr once suggested that we should live with the newspaper in one hand and the Bible in the other. Today—tamed cynic that he was—he would probably call for PBS television on the left and the Internet on the right (with MacScripture booted up). It is an ancient image. John Wesley wrote of cross-eyed Christians: one eye fixed on God; the other ranging steadfastly over the world. It is the vertical bisecting the horizontal, establishing direction and meaning. It is the union of principle and practice, theology and ethics, God and the world.

However difficult the ethical life is to practice, we understand this, and feel comfortable in its neatness. For if God does exist, and if divine will makes guidance possible, then in God all things do move and have their being, and our anxieties are redeemed. Life does mean, and mean intensely, as Browning wrote, and to find its meaning is our meat and drink.

Religion is the name we give to this meaning: the point of intersection of spirit and world. Religion puts it all together, centers us and transmutes our mortality into activity that matters. And the more fragile our existence becomes, the more desperately we search for that centering presence. Whenever chaos threatens, there is ready ground for divinity.

Yeats' image of the Sphinx is resurrected on this ground—our *Spiritus Mundi*: the rough beast bestirring itself somewhere in the sands of the desert, as "things fall apart" and the "blood-dimmed tide is loosed upon the world."[39] The lion body (*mundi*) with the head of a man (*spiritus*) "slouches towards Bethlehem" to be born in a bizarre second coming.

The entire poem was widely quoted by the Cassandras in the academy, and that last phrase became the title of Joan Didion's essays on the sixties (*Slouching Towards Bethlehem*). No one could doubt that things were "falling apart." Even a one-handed Niebuhr could interpret such headlines: exponential population defended by militant self-righteousness-to-life groups, fossil fuels disappearing, freon apocalypse, AIDS as the new plague, Asia falling into the hands of the people who live there, the Ganges flowing West, America declaring itself the winner in the Cold War and plunging straight into a Hot Peace in Iraq, Palestine, South Africa, Russia, and Bosnia, economic fire on the Pacific rim, and one president after another—from Eisenhower to Clinton—masquerading at "the ceremony of innocence."

Nor were our religious notices any more sanguine: fundamentalists mindlessly believed everything while religious liberals systematically explained everything away. It is an instructive metaphor that Christendom took ill in

1453 and survived into a twentieth century ravaged by the virulent strains of Marxist dialectic, Freudian analysis, and radical empiricism.

On August 6, 1945, at precisely 8:15 A.M., black rain at Hiroshima streaked our ethical arrogance. Were we a secular state motivated by raw power and governed by technical possibility? If so, then the vector of the twentieth century could be charted: industrialization, urbanization, technocracy, and geopolitics. The "second coming" would be from the *Spiritus Mundi*: the one world of mortality and chaos, the secular arena of heavy, limited, anxious freedom. And *this* Second Coming bestirs itself not beyond the stars, but in the sands, the real desert fox—a shape moving with animal body and fierce fantasies, its thighs made of earth, its soul of soil, now waking, now walking, now aborning in Bethlehem.

Is this credo too left-handed? Too much newsprint and not enough Holy Writ? Let me hasten to confess that I am a Christian, having full clergy credentials in the United Methodist Church, teaching for thirty-seven years in Methodist-related colleges, and publishing—now and again—my understanding of the Christian faith.

I began my ministry in Texas as a naïve fundamentalist fellow traveler, accepting what I was told by the Church's hierarchy and their cadre chairmen in the universities. Sensing a deep need to measure out the frontiers and limits of orthodoxy, I earned my doctorate at Harvard, writing a thesis under the guidance of Richard R. Niebuhr on *essential doctrine in the theology of John Wesley.*[40]

But despite such immersion in theological tradition, I still had never faced the central challenge of religion itself: to meet the deep desire of human beings to submit to authority, to transcend the body, and to achieve life after death. That is: to delineate the nature of religion.

The "Great Awakening" of the sixties began my real introduction to God, as we went slouching toward revolution, and my affiliation with Callison College of the University of the Pacific began my introduction to cultural inflections on religion.

Callison was a cluster college born out of the new sixties mandate for widening our intellectual and social world. Its motto was banal and pretentious but emancipating enough: "Education for Global Responsibility."

Part of that education was the innovative requirement that *every* student spend the entire sophomore year studying in a non-Western country. Our first program was in Bangalore, India, from 1967-1970. In 1968, I was flown to Bombay as a guest of Air India, and along with my faculty colleague, Dr. Gilbert Schedler, toured major sites and educational centers in northern India. We were there to greet the charter class as they arrived in Bangalore. It was my first living exposure to a non-Christian culture—unless you count the Baptists in Waco, Texas.

In 1971, the university moved our non-Western program to Kyoto, Japan. In 1974-75, I was asked to join the resident faculty, as a liaison between our west and east campuses. That residency changed the way I thought about God and the relationship between body, mind, and spirit.

I was no Will James—and certainly no Richard Chamberlain dissolving into *Shogun*. But there was a transformation. I was a Westerner—a Christianized, Texas Californian living in Eastern, syncretistic, traditional, religious, secular Japan, where the world began when Amaterasu was tempted from her cave, and began again in the ashes of Hiroshima.

One hears with romantic intrigue engaging accounts of Zen gardens, the arts of archery and tea; one envisions tranquil monks, colorful festivals, graceful pagodas soaring toward the sacred sun—and then is jarred by the reality of polluted cities and seas, virulent Yakuza gang crime, lightning blue and white bullet trains, electronic walls of Jericho, cultural insulation, a super-technical, fragile power that hosted the Olympic Games and the World's Fair only a *generation* after the Bomb. For an instructive encounter with religion for the twenty-first century, one could have done worse than slouching towards Kyoto.

There the rough beast assumed remarkably various forms: the activism of the politically-minded Soka Gakkai, the use of *zazen* to train business executives, the frankly materialistic decree of Perfect Liberty Kyodan, the revival of non-bushido Shinto, the emergence of Taoist feminine dominance, the new internationalism of Japanese cinema, the disarray of Marxist ideology, the new pentecostalism and the old Christian mysticism.

It was a wildly pluralistic scene with a single permeating consciousness—insular, ancient, nature-dominated Japan, and a single permeating setting—international, secular, transistor-dominated Japan. After revolutionizing in the sixties and slouching through the seventies, by the eighties I was willing to call myself a radical, secular Christian, slightly but significantly Japanized—a kind of Zen Methodist—with the *Mainichi Daily News* in one hand and the *Diamond Sutra* in the other. It was becoming increasingly clear to me that the beast aborning could be suggested by three words: relativistic, immanent, and immediate.

NAMING THE RUDE BEAST: RELATIVISM

During the sixties, the college campuses were riot with relativism, and "do your own thing" was the sociological equivalent of *think* your own thing. Allan Bloom struck gold (as well as nerves) in the late eighties with his ivy-covered diatribe against this voluntary intellectual poverty. He entitled it *The Closing of the American Mind*, and it became the biggest publishing surprise since *Zen and the Art of Motorcycle Maintenance* in 1974. Both books dealt with the idea of "quality": how can we know that what we know is worth knowing? Bloom rearranged his old lecture notes on ancient Greeks and nineteenth-century Germans, and threw them at the revolting generation that took over his office at Cornell in the sixties. Pirsig had a nervous breakdown, left teaching and Minnesota on a motorcycle with his estranged son, and rode West to El Dorado—ending at Shunryu Suzuki's Zen Center in San Francisco, with a notebook full of therapeutic musings on the things that matter most.

Zen couldn't be further from Plato, just about as far as Kyoto is from Athens. Zen is instrumentality—the practice. Plato is abstraction—the thought. One gets the impression that, for Plato, the perfect motorcycle works perfectly because it never has to roll across an imperfect highway—rather like the ontological argument for God, where God is proved to be by definition rather than by any empirical evidence.

In Japan I left the abstraction of a "right" religion and lived in the midst of "instrumental" religion. It is an old—and accurate—epithet that the Japanese are born Shinto, die Buddhist, and, on December 25, celebrate Christmas. I was forced to consider what never was an issue for me in America: what, after all, *is* religion?[41]

A young girl is seated in front of a goat. A glistening black man passes a razor-sharp knife over her throat, then slits the animal's throat—the girl emitting unearthly bleating and the goat seeming to cry like a sobbing child. *This is religion.*

The Indian Congress, ready to vote on independence from England, pauses while a thin, brown, bespectacled man retires for meditation. The British Empire waits while Gandhi prays. *This is religion.*

A small commune gathers around a flagpole as the Rokuna-Gyogo flag is hoisted to the prayer of Tenko-san: an oath to clean every toilet in Japan. *This is religion.*

A bull is brought out over a grate in ancient Phrygia. The priests dance wildly about, seizing a live scorpion and jamming it against the genitals of the bull. The bull roars—as well he might—the priests quickly cut its throat and bathe in the thick hotness that pours out through the grate—washed in the blood of the bull. *This is religion.*

The monks sit, backs perfectly straight, heads rigid, eyes seeing and unseeing, feet crossed onto thighs, in disciplined, frigid silence broken only by the swish and slap of the Roshi's stick off some offered shoulder. *This is religion.*

The huge shock of white hair above eyes penetrating the depth of culture is brushed back, while measured teutonic tones define God as the unconditioned—and students wait austerely and pretentiously for the final world of autonomy. Outside the white, steepled building, bushes are on fire and not consumed—as autumn leaves turn the ground holy. *This is religion.*

A young boy picks up a basket, sweat popping and hand trembling as he reaches for the rattlesnake, the boy's eyes wide with fear and faith as the rattle sounds and the Tempter whispers. *This is religion.*

The woman softly murmurs in verse: "To caress my lover, my body exploding with desire—this my temple entire—and my God." *This is religion.*

The outrageous curls tumble over his ears, the faithful shake at his feet, possessed and healed by the Spirit, the erotic lips intone the benefits of Jesus the Crucified: "He was hung-up for our hang-ups." *This is religion.*

The doctor gazes on his patient with arrogance and humility, and the pain eases at last in the shining black African face. "The Lord Jesus sent me," he says. *This is religion.*

The eyes glaze, the hooks pull the skin straight out from the body, the skewer is shoved through the cheeks and lip, as the faithful climb the eighty stone steps to the cave of Shiva, quivering and sweating with gratitude and supplication. *This is religion.*

The razors slice the scalp, the face runs red as the pilgrims march in celebration of their murdered Arab leader. *This is religion.*

What *is* religion? A Haiti sacrifice? A Hindu prayer? A Japanese menial labor? A taurobolium? *Zazen* at Daitokuji? A Harvard Chapel address by Paul Tillich? A Tennessee snake-handling service? Lenore Kandel's *Love Book* invocation? Marjoe's pentecostalism? An Albert Schweitzer healing? The festival of Thaipusam in Malaysia? The Shi'ite ritual honoring Al-Husayn?

This complexity can be sorted out into two simple categories: unfriendly and friendly.

Unfriendly Religion

Religion, said Mark Twain, is a dangerous thing—if you get it *wrong.*

It's enough to unleash Niebuhr's cynicism on immoral society everywhere. On the one hand we have Jim Jones' lethal communion service in Guyana, David Koresh's seventh seal apocalypse in Waco, and the Ayatollah Khomeini's bizarre school of literary criticism. On the other hand, we have the scorched earth policy followed by the ancient Hebrews in dealing with the Canaanites—whose land, they claimed, had been deeded to them by the Creator of the land itself. Then there's David's strange idea of mercy in executing only one-third of all the Moabites (in honor of his great-grandmother Ruth), and Paul's misogyny tucked in safely behind salvation by faith alone, as all real women were transformed into spiritual "men."

One could make an argument that it is impossible to get religion right—which was, by the way, Mark Twain's point.

I see four ways to get religion "wrong."

1. Religion as Projection

Religion is a harmful illusion which has impeded the full maturity of human beings. Giuseppe Sergei thinks it almost clinical: "the pathological manifestation of the protective function based on nature and her laws." The classic statement here belongs to Sigmund Freud: "Religion consists of certain dogmas, assertion about facts and conditions of external (or internal) reality, which tell one something that one has not oneself discovered and which claim that one should give them credence." Freud further shows how religion is born as a bulwark against human helplessness: "the child's defense reaction to his helplessness gives the characteristic feature to the adult's reaction to his own sense of helplessness."[42] This is illusion, but not necessarily error, since illusion is the result of wish fulfillment—a point refined by Erich Fromm in *The Art of Loving*.

The wish is almost irresistible. When little daddy on earth demonstrates clay feet by failing to be omnipotent, omniscient, and immortal, Big Daddy in the sky "walks out on space" to take us by the everlasting hand.

Invulnerability is not standard equipment on mere mortals, and we don't even get warranties on the disposable parts we are given. Surely any rational person can see this and should give up God the way growing children give up Santa Claus. William James certainly agreed that some religious beliefs may be pathological and called such believers "sick souls,"[43] but he contended that it might not be fair to define religion strictly in terms of its worst case. It would be misleading to judge chemistry by the alchemists, or astronomy by the astrologers, or modern medicine by witchcraft. No question that bizarre and sick things are done in the name of religion, but we may rightly ask if religion is *necessarily* pathological.

I would suppose that monotheism is the presupposition of modern science: if we live in a multiverse, then it is quite silly to look for principles which might apply everywhere. And as a matter of fact, scientists must believe that the world is worth investigating, will allow a systematic inquiry, and will in some sense reward intellectual discipline. These are unprovable assumptions, scarletly-lettered by John Updike in *Roger's Version*.[44] Here Dale Kohler, the pimply-faced computer hacker, feels that God can be deduced through mathematical calculation—the intersection of body and spirit here being the newest of the Big Daddies, the computer.

Everywhere we look, "finely adjusted constants" assemble into a world we can recognize, with no reason for being except that *God made them that way.* Science writes with a luminous pencil against the dark night of unbelief: God made Heaven and Earth. The irony is that it is Roger, the Divinity School professor, who doesn't believe. But to refugees from seminary this is actually not surprising. The study of the early theological wars will suck the juice right out of the ripest faith.

Naturally the simplest reply to Freud has always been: so religion is a wish fulfillment—so what? I might wish that the sun will rise tomorrow but that doesn't make it not so. Of course. Freud has already conceded that. The problem is to mesh our wheel of wishing with reality, instead of spinning uselessly in never-never land.

Christians have objected that Christianity is scarcely a wish fulfillment, since it led to the cross for its founder and to sacrifice and martyrdom for his followers—at least *some* of them. Others seem to live quite comfortably—a fact that led Nietzsche to declare that the last Christian died on the cross. Calvin insisted that no one knew whether salvation for them was in the inscrutable will of the Almighty, and wrote into the church vows this question: Would you be willing to go to hell for the sake of God?[45]

2. Religion as Convention

Here religion is defined as a deliberate device of the priesthood to control the masses by capitalizing on our ignorant and superstitious fear of the unknown. Fascist as this sounds, it is masked as benevolent: instituted for a special class perhaps, but capable of including the whole society. David Hume, for example, tells us that the origin of religion is human *angst:* "The anxious concern for happiness, the dread of future misery, the terror of death, the thirst for revenge, the appetite for food and other necessities."[46] So the natural history of religion, according to Hume, is (1) polytheism, (2) monotheism, (3) deism, and finally, quite naturally, (4) atheism.

What is beneficial about this diminution of transcendence? Religion acts as a progressively useful insulation against inevitable human suffering. As the natural history unfolds, the many gods (1) coalesce into the one (2) who recedes into emeritus status (3) and, finally, abdicates into pure randomness (4)—leaving us to create, if we will, on our own.

For those who need some convention to stave off social and personal chaos, there is the most ironically altruistic group in history: the priests, for heaven's sake. Dostoyevsky gives us a terrifying version of this "benevolence" in *The Brothers Karamazov*, creating for us the legend of "The Grand Inquisitor" in the Cardinal of Seville. And the tale is told by Ivan, the non-believing Karamazov.

Christ had reappeared in Seville and was promptly imprisoned by the Inquisition. Late at night, the Cardinal—whom Ivan describes as also an atheist—visits Christ in the dungeon, and attempts to justify to the Savior his suppression of intellectual and religious freedom in Spain. Describing the believers whom he and those who practice his priestcraft had deceived, the Cardinal insists: "And all will be happy, all the millions of creatures except the hundred thousand who rule over them." For only they who unctuously guard the mystery shall be unhappy.[47]

An inspirational sacrifice indeed! All those thousands of millions of happy children and only a hundred thousand or so sufferers who continue to "take upon themselves the curse of the knowledge of good and evil." At death the believers will find the nothingness of death, but they will live and die in peace. The secret—that there is no God—will remain the cross that only the priests will have to bear. The Grand Inquisitor even condescends to tell Christ that he, too, "prized the freedom with which thou hast blessed men," but that he—like some Iberian Buddha—woke up:

>...I awakened and would not serve madness. I turned back and joined the ranks of those who have corrected thy work.[48]

In the beginning was the Word and the Word was made palliative: perfect fraud casts out fear. Religion keeps society from panic, rather like the airline captain whose casual voice, announcing "some slight turbulence," belies the crash to come. Perhaps the little girl who thought that Jesus was crucified by Pontius the Pilot was really a first-rate critic of church history.

3. Religion as Inhibition

Lucretius was saying it fifty years before any of the holy ones slouched towards Bethlehem. In *De Rerum Natura* in 51 BCE, he wrote that religion is "the fear of the gods, which is the cause of all evils." Salomon Reinach calls it "the sum of the scruples which impede the free exercise of the human faculties." And one would certainly expect William Blake, walking about in the *Garden of Love*, to be unfriendly to this understanding of religion:

>And Priests in black gowns were walking their rounds,
>And binding with briars my joys & desires.

Is there *anyone* who doesn't resonate with these rhymes? Who *are* these people who live in mortal terror that someone somewhere is having a good time, who volunteered for prison and want us to join them? They always remind me of Nurse Ratched in *One Flew Over the Cuckoo's Nest*: masquerading as angels of mercy, they impose on us the "therapy" of control.

As a young evangelical in the South, I recall memorizing one thousand verses of scripture, all organized for the intstant they were needed—most particularly when adolescent desire sprang up. How many times I quoted 1 Corinthians 10:13, repeating it like a mantra: "There is no temptation taken you, but such is common to man. But God is faithful, who will not suffer you to be tempted above that you are able, but will with the temptation also make a way to escape, that you may be able to bear it."

I am not saying that roads shouldn't have stop signs on them when traffic is dangerous. My mantra was probably safer than a condom, and it has a lifetime guarantee. But who is to say just *what* temptation should be resisted?

If we are so determined to allow someone else to run our lives, then we ought to convert to the perfect desert religion. Authority was just warming up with Moses on the mountaintop and Jesus on the Mount. God got it exactly right with Muhammad of Mecca. The proper climax of complete systems of inhibition is Islam, where the very name of the religion means "submission."

4. Religion as Explanation

Cosmological arguments for God to the contrary, religion which attempts to "explain" the world is looking for serious trouble with any legitimate scientist. The effort to square Genesis with evolutionary theory or the Qur'an with the Big Bang seem to me somewhere between misguided and pathetic. Genesis is not an explanation, it's a theological commentary on the Babylonian creation story, which in itself was an effort give meaning to Mesopotamian life.[49] And the Creationists are worse than the De-mythologizers. They want Genesis taught as science in the biology departments of the schools. How far is it to Revelation taught in History, Jonah in Marine Biology, Ruth in Sociology, and Exodus in Political Science?

But, if not an explanation, religion does insist that life has direction. Carol Ochs reminds us that religion always answers three questions:[50] Where did the world come from? Are we worth anything in the world? What in the world should we do? These questions translate as cosmology, salvation, and ethics. When religions address the first question, they are interested not in atoms, black holes, quasars, or magma boiling about in the ring of fire. They are interested in the gods: the contact points between the awesome power of the universe and the tiny participant in that power. Asking where we came from is another way of asking why we are here, and asking why we are here is another way of asking what we should be doing. Genesis belongs in ethics, not biology.[51]

Every time we human beings cannot figure out how something works, we are tempted to invent a *deus ex lacuna.* The more we know, the less we believe, until we finally believe nothing. In the now-famous television series, *The Power of Myth,* Joseph Campbell was asked by Bill Moyers if he had faith. Campbell replied that he didn't need faith; he had experience. Campbell understands myth not as an explanation of the world but as a psychic narrative, a kind of public dream symbolizing our own reality. Myths are not about the gods; they are about us. Religion is metaphor, not chemistry.

Karen McCarthy Brown echoes Ochs' approach. She tells us that religion's "…primary function is to provide a comprehensible model of the world and to locate the individual safely and meaningfully within it…"[52] Brown's definition is particularly interesting for an analysis of body, religion, and gender domination: "When the mind and the spirit are cut off from the body, women become magnets for the fear raised by everything in life that seems out of control. The degree to which control is exercised over women is therefore a key to the profundity of stresses felt by most persons and groups."[53] Brown is also speaking in the context of fundamentalism, for that phenomenon, she says, "is a product of extreme social stress."

This is all very unfriendly, and, I would hope, unnecessary.

Friendly Religion

I see five ways to get religion "right."[54] Wallace Hamilton, who forty years ago mesmerized Florida's first drive-in church at St. Petersburg, once gathered up a list of the definitions of God:

> So men have peered into the darkness, listened in the stillness, looked into the cold, silent depth of space, and have come back with halting half-words about the great "Other." Who goes there? Aristotle said, "The Unmoved Mover," Spencer said, "Eternal Energy"—energy with a capital "E." Huxley said, "The unknown Absolute." Arnold said, "The Power not ourselves that makes for righteousness." The Arabs, it is said, have a hundred names for God, and we in the western world have almost matched it. "First Principle"—"Process of Integration"—"Cosmic Organism"—"Life Essence"—"Fundamental Substance"—"Principle of Concretion"— "Divine Architect"—"Sum Total of Accumulated Idealism"—"Élan Vital"—"Life Force"—"Supreme Intelligence"—"Stream of Tendency"— "Judge"—"King"—"Almighty"—and on and on, all the way up to the "Big Boss" or the "Man Upstairs." Who goes there? An African chief said, "We know at nighttime Somebody goes among the trees, but we never speak of it."[55]

I'm going to risk speaking. It's early and there's still light in the forest. The following is my gathering up and labeling of these infinite definitions of the infinite.

1. Intellectual

Religion is what you believe. It is an assent to a proposition or a series of propositions about the universe: the thirty-nine of the Church of England, or the twenty-five of the United Methodist Church, or the twenty-one of Perfect Liberty Kyodan, or the four of Mahayana Buddhism, or the two of Islam, or perhaps the zero of Zen. Religion is our model of the essential world to which we point when the question arises: *What* is it all about?

Sir Edward Tylor called religion belief in living spirits; Herbert Spencer, a hypothesis. Edward Caird is typical: "man's ultimate attitude toward the universe, summing up the meaning and purport of his whole consciousness of things."[56] Funk and Wagnalls give us a rather spooky definition: "A belief in an invisible superhuman power, together with the feelings and practices which naturally flow from such a belief."[57] Georg Friedrich Hegel termed it a finite apprehension of the Absolute—an approximate conception or mental picture (imaginative) of the truth about ultimate reality.[58]

Max Müller said it well enough: religion is "a mental faculty or disposition, which, independent of—nay in spite of—sense and reason, enables man to apprehend the infinite under different names and under varying guises."[59] *Religion is theology.*

2. Volitional (Psychological)

Religion is what you want. It is voluntary activity beyond reason and acceptance of propositions about the world. It locates the mainspring of human life in the will, where logic is transcended by desire. James Montgomery's hymn expresses it vividly:

> Prayer is the soul's sincere desire, unuttered or expressed
> The motion of a hidden fire within the human breast.[60]

It is Augustine's restless spirit, Pascal's reason of the heart, and (in religious oxymoron) Siddhartha's *cessation* of desire. Henry Nelson Wieman in *Psychology of Religion* calls it "devotion."

Immanuel Kant sums it up: there is nothing good but a good will.[61] We crave happiness first and unconditionally, but it is not the object of our rules. That object is "worthiness to be happy." *Religion is psychology.*

3. Emotional

Religion is what you feel. It is a primordial response to being in the world, a profound awe before the presence of life and death. Allan Menzies calls it "the worship of higher powers from a sense of need."[62] J. M. E. McTaggart wrote: "Religion may best be described as an emotion resting on a conviction of a harmony between ourselves and the universe at large." Rudolph Euchen defines religion as the "mystical experience in which the oppositions of life are transcended."

Rudolph Otto gives us the best description of the feeling of mystery and awe created in humankind by the impression of what he called the "Numinous." [63] This "tremendous mystery" may come as only a " gentle tide" and be metamorphosed into a lasting attitude of the soul. But it also may "burst up in sudden eruption." It may become "the hushed, trembling, and special humility of the creature in the presence of whom or what? In the presence of that which is a mystery, inexpressible and above all creatures."

Mircea Eliade speaks of a location for this awe. [64] He calls it the *Axis Mundi,* the center of the world, where that special feeling communicates that the universe is benign, orderly, and *for* us. This is the genesis of all sacred spaces, the very spot(s) where creation or redemption began: Mt. Zion in Jerusalem, the Konrodai at Tenri-shi, the Kaaba in Mecca, the Black Hills of the Dakotas, the Ganges at Benares. "To us, it seems an inescapable conclusion that *the religious man sought to live as near as possible to the Center of the World.*" [65] It is the Dionysian festival in Greece and the Kasuga shrine matsuri in Nara, Japan. It is Otto's "mysterium tremendum" and Ninian Smart's "mystical consciousness." It is the sound of Gregorian chants in St. Peter's, the 108 bell tones at Shogatsu in Kyoto, and the ancient Jew before the stars. It is Ferlinghetti's "rebirth of wonder."

Friedrich Schleiermacher's defining sentence is classic: "The essence of the religious emotions consists in the feeling of absolute dependence." [66]

This is not the wave of goodness that floods the Marin County pseudo-Taoist watching the sun go down from his hot tub. The translation should indicate "consciousness": a dependence on something which determines us and which we cannot determine in return. *Religion is worship.*

4. Axiological

Religion is what you value. It is the process of deciding what is worth doing, the architectonic choice, the self-conscious awareness of perspective. Reality is seen as the summation of values merging into an absolute good for which the universe as a whole exists. Harold Höffding says: "That which expresses the imminent tendencies of all religions is the axiom of the conservation of values."[67] Nevius writes: "A thing has value when it possesses the power to satisfy us; and what we term human values may thus be regarded as built into the structure of man's own life and his social needs." So Nevius concludes: "Religion is the effort of man, conscious of these values, to possess them."[68] William K. Wright is a close-to-the-vest sociologist: *"Religion is the endeavor to serve the conservation of socially recognized values through specific actions that are believed to evoke some agency different from the ordinary ego of the individual...."*[69] William James must have been unduly influenced by the epistle of the same name when he suggested that religion is "to visit orphans and widows and keep oneself unstained from the world." John Wesley never tired of ringing the theological changes on this "social" holiness:

> "What, then, is religion?" It is happiness in God, or in the knowledge and love of God. It is "faith working by love," producing "righteousness and peace and joy in the Holy Ghost." In other words, it is an heart and life devoted to God; or communion with God the Father and the Son; or the mind which was in Christ Jesus, enabling us to walk as He walked.[70]

Sometimes single words seem to sum up the axiology: J. G. Frazier's "propitiation," James Leuba's "appeal,"[71] W. K. Wright's "endeavor,"[72] J. Milton Yinger's "effort."[73] A very recent text, introducing religion in college classes, is determined to challenge student ethical behavior:

> Accordingly, in *Exploring Religious Meaning*, we will define *religion* as *any person's reliance on a pivotal value or a group of related values in which that person finds essential wholeness as an individual and as a person-in-community.*[74]

John Dewey's reduction is still welcome: the religious life—he proposed that we drop the word "religion" since it implies a static metaphysic—is "Any activity pursued in behalf of an ideal and against obstacles and in spite of threats of personal loss because of conviction of its general and enduring value is religious in quality."[75] *Religion is ethics.*

5. Operational

Religion is what you do. It is the activity that you participate in when you participate in religious activity, which is to say that all definitions are circular—or at least nominalistic. It is as if Robert Frost were to change the terms of his famous definition of tennis: tennis is what we are doing when we are playing tennis. Religion is your function in the community: the witchdoctor in the tribe, the priest in the temple, the rabbi in the synagogue, the pastor in the Protestant pulpit. The IRS will recognize this definition, and will honor my deduction for the *Journal of Religion* but not *Playboy* (unless I can convince them that it is a theological journal for frustrated Methodists).

William Irvin Thompson gives us an entire theory of civilization in one balanced sentence: "Art is the opposite of the State; Religion is the opposite of the Military."[76] The four roles of tribal community (Headman, Hunter, Shaman, and Clown)—and there only four in human organization—have clearly differentiated functions: to lead, to conquer, to divine, and to imagine. These four roles translate into institutions activating "certain values" in conflict with other institutions. "Human society becomes...a many-body situation in which values can only be achieved in conflict with opposites."[77] Headman into State/Government; Hunter into Military/Industry; Shaman into Religion/Education; Clown into Art/Media. *Religion is sociology.*

And So..........

A penetrating definition of religion should contain portions of all five of these dimensions. Sri Aurobindo is especially clear about this. In *The Life Divine* he writes:

> If it is merely some part of ourselves, intellect, heart, will or vital desire-self, which, dissatisfied with its own imperfection and with the world,

strives to get away from it to a greater height of existence, content to leave the rest of nature to take care of itself or to perish, then such a total transformation would not eventuate....[78]

Aurobindo is speaking of a "change into higher consciousness or state of being" which is not only "the whole aim and process of religion, of all higher askesis, of Yoga,"[79] but is in fact the direction of life itself. It is "the secret purpose" at the heart of all endeavor.

My own definition is as follows: *Religion is the total response (celebration, articulation, and social activity) of our whole nature to that which we consider to be ultimately significant in life.*

Everyone will quickly recognize the influence of Paul Tillich here. His own summation of these diverse efforts at definition has the stunning qualities of being simple, instructive, and emancipating: Religion is that which concerns us ultimately. I learned from him that religion has no special place in the world, but it is, quite literally **and** symbolically, everywhere: that the religious sphere is that which interpenetrates all other spheres. It was a liberating moment when I read Tillich's thesis sentence in a volume of essays entitled *Theology of Culture:* "Religion is the substance of culture; culture is the form of religion."[80]

It should be obvious, then, why I consider "relativism"—or at least genuine pluralism—theologically correct. No religious experience can finally be categorized and "handled." What we see is the enormous richness and variety that is religion—indeed why Andrew Greeley calls it "persistent." The quest for meaning and desire for security does not end when we pronounce God dead. That obituary only means that one approach has closed off for us and a new, more imaginative, more authentic, way of centering must be found. I am only beginning to understand that Voltaire was not putting down religion when he said that, "if God did not exist we would have to invent him."

All of our religious life forms are "inventions," but the assumption that we can live without them has no support in history or contemporary sociology—or even psychology. If secularism means that men and women do not need rituals and symbols of their faith, then it is both arrogant and ignorant.[81]

Nevertheless, the recognition of context—of the legitimacy of alternative claims to truth—is the *sine qua non* for exploring religion. No one ever mentioned this to me in Texas. The only reason to investigate Buddhism during my southern education was to see how wrong it was. We spoke with utter condescension of Asians who sang "Onward Buddhist Soldiers," because their "faith" couldn't inspire *real* music. That's why we taught the little children— we called them Sunbeams—to sing verses like this:

One door and only one, and yet its sides are two.
Inside and outside: on which side are you?
One door and only one, and yet its sides are two.
I'm on the inside: on which side are you?

Stumbling on the shrines of Kyoto tends to multiply the doors, because religious pluralism is a way of life in Japan. Nearly every Buddhist temple has a torii or two. Saicho, the founder of Tendai Buddhism, is said to have stood before a Shinto shrine and chanted this Tanka:

> *Nanigoto no owahimasu kawa shirane domo katajikenasa ni namida kokoruru.* (I do not know what it is, but I cannot but have tears in the awareness of something holy and graceful.)[82]

John B. Cobb, Jr., the Christian process theologian, has stood before Western audiences and articulated this relationship: "While Christianity is Buddhized, Buddhism can be Christianized."[83] The way to unity it seems is not by amalgamation, but by understanding what is truly special about each—and how that uniqueness enriches us. Even the unity *within* a tradition is plural.

What could be more absolute than the Christian claim to the crucifixion and resurrection of Jesus? Yet, in Aomori Prefecture in northern Honshu there is the grave of Jesus Christ. This is no tourist trick—nor another bizarre *pesher* reading of the Dead Sea Scrolls by Barbara Thiering. It seems that some Japanese Christians, having escaped the sixteenth century persecution (in response to their discovery that the Jesuits had domination in mind),[84] fled to offshore islands, and in that isolation developed their own traditions. Jesus, they taught, escaped the cross—as *they* did—his younger brother being killed in his place. Eventually the Nazarene made his way to Japan, where he died a natural death, and was buried—far off the tourist trail.[85]

"What is the sound of one hand clapping?" asks the famous koan of Hakuin Zenji. Right and left hands pounding together produce sounds—which is to say—if it *could* be said: dualistic thinking is the basis of conventionalized thought patterns (mind vs. body, good vs. evil, male vs. female). But the sound of truth is beyond such distinction and not finally available to discursive approaches. "If you meet the Buddha, kill him," runs another Zen saying. One thinks of Isaiah: "In the year the king died, I saw the Lord." In the death of absolutes, I began to live.

The rough beast bestirs itself in the sands of Egypt. And though we must name him, he shall be forever nameless.

DISSOLVING THE RIDDLE: IMMANENCE

There is a second characteristic of my emerging understanding of religion, particularly the Christian faith: it is radical immanence. By immanence (the doctrine of complete presence), I mean to deny any split between God and human life, any distance to be traversed by some spiritual exercise or exorcism. It is precisely this understanding that produced what Joseph Campbell called "the confrontation between East and West.[86] The East, according to Campbell, emphasizes the continuity, indeed the unity, of cosmic creative energy and mankind. The West, through Judaism, Christianity, and Islam, tends to name God "transcendent"—"Wholly Other" in Rudolf Otto's famous phrase.

Ken Wilber—a brilliant interpreter of the evolution of consciousness—understands the profound implications of this orthodox Western view of God. In *Up From Eden* he tells us that this is not simply a psychological Other (separation by time), or epistemological Other (separation by ignorance), but an ontological Other (separation by nature).

> God and man are forever divorced—they are not, as in Hinduism and Buddhism, ultimately one and identical. Thus the only contact between God and man is by airmail....God's contact is by contract. Across this gaping abyss God and man touch by rumor, not by absolute union (samadhi), and thus history was viewed as the unfolding of this contract, this covenant, through time.[87]

Both the Judaic and Christian sacrificial apparatus was arranged to "bridge the gap," placate the offended Creator with offerings ranging from doves to righteousness, and failing in all of these, finally gave us the startling image of a God sacrificing Himself for all humankind: "He, who was the Son of God, became man, that we, who are sons of men, might become sons of God"—so runs an ancient Christian epigram. The sense Christians have tried to make of this is excruciating [quite literally] history.[88] Islam opted out of the sacrificial paradigm altogether, and protects God's complete otherness by emphasizing Muhammad's—and Jesus'—complete humanness. If Christianity is Judaism for Gentiles (the whole human race is the chosen people), then Islam is Moses speaking Arabic (the law has now been fully revealed).

The essence of Christianity is the Incarnation; and, interpreted in traditional transcendent terms, makes it clearly exclusive—what Kierkegaard tagged "the scandal of particularity"—turns it into the rival of every other religion. But in immanental terms, this Incarnation delightfully denies the claims of any "wholly other" ideology—and one can easily understand why men permeated with a consciousness of discontinuity would feel offended by the revolutionary claim that "I and my father are one." It has remained, ironically enough, for the mystic tradition of Christianity (St. John of the Cross, Teresa of Avila, the author of *The Cloud of Unknowing)* to keep alive this sense of oneness with the divine. Indeed, the mystics, by turning the cross into a Christian koan, may have become the carriers of the Incarnational tradition.[89]

But the Wise Men that came to celebrate the Savior were not from the West—as Campbell, William Johnston, Huston Smith, Jacob Needleman,

Father LaSalle, Alan Watts, and a host of new age types will be glad to point out. The East, they tell us, specializes in continuity—in ways to be one with the One. *Buddha*, of course, simply means "one who has come to his senses." Not a bad image that: the one who woke up.

For a towering effort to make the men of the West wise, few match D. T. Suzuki's exposition of the Buddhist tradition, particularly the Zen community. In an article on the role of nature in Zen Buddhism Suzuki writes, "Nature is the bosom whence we come and whither we go."[90] "Nature produces man out of itself, Man cannot be outside of Nature." "I am in Nature and Nature is in Me."[91] This remarkable unity between Man and Nature is then contrasted by Suzuki to the Biblical view of the human condition following the fall in Eden. Man is here against God, Nature is against God, and Man and Nature are against each other: God's own likeness (Man), God's own creation (Nature), and God himself—all three are "at war." Even God is against Man, since being All-Knowing, he knew Adam would sin before he actually did. In recounting to Moyers his own meeting with Suzuki, Campbell adds a wry Suzuki assessment of the Biblical view: "Very funny religion!"[92]

Hiroshi Teshigahara is an artist and collector of art in Japan, the son of a famous designer of gardens. In 1964 he made a film, *Suna no Onna* (*Woman in the Dunes*) which now has assumed classic status—chosen as one of the ten best films for demonstrating Japanese artistry to the American public, for example. Whatever its critical acclaim, *Woman in the Dunes* is a powerful evocation of Suzuki's "difference" between East and West. Dennis Giles, in fact, demonstrates that the film can be experienced as a Taoist document.[93]

The ancient Chinese symbol for *Tao* consists of three parts: road, head of a chieftain, and foot. *Tao*, then, is the way that a man follows, the natural process, the path that all things—when they know themselves—follow. To be "in the *Tao*" is to be in harmony with—not in conflict against—the natural order of heaven and earth. The *Tao* is yielding, flowing—like water in a valley, like sand into a pit. There in the valley, according to the *Tao Te Ching*, the mysterious female (the passive, graceful nature of existence) overcomes the overt male (the active, dominating nature of life). Or rather, the two fit together, concave and convex, yin and yang, soft and hard, reception and penetration.

The male of the film [nameless] is an entomologist, a scientist who lives by classification and logical order, who invades the hills of sand with his notebook, insect nets, camera, and Western clothes. In the evening, he is led by villagers to a place for rest—to a deep pit in the dunes, inhabited by a woman. There he is lowered by rope ladder, thinking his adventure in the valley will last only one night. He must return to Tokyo in the morning, continue his work of categorizing the world of living things—make a name for himself—win a prize—write a scientific treatise. Achieve.

But he, who captures insects and immobilizes them on observation boards, is now captured and immobilized in the valley of the female. He finds that he cannot escape from the pit, for the rope ladder has been withdrawn, and every effort to climb up the sides of the pit bring sand cascading down. The Western clad scientist is caught in the pouring sand and ridden to the bottom of the pit. All the powers of his logical mind are brought to bear on escape, and, even when he finally struggles to the top of the dunes with his carefully constructed rope, he is trapped in quick sand, rescued by the villagers and returned to the pit.

Gradually the scientist's anger, cleverness, and deceit gives way to the flow of the woman: her acceptance of the pit, her body of sand, sweat, and quiet passion, her overwhelming humanness. He burns his insect collection, tries to bribe the villagers (to allow him periods of time above the pit) by copulating with the woman under the light of torches and lamps, urged on by their erotic drumming. When the woman recoils from this *unnatural* act, they both prostrate themselves, impaled by the beams of light, like the insects he had just destroyed. Digging his own small pit, the man attempts to trap a crow, but, peering in his trap, finds water instead. He has accidentally discovered that the sand can act as a pump and provide water: complete wetness out of total dryness.

The woman becomes pregnant, and when about to miscarry, is taken from the pit. We are left not knowing whether there is to be life or death: only with the reflection of a very young boy who is looking down from the edge in the man's "well" of serendipity. The villagers, aiding the woman, leave the ladder of rope, and the man, dressed now in traditional Japanese clothes, climbs to the sea—looks without anxiety, and returns to the pit. It has been seven years since that first night. He who was captured is now free. The film ends, and with it, once and for all, the attraction of transcendence. One can only run the film again.

"Transcendence" means to "climb across," precisely what our scientific, Western, competitive culture has institutionalized as the super good. Immanence means to "remain within"—precisely what our natural, Eastern, religious culture has celebrated as the "way of the gods." It is this perpetual state of war that lies at the root of Western man's need to conquer nature rather than share her benefits. "Have dominion," says the Lord God. "Multiply"—but be sure to give me the first fruits to assuage my anguish at producing you.

We ought here to make further distinctions. As the rough beast rests now in the dunes of central Honshu, tranquilized in the rebirth of the moment, we can sketch out the dimensions of immanence.

Immanence as Present Awareness

The "East" is useful as imagery and rhetoric, but this symbol requires me to be more exact. I choose Kyoto over Benares, Zen over Yoga, and, for that matter, Soto Zen over Rinzai Zen. Of course the yogi's ascension from the lower part of the body to the cosmic consciousness in the "thousand-petaled lotus" has a rhythmic, attractive beauty,[94] and it has occurred to me that this yogic ascension from the base of the spine through seven chakras is the origin of the old Hindu rope trick. Remember? The magician causes the coiled rope—the kundalini—to rise up straight to the ceiling. A boy then climbs up the rope and disappears at the top, the rope falling to the ground. Magic and religion together again, just as Frazer said. Certainly Yoga consciousness and Zen consciousness seem similar: supra-conceptual, imageless, wordless, unearthly silent.

But the scientific work of Dr. Tomio Hirai at the University of Tokyo (*Zen Meditation Therapy*)[95] in conjunction with the theological analysis of Dr. William Johnston of Sophia University (reported in three books, *The Still Point, Silent Music: the Science of Meditation,* and *Christian Zen*)[96] presents an important distinction. Johnston writes:

> EEG experiments have shown that if you make a noise, the Zen meditator hears it; if you flash a light, he sees it; if you stick a pin in him, he feels it. This is because his meditation is very much geared to the here and now, to a total presence to reality. In this sense, Zen is extremely incarnational. On the other hand—other body?—, when the yogi enters into very deep meditation, he hears nothing, sees nothing, and feels nothing. So much so that one researcher writes that "the control of attention achieved by the subject is so intense that neither flashing light, sounding gongs, vibration or the touch of hot glass test-tubes could disrupt the state of concentration and cause alpha-blocking."[97]

This *attentive* aspect of Zen does not take us to any *transcendent* Buddha, but provides a discipline for the keenest possible perception of the present moment. A *New Yorker* cartoon presented it perfectly: an evangelical white Christian holds a sign reading "Jesus Is Coming," while a bemused Japanese upstages him with a sign reading "Buddha Here Now."

Immanence as Union of Body and Mind

A primary notion carried by early Greek thought and dominating Western intellectual and religious history is the radical split between body and mind (or spirit). From Plato to Descartes, from Augustine to Hugh Hefner, this division has ranged from thoughtful to profitable. Today, this split is being challenged everywhere and subjected to sophisticated theological analysis by the body intellectuals, particularly by the respected Chicago theologian Sally McFague. In her ecological theology, *The Body of God*, she "corrects" the anatomy of ontological schizophrenia:

> But both of these terms, *spirit* and *body*, are, as we have emphasized, backside, not face, terms.[98]

God is simply not available to us "in or to our categories," she says. Transcendence means this and not some superperson—like GOD yelled in a loud voice. It is rather, I suppose, like the second form of Anselm's ontological argument: God is greater than can be conceived. This is why Tillich was so impressed by the argument: it is no *argument* at all, but a *definition* of what we mean by the word "God." As Campbell puts it in "Masks of Eternity": God is "beyond all categories, beyond being and non-being, beyond all form."[99] McFague goes on to defend a kind of reverent relativity:

> It is what God is when God is not "being God"; it is the mystery, the absoluteness, that relativizes all our notions and models of God; it is the godness of God; it is the silence that surrounds all our paltry and pathetic attempts to speak of God; it the big no to all our little yeses. [100]

And it is this "transcendence" that encourages us to retain the trinitarian formula, insisting that we examine both the spirit and the body as aspects of our model of the universe. This is why I have retained it as the structure of this book, except that I see "transcendence" as an adjective and not a noun. I take Chalcedonian Christology (Jesus as *both* divine and human)[101] as the actual state of affairs in thinking about God, with the crucial addition of genital incarnation and not some ecological abstraction that denies the body while seeming to affirm it. A deep tradition in Japan also denies this split and has developed agile communities to promote the union. These are the various martial arts: *kendo, judo, karate, aikido,* and in particular, *shorinji kempo.*

The name *shorinji* is simply Japanese for Shaolin temple in Honai Prefecture in China, where Bodhidharma, the sixth century Buddhist worthy, is supposed to have introduced priests to an art form combining physical defense and spiritual discipline. *Kempo* points to the fundamental unity of Ken and Zen, the body of action and the mind of composure.

This knowledge is the middle way, the golden mean, the perfect oneness of body and mind, symbolized visually by a circle made of two flowing lines—recognizable to us all as a swastika [jarring to eyes that remember what demonic use was made of such an insignia]—appearing on every Shorinji Kempo training hall and on the white practice uniforms.

This immanental tradition has so permeated Japan that it has helped make it one of the most physically conscious nations on earth: massive sports programs through the school, colleges and professional ranks; omnipresence of dojos and martial artists in the streets, parks, temples and shrines; company lunch break exercises—and those company sponsored trips for week-end *zazen*, a body building exercise if there ever was one. If there's anything harder than a Calvinist's head, it's a Zen Master's abdomen. Buddha, I decided after a weekend of *zazen* myself, wasn't tranquil: he was paralyzed from chronic *kekkafuza.*

But the seated figure is no joke. Is the Buddha's gaze tranquil or merely empty, as Arthur Koestler has suggested? Not a lotus but a robot: sitting there all these centuries, emitting alpha waves, bemused by hordes of tourists, fixed on film, his gaze bland and pitiless as the sun, indignant birds fluttering above his torpid torso while the world frets for enlightenment?

Or is he stirring now—his hour come round at last?

EMBRACING THE MOMENT: IMMEDIACY

There is a third and final contour that I see to this rough, slouching religion, which can be labeled "radical immediacy." Jacob Needleman, in his primer on "the teachings of the East" entitled *The New Religions*,[102] pointed out that one of the main reasons why the young people turned "inward" to so called "exotic" forms of religion was precisely because Eastern teachings have preserved the *instrumental* aspect of religion. Meditation techniques, physical and psychological exercises, the need for guru or sensei, all tend toward what Needleman named "the return of the practical." In their genesis the mainspring of religions in the West, he claimed, *was* instrumental (holy habits by the handful!), but gradually—and bizarrely—the West started forgetting: began reading prescriptions and diagnosing disease, but stopped taking medicine.

> It is impossible to say when this forgetting of the fundamentally instrumental nature of religious forms began in the West. But obviously the general clergy—priests, ministers, and rabbis—forgot it quite as much as their congregations. No wonder the young became disillusioned with religion. They heard exhortation, commandments, prescriptions by the basketful, but nobody was telling them *how to be able* to follow them.[103]

Methodism—I'm happy to reconfirm—was born out of exactly this lapse of memory by the Anglican church. Wesley daily inveighed against "having the form, but denying the power"—and "how to be able" is a fine translation of practicing the Christian way by "method."

But the New Religions of Needleman are not as much to my point as the "new religions" of Japan, which he doesn't mention. By "new religions" I refer to the religious communities that have arisen specifically in the twentieth century and received their main impetus after World War II.[104] They feature syncretism, charismatic leadership, spectacular building programs, highly energetic missionary programs, political activity, but most centrally a body of teaching designed to facilitate living in the real world as it exists. There are a host of candidates bursting forth in crowded Japan, and McFarland labeled the phenomenon nicely as "the rush hour of the gods"—referring to Tokyo's incredible commuting crush and not a pun on the name of America's former ambassador to Japan. [105]

Once again, distinctions are in order, God being in the details.

Soka Gakkai

As early as October 26, 1954, the *Asahi-Shimbun* in Tokyo reported on an "army-like organization" with a "religious mission" called Soka ("value creating") Gakkai ("academy"). The paper's account was virtually the first public look at what has become one of the most successful evangelistic enterprises in the entire history of religion. Claiming an orthodox tradition of seven hundred years (allegiance to a thirteenth century Buddhist priest named Nichiren), Soka Gakkai was first registered as a religious Hojin (juridical foundation) in May, 1951. It was actually established by Tsunesaburo Makiguchi and Josei Toda in 1930, but suppressed and almost destroyed by the military government. In 1960, Mr. Daisaku Ikeda became its third president. In 1999, he is still head of the organization known world wide as SGI (Soka Gakkai International), and author of at least thirty-two books, ranging around the human revolution wrought by Buddhism in *action.* Termed a "muscular Buddhist" by the Associated Press, he lifted Soka Gakkai into international prominence with his interviews of world leaders (Kosigin, Chou En-lai, Kissinger, President Clinton, Pope John Paul II, etc.). In June of 1995, SGI hosted a city-wide program in San Francisco, synchronized with Clinton's presence at the 50th anniversary celebration of the United Nations.[106]

For the Japanese, this gigantic religious body has provided a social collectivity ideally filling the vacuum left by the demise of the Emperor cult and totalitarian social system it represented. For the secular world, it provides a remarkable example of the ideology of immediacy. Noah S. Brannen comments in his book, *Soka Gakkai: Japan's Military Buddhists,* that this is "the religion of here and now"—not given to conversation about the blessedness of the beyond, but instead preaching "instant freedom from sickness and poverty."[107] John Roderick of the Associated Press wrote simply that Ikeda believes in getting things done without armchair philosophies, that Ikeda deeply admired both Mao and Chou, contrasting their sense of purpose with Japan's floundering and—in the case of Tanaka—corrupt administration. As Mao's monstrous behavior has dethroned his "divine" status in China, Ikeda invokes Buddhism to ensure that he will never fall from grace.

The consistently horizontal dimension of Soka Gakkai is saved from fascism by Buddhist compassion, delightfully illustrated by Ikeda in his parable *The Princess and the Moon.* A little girl discovers by means of a magic night visit to the craggy country of the moon that everyone is actually good inside—and that she will be treated like a princess in the very act of looking for that goodness. Ikeda's story evokes gentleness, reverence towards life, healing powers of nature, and kindness to others—all helped along by the moon's emissary, a great rabbit: a kind of Buddhist Alice in Lunarland. His story invokes the ancient Asian wisdom that what is inevitable for each of us is happiness.

In his New Year's message to SGI, given in Tokyo on January 2, 1999, Ikeda still dispenses this hope: "There is no way that you who are working so hard for [these values] will not be protected by the Buddhist gods and by all the Buddhas and bodhisattvas throughout time and space—the protective functions of the universe."[108] Here the "twenty-first century" radiates as a symbol of the simple, active present: our school of value created out of the reservoir of human energy, becomes now the center for a peaceful, global unity. And twenty-five million sing *"Shin Seiki no Uta"* ("The Song of New Century").

Perfect Liberty Kyodan

Perfect Liberty Kyodan (usually abbreviated PL Kyodan) traces its history, not to Buddhism, but to Tokumitsu Kanada, a Shinto priest of the *Mitake-kyo* sect, who in 1912 founded his own group known as *Shinto Tokumitsu-kyo.* His successor was Tokuharu Miki, who in 1931 established the *Hito-no-Michi Kyodan* ("the Way of Man")—renamed Perfect Liberty Kyodan after World War II by Tokuchika Miki, the visionary third leader. The English phrase in the title is intentionally international and conveys, according to PL propaganda, "world-wide propagation for peace and welfare of mankind" as the ultimate goal of PL. [109]

PL specifically advertises itself as a "modern religion for modern men" under the theme of "Self Liberation," abbreviated appropriately to "Self-Lib." It is unashamedly *direct* in its appeal to materialistic contemporaneity. Its Vatican in Tondabayashi (near Osaka) contains the largest one floor auditorium in the world, a fountain gracing the main white marble shrine (*Seiden)* with the world's tallest jets of water, the five hundred and ten feet Peace Tower completed to coincide with the Osaka World's Fair in 1970 (and preserving the name of every known war dead in the history of humankind on microfilm), its prize golf course the site of Japan-America championships, its theater troupe booked for international tours, its retreat center housing eight hundred guests overflowing with religious tourists like Marcus Bach—looking for the dynamic that makes this four million member organization live.

The precepts are short, simple (*exceedingly* simple), practical, gently sexist, a blend of Shinto, Buddhist, and contemporary insights: "Life is art" (1), "Man is a manifestation of God"(3), "Strive for creating mutual happiness" (10), "There is a way for men, and there is another way for women" (13), "Act when your intuition dictates" (19), "Live in Perfect Liberty" (21).[110]

I never saw any religion so guiltless about recreation. PL is known in Japan as "the golf religion" and they accept such derision graciously. The headquarters in Tondabayashi also contain dormitories specifically for "caddiettes," three hundred young girls paying their way through PL high school at Seichi by serving as caddies in four hour shifts. They would have delighted the heart of Walt Disney—or Jerry Falwell for that matter—with their smart blue slacks, orange windbreakers, and white headbands bearing the large block letters PL. The girls are typical of PL ethos. A Japanese industrial executive said it straight out:

> The reason I enter the competitions in spring and autumn every year is so that I can not only golf for itself but also to indulge in a fresh mood. The services of the caddies of the PL links are beyond expression. They attend to us with warm hearts of their own accord, and speak with affection. They are not motivated by someone else, but by their natural dignity. Their kindness I have never met before, and it quite overwhelms me.[111]

I watched some of that "fresh mood" develop out on one of the courses and it just about convinced me to take up golf again. Ah—to play around the rolling hills, far from the tumult and shouting of sexual harassment suits: to swing, to roll, all in the guilt free air of natural dignity. What man wouldn't play this open golf: heaven on earth—a Master's with a mistress.[112]

And yet "golf religion" is a revealing phrase for PL. They deeply believe that all life is art—that serving tea, working with computers, playing championship baseball [they won the Japan high school championship the year after my visit], researching cancer cures, riding monorails, learning tribal dances, promoting world peace, hosting wide-eyed *gaijin* slouching towards Kyoto, is all part of "living radiantly in the sun"—their twenty-one precepts shooting out in a golden wheel sunburst as the final symbol of Perfect Liberty.

And their greatest celebration takes place the first of August—the anniversary of the death of the founder. How do they do it? Great lugubrious chanting? Solemn rites of commitment? The tolling of bells perhaps? Of course not. The death of the founder is brought to the attention of central Japan with the greatest fireworks display in all the world—with the possible exception of the magnesium rocket cloud layered over the Charles River climaxing the latest Boston Civic Independence night—accompanied by colossal columns of water hissing far into the carnival sky. Instant astral display for instant religion. Palpable ritual of immediacy. *Sic **non** transit gloria mundi.*

Now this *is* getting left-handed: all dailies and no eternals. And yet—at the risk of adding to the world's oxymorons—I see no future at all for religion that doesn't work right now. Instant religion used to be a joke—rather like a student of mine who once gave me a bottle labeled "religion," all stuffed with tiny pellets she called "gos-pills:" each filled with the scriptural dose for the day.

Rude and silly—right? But Christianity has been guilty of mediating the postponed life, and many of us are running out of time. All of us are. Religion has to be practical to be anything at all. Jesus' answer to John's question is instructive. "Are you the one?" the Baptist wanted to know. Tell John that the lame walk, the blind see, the prisoners are free. Perfect Liberty and Value Creators abound.

Perhaps such passionate intensity is doomed to drown in blood tide—and the spirit of the world is tenuous and troubling. Still I celebrate this birth about to be and is, this rough beast moving: relative, immanent, and immediate.

But how? With fireworks and fantasies? Personality cults and hot-wired humanism? Simplistic Dale Carnegie chanting? In Japan I saw many festivals: wild sake-inspired dancing at Omi Hachiman, the solemnity of Aoi, the colorful purgation of Shogatsu, beans hurled at Asakusa, coins churning up good favors at Ebisu, one hundred thousand marching in the sun to the sea at Kobe while eight hundred thousand watched in wonder.

Yet the most appropriate rite for me took place in a small shrine on Mt. Yoshida, just up the street from our home in Kyoto. An old Japanese man, with a musical instrument tucked under his arm, the only person at the shrine, walked up to the front where one usually rings a bell and claps to get the attention of the gods. He stopped just for a moment, bowed slightly, and then—tipped his hat.

It was this informality with the gods, this familiarity with the center of life, this politeness toward the presence of the sacred, that alchemized for me all those Japanese ceremonies into substance. Their "real" religion, that somehow tied together the many programs for peace, continuity between the gods and men, love of nature, the livability of Tokyo, the miraculous social honesty, drinking tea, and the girl caddies of Tondabayashi, …their religion was courtesy. Our family was never treated so well, by so many, for so long, in our lives.

I fully realize that there is a very dark side to Japan, presented with chilling force in the PBS documentaries "The Sword and the Chrysanthemum: Violence in Japan," and "Whitepaper: The Japan They Don't Talk About." And Patrick Smith's 1997 prize-winning book, *Japan: A Reinterpretation*, is a sustained deconstruction of the "simple" universe that drew Americans in the 1970's "in search of the 'secrets' behind Japan's economic miracle."[113] But we must still account for its incredible emergence as a world power from the devastation in 1946, and a profound part of that account—whether we like it or not—is that Japanese are simply better than most at being together. In truth they may not even understand what individualism is.[114]

Father William Currie—my translator at Teshigahara's office—once tried to teach literature at Sophia University in Tokyo using Wylie Sypher's book, *The Loss of Self in Modern Literature*. After weeks of blank stares from the class, he finally realized that his students couldn't comprehend the text because they had no idea what a "self" was. If Tillich is right that culture is the form of religion, then the religion of Japan is being Japanese. Could then that form—that incredible ability to be together—be widened out to include the Koreans? The blue eyes who have learned the mysteries of Japanese consciousness? The women who cannot or who chose not to have children? The nail that sticks up be left alone in its loftiness? If that inclusiveness and toler-ance were grounded in substance, Ikeda could be correct. Perhaps Japan does possess the secret for the world of the twenty-first century.

One might call it the etiquette of belief. In the crush of pluralism and competing claims, I bow. Carrying what talents I possess, whatever instru-ments I have learned to play, lumbering, slouching, loving—angered by my ineptitude at being human, seduced into taking emeritus inventory in terms of power over people and capital, Internet in one hand and *Tao Te Ching* in the other, I pause here at this shrine of thought, pursuing a history of lived con-versation about things that matter most in a day when things fall apart. I pause and tip my hat—aware that the entrance to this shrine is shadowed by a rude beast that knows no absolutes, harbors no security, and seeks new birth this very hour.

CHAPTER TWO

JESUS IS COMING AGAIN AND AGAIN:
THE BODY AS CHRIST

SOME [SAY] THAT EVER 'GAINST THAT SEASON COMES
WHEREIN OUR SAVIOUR'S BIRTH IS CELEBRATED,
THE BIRD OF DAWNING SINGETH ALL NIGHT LONG;
AND THEN, THEY SAY, NO SPIRIT CAN WALK ABROAD;
THE NIGHTS ARE WHOLESOME; THEN NO PLANETS STRIKE,
NO FAIRY [TAKES], NOR WITCH HATH POWER TO CHARM,
SO HALLOW'D AND SO GRACIOUS IS THE TIME.
                    SHAKESPEARE

WE AWAKEN IN CHRIST'S BODY/AS CHRIST AWAKENS OUR BODIES
                    SIMEON THE NEW THEOLOGIAN

ORTHODOXY IS THE DEATH OF INTELLIGENCE
                    BERTRAND RUSSELL

The new birth and the second coming: echoes of Nicodemus, the Great Awakenings of American history, and the fundamentalists. Anyone who thought the fundamentalists dead in 1925 started believing in the resurrection in 1980. They were back, alive, politically powerful, and despite their scandalous sexual behavior in the late eighties—not to mention their political witch hunt mentality in the late nineties—still represent an authentic American consciousness, one-third of *all* the American consciousness.[115] No one interested in locating the religious imagination can ignore them. In the mid-nineties exhaustive studies (three volumes) of fundamentalism's place in American life and thought (by Martin Marty and R. Scott Appleby) were published by the University of Chicago Press.[116] As the nineties began, John Shelby Spong, an Episcopal Bishop—possibly under the influence of mystical visits from the beyond by Bishops Robinson and Pike—entered the arena against the neo-literalists, with a series of books "re-thinking" the major doctrines of the Christian faith. "Re-thinking" means asking a lot of disturbing questions.

Was Paul a misogynist? Did Mark use bad grammar? Did Matthew mistakenly have Joseph and Mary's hometown as Bethlehem? Is John's gospel anti-Semitic? Is gang rape allowed in Genesis?

If you answered yes to all the above questions—and you certainly could—does this mean that the Bible is not true? Yes, say the fundamentalists. Nonsense, says the incisive Bishop from Newark, who claims that sex "drove" him to the Bible, and forced him to demonstrate why a proof-text was a pre-text in understanding God's Word.

> Because I believe those words to be in touch with something eternal, transcendent, and holy, I want to rescue them from the hands of those who by claiming too much will finally accomplish too little.[117]

Spong is no cynic, no left-over Marxist, no Anglican version of Madelyn Murray O'Hair, and his book is no exercise in therapy for a frustrated free thinker. He acknowledges his debt to his literalist Presbyterian grandmother for taking the Bible seriously and is, in fact, an evangelist for what Wesley called the uniting of "knowledge and vital piety." He has done his homework thoroughly, and he writes with razors.

A great deal of very sharp homework is being done these days, most particularly the Jesus Seminar. Co-chaired by Robert W. Funk and John Dominic Crossan, with John Spong as a fellow traveler, the Seminar published the results of a nine year scholarly pursuit of the historical Jesus, entitled *The Five Gospels:* the four we know plus one of the twenty or so we don't know, The Gospel of Thomas.[118] The Seminar [almost one hundred biblical scholars] is famous (and infamous) for daring to vote on what Jesus actually said, and print the results in the gospels themselves: **red** (authentic), **pink** (probably), **gray/blue** (probably not), **black** (somebody put words in his mouth for sure). Whatever virulent criticisms are leveled at their work,[119] the Jesus Seminar deserves careful study (and high praise) for addressing most directly the central issue in religion: **the question of authority**. And it does its work in a decade calling for mindless surrender to the faith of our godfathers.

ELMER GANTRY IN PRIME TIME: AUTHORITY

It may not be "portentous and a thing of state" that the millennium ends with the year of rabbit, but it is certainly interesting to me. The Asian calendar declares a year of the rabbit every twelve years—1975 being that transforming religious odyssey in Japan. And for anyone studying religion in American life, 1987 was a warren of sin and synchronicity.

First, the leading Democratic presidential candidate hopped off to Bimini with a comely playmate (Donna Rice) on the good ship *Monkey Business* (the actual-in-your-face-name of the boat). Then the newest Republican candidate (the ingratiating evangelical, Mr. Robertson—the one with the "elfin smile") conceded that he and his wife were married only ten weeks before the birth of their first child, and Oliver North showed up at the Iran-Contra hearings with a loyal secretary—who shredded any suggestion of funny-bunny office behavior. Oral Roberts announced an astounding new way to raise funds at his church college, piously whining that if he didn't receive multiple millions by March 31, God would call him home. In October the stock market bulls turned into scared rabbits, scampering into the bush with a quarter of my retirement money—a hare raising tale by anyone's standards. And the November issue of *Playboy* (where the Bunny icon is legendary), featured Jessica Hahn outside on the cover, and on the inside on the uncover her version of the encounter with Jim Bakker—the Peter Cottontail of television evangelism.

The Scandals of 1987 revealed some fundamental flaws in American consciousness: from Bimini to Contra-Gate, from Wall Street to Pearly Gate. The Bakker Affair was the most public *religious* scandal in US history and precipitated a "holy war," the likes of which our country hadn't seen since the 1920's, when the Fundamentalists met the Modernists in Dayton, Tennessee, and Sinclair Lewis immortalized the struggles between sex and power, money and salvation in his novel *Elmer Gantry*—between loving God and seducing your neighbor, between serving the Almighty and serving the Almighty dollar.[120] Sinners in the hands of an angry author.

Now the cycle of twelve has brought us to 1999, the resolution of the most public *political* scandal in US—perhaps even world—history. Sinner in the hands of an angry congress.

The Fundamentals

I know something about fundamentalism and evangelism. I *was* a fundamentalist, a Jesus cowboy in the Holy Ghost corral, with ten gallons full of glory, a radio show out of Ft. Worth called "Impressions for Eternity" [that lasted for eighteen months], a revival preacher and singer all over the South, a shoutin' Methodist, a Bible bigot right out of *Inherit the Wind*. I was a fast drawin' gospel gunslinger—with the Old Testament on one hip and the New Testament on the other, firing biblical bullets at the ungodly. Romans 3:23—*Bang*! "All have sinned and come short of the glory of God." *Bang* !

Back in Texas, I was on William Jennings Bryan's side in the "Monkey" trial. My baccalaureate preacher in high school in Dallas was the Rev. W. A. Criswell, the *then* new pastor of First Baptist—the largest Baptist church in the world. I can still remember his tirade in 1945 against evolution. Cut off a dog's tail, he shouted, and her offspring will have a tail. And the sons of all tailless bitches will still have a tail.[121]

By now we should have the nomenclature straight. There are *evangelicals, charismatics, pentecostals,* and *fundamentalists*. They are distinct if not always separate (rather like Kant's distinction between the phenomenal and the noumenal world). Classical orthodox Christians usually place the emphasis in their theology on the first person of the Trinity—from the City of God in Augustine to the Glory of God in Calvin. Evangelicals shift the emphasis to the second person, to the saving work of Christ. This is why the Wesleyan revival in England was called *evangelical*—as well as the second great awakening in America under the work of Charles Finney in the 1830's. *Pentecostals*, wrapped in tongues of fire, are territorial with the third person—the spirit.

Evangelical is a name accepted by many denominations, but clearly the largest of them is the Southern Baptist Convention, with fifteen million members, including Billy Graham, Jimmy Carter, Pat Robertson, and Jerry Falwell. *Charismatics* obviously emphasize the third person of the Trinity, *charisma* deriving from the Greek word for *oil*—symbolizing the spirit. *Charismatic* means "anointed" and, hence, the phrase "filled with Spirit."

A generation ago the Roman Catholic Church, mindful of the ancient Montanist heresy (the spirit undermining clerical authority), was suspicious of the charismatic movement within its own ranks. Today—even as Pope John Paul II rides in his Pope Mobile in Mexico City—the hierarchy is deeply concerned over the loss of four million Catholics a year, mainly to the churches that emphasize the Witness of the Spirit: Pentecostals and Evangelicals (the erosion in Brazil is epidemic). Msgr. Francis Olivier calls the Pope's 1999 visit part of the "new evangelization," and points to the Church's recent stand on the natural rights of immigrants—even "illegal" immigrants—as evidence of this concern for recovery.

The word *pentecostal* is derived from Greek *pentikosti*, meaning the fiftieth day after Passover. In the Hebraic tradition it was called the Feast of Weeks—a kind of thanksgiving for the wheat harvest [and the stone tablets given on Sinai]. The Christians "baptized" this tradition to celebrate the ecstatic event recorded in the second chapter of Acts, when the Holy Spirit descended and all began to speak in tongues. Modern Pentecostals had their beginning in 1914, when a gathering of pastors formed the Assemblies of God, emphasizing the baptism of the Spirit and the gift of tongues (glossolalia)—and known disdainfully by the staid upper crust churches as Holy Rollers.

The largest Christian church in the world is Pentecostal: the Yoido church in Seoul, Korea. In April of 1989, I was invited to address students at Beijing University on the subject of "American Freedom" —one week before the death of Hu Yaobang and the consequent demonstrations. We left Beijing from a train station that looked like a war zone, heading south for Tian, Nanjing, and Shanghai. By May we had flown to Korea, straight into another student revolution—this one staged outside Yonsei University. Because of the presence of a U.S. Army base in Seoul, we were able to look at *Nightline* covering the chaos in China. It was surreal: sitting inside one revolution watching another.

Yonsei was founded by Presbyterian missionaries and represented the powerful Christian strides made in Korea, by far the most Christianized of the East Asian nations: 30% of the populace and over 50% of the Korean army. We were told by Dr. Underwood—whose grandfather is revered by Korean educators—that visiting Dr. Paul Yonggi Cho's Pentecostal church would be memorable. I had understood that it had over 50,000 members and I could hardly wait to hear all those Koreans speaking in tongues.

On Pentecost Sunday, 1989, my wife Pat and I attended that church. And the numbers were even more astounding than we had been told. Not 50,000 but **500,000** members—and growing at a rate of 11,000 per month.[122] The sanctuary seated 25,000, with overflow in other buildings of 6,000—and seven services a Sunday, and simultaneous translation in six languages. As we sat stunned by the sheer size of this operation, the woman next to me starting speaking in tongues—or so I thought—until Pat pointed out that she was praying in Korean. It was still exotic enough: charismatic Korean is close enough to glossolalia to qualify for any witness of the Spirit.

Fundamentalism is strictly a twentieth century word. It is a most enjoyable indoor sport to put fundamentalists down—and I play it as often as possible. We used to say that fundamentalists had very little emphasis on the "fun," lots on the "dam," and none at all on the "mental." But it began not as redneck religion in the backwoods of the Bible Belt, but with great intellectual respectability—with Professor Benjamin Warfield (high emphasis on reason) and Dr. J. Gresham Machen (careful scholarship in Greek New Testament studies) of Princeton Theological Seminary. The movement derived its name from the Stewart brothers and Torrey Dixon, who between 1910 and 1915 wrote a series of twelve pamphlets called *The Fundamentals*. They can be summarized quite neatly—an adverb which should be added to the famous four in the Chalcedonian creed—in five points.[123].

What is a Christian? Let's get clear about this and cut through all the liberal mish-mash mythology. Here is a "bottom line gospel" approach to theology—a revisionist *kerygma*:

1. **Plenary inspiration of the Bible**. The authority of the Word of God is total, preferably the King James Version, since the originals would be difficult to read if anyone ever found them.

2. **The Virgin Birth.** This miracle announces the Divinity of Jesus. Mary is only the conduit of the Divine Child, and must not be an object of devotion. Fundamentalists wouldn't be caught dead—or resurrected—preaching a sermon about the Holy Mother.

3. **The Substitutionary Theory of the Atonement.** Jesus' shed blood on the cross atones for all our sins—does for us what we could never do for ourselves. When I was a boy in Dallas, I listened "religiously" to the First Assembly of God broadcast, which always opened with the hymn, *There Is a Fountain Filled With Blood*—drawn from Immanuel's veins. And

sinners—especially young men with juices just beginning to flow—plunged beneath that flood, lose all their guilty stains. Sonorous slaughter house theology.

4. **The Physical Resurrection of Jesus.** The stone was rolled away and a formally and really dead Jesus—not a swooned, or drugged Jesus—came out alive and take *that* Pilate. The Lord [not a myth but the Messiah] is alive and so are we.

5. **The Second Coming.** This means *judgment* day. If you missed him the first time around, you won't the second. Every eye shall see him, and the hosts of heaven will shout as he comes with *Word* written in blood, and a thousand years of his kingdom will be inaugurated, before the devil is loosed and then cast into the lake of fire—along with all the rest of the secular humanists who can't take a heavenly hint.

The Special Creation of Fundamentalism

The great enemy of the fundamentalist has always been the secular humanist—known in the early part of this century as a modernist: the person who does not believe in supernatural intervention in human history and whose highest authority is therefore human reason and the scientific method. Each one of these doctrines had long been part of the Christian Church's orthodoxy, all the way back to Augustine. But these *fundamentals* were responding to the specific intellectual challenge of nineteenth century Europe.

Plenary inspiration was an address to the Graf-Wellhausen thesis that the Bible came to be in its present form by a selection and editing process, much the way a film is put together by editing different sequences from a large selection. The emphasis on the *Virgin Birth* was a response to the work of Albert Schweitzer, who had concluded his scholarly quest for the historical Jesus by declaring that Jesus, as a human being, was forever lost behind mythical stories of his origin and ministry. *Substitutionary Atonement* was an answer to the work of social gospel advocates, represented in America by Charles Sheldon and Walter Rauschenbusch, who insisted that to be a Christian was to become Christlike and follow "In His Steps."[124] *Resurrection* was a denial of the theories of David Strauss in 1836, who suggested that every miracle could be explained rationally, that Jesus walked on stones just covered by water near the shore, and that he hadn't died at all on the cross. He had, it was suggested, only fainted, and was then revived by the cool air in the tomb. *The Second Coming* laid the axe to theories of progress out of France, where Coué—not having the lethal example of Nazi Germany, the Serbs in Bosnia and Kosovo, or the insanity in Rwanda at his disposal—

declared that men were getting better and better with each new generation.

A coalition of fundamentalists and main stream Christians was formed under the colorful preaching of Billy Sunday (the former Chicago White Sox center fielder), and the populous oratory of William Jennings Bryan (Secretary of State under Woodrow Wilson—and multiple Democratic candidate for the presidency). This revivalism spawned one of most flamboyant and scandalous of the Pentecostals, Aimee Semple McPherson, insinuating her Angelus Temple in Los Angeles. Her ecstatic preaching (and life style) attracted a huge national following, including a young Hispanic who preached on the street for her, and developed his acting skills under her inspiration—later to be known as Anthony Quinn. She was the model for Sister Sharon Falconer in Lewis' novel, so wholesomely played by Jean Simmons in the film version of *Elmer Gantry.* [125]

In 1925 this modern "Great Awakening" had its Armageddon. A law against teaching evolution had been enacted in Tennessee, and the consequent Scopes trial in Dayton was archetypal: a clear battle between God and the Devil, Good and Evil, Fundamentalist and Modernist, Revelation and Reason, the Bible and Secular Humanism. William Jennings Bryan was the champion of the fundamentalists and Clarence Darrow, the humanist lawyer from Chicago, spoke for "the right to think." H.L. Mencken, the famous (and acerbic) journalist in America, covered the event, with obvious bias in favor of young Scopes—the biology teacher who challenged the law. We know the trial through Stanley Kramer's film *Inherit the Wind,* starring Spencer Tracy, Frederic March, and a non-dancing Gene Kelley.[126]

The event was publicized by radio—and the national media exposure embarrassed the fundamentalists, broadcasting Bryan's incompetence in the face of Darrow's questions. Why would a flood kill all the fish in the sea, since by and large they seem to respond rather well to water? Why, if day came before night, was it only a "day" ahead? How could there be evening and morning on the first three days of creation, since the sun wasn't created until the fourth day? Why would making the sun stand still lengthen a day, since the sun is always standing still? Bryan died a week after the trial from indigestion and coincidence.

In 1927 Sinclair Lewis published his "Preacher Book"—a vicious and unrelenting portrait of a con-man from Kansas named Elmer Gantry: slithering his way through Baptist preaching, revivalism, plagiarism, hypocrisy, sexual exploitation, and Methodist redemption, only to be conned himself by a church secretary, who allowed herself to be filled with the spirit *and* Elmer Gantry. Billy Sunday, the chief personal target of Lewis' book, found himself defensive and suddenly out of favor with mainstream America. Fundamentalism retreated to the rural catacombs.

In the period just after World War II—in our return to normalcy—America also returned to the old time religion. Billy Graham rose up on the power of mass evangelism and radio to call America to its "Hour of Decision." Then realizing the astounding power of "religious" TV—Bishop Fulton J. Sheen's

"Life Is Worth Living" telecast had replaced Milton Berle as the most popular prime time program—he allowed his evangelistic crusades to be televised. It was at the height of Graham's national influence that *Elmer Gantry* was made into a film.

What the Serpent Offers the Innocent

The real theological original sin is **literalism**. So says Spong in this assault on the numbing superficiality that cripples Christian intelligence.[127] He also writes as a former fundamentalist—now turned Anglicanized visionary—who has not lost his love for scripture. "A literalized myth is a doomed myth. Its truth cannot be rescued." Literalism is "nothing less than an enemy to faith in Jesus Christ."[128] Not to mention common sense. If Noah gathered all the animals of the world in that tiny boat, did that include kangaroos—which no one knew existed until centuries later when Australia was discovered? If Jesus' gravecloths were left in the tomb, did the resurrected Jesus wander around naked?

This is not abstract scholarship, written in the safe confines of academe. Bishop Spong works in the trenches, often among those predominantly oriented towards literalistic Christianity. And liberals, he warns, need not feel too smug about their own cavalier dismissal of the biblical heritage: "Fundamentalist Christians distort the Bible by taking it literally. Liberal Christians distort the Bible by not taking it seriously."[129]

The point of departure is clear: the Jesus story is evangelical mythology, constructed out of units of tradition—including both personal and communal memory—enabling the reader to see the "reality of God in Jesus."[130] Just as Wellhausen had said, the gospel is a *midrash*, suggesting the meaning of the Christ. The gospel writing is not a documentary, with some early home movies of Nazareth edited in with telecasts of the Sermon on the Mount.

The story has to start somewhere. Mark begins with the baptism. John with creation itself. Matthew and Luke decide that birth is not a bad place to open the narrative of the new Joshua: "The first building block in constructing the non-human Jesus of later Christian mythology...."[131] It is a magical world of virgin births, exotic visitors, cosmic singers, wicked kings, mystified husbands, astral displays, an infant messiah, and a woman who has become the queen of heaven.

Spong wants to re-enter that world at a new level of understanding that will help us all be born again—make that "empowered to serve God." Inspired and informed by Dr. Raymond Brown at Union Theological Seminary (*The Birth of the Messiah*) and Jane Schaberg of the University of Detroit (*The Illegitimacy of Jesus*)—as well as an earthly host of scholars from Harvard, Yale, and Oxford, Spong quite literally—pardon the word— becomes a wise man from the West, journeying to Bethlehem bearing the gift of insight. The birth stories are then read backwards as literary prolegomena to the Easter story: "From the Scandal of the Cross to the Scandal of the Crib".[132]

Whatever was intended by the birth stories, we have paid a price for them, including both patriarchal nonsense and virulent Gnosticism. There are treasures (in exquisite earthen vessels) that compensate, but we must be aware not only that ideas have consequences, but that mythologies may also be myths.

What do Fundamentalists Want?

What is at stake in these discussions? The fundamentalist fantasy is constructed with five desires that seriously challenge human freedom and the Christian faith itself.

Certainly Fundamentalists Want Certainty.

The fundamentalist mentality has an extremely low tolerance for ambiguity: what the Bible says ends the matter. We remember that innocent Bible School song:

> The B I B L E, Yes that's the Book for me,
> I stand alone on the Word of God, the B I B L E.

As Professor Albert Outler at Perkins School of Theology used to put it, fundamentalists exchange a **papal pope** for a **paper pope**. Evangelist Sam Jones once said that he would believe the Bible if it had reported that Jonah swallowed the fish. We have as much evidence that Jesus walked on water as that he walked on the land, he used to shout. This is why many evangelicals can be so confidently opposed to evolution, as well as the ordination of women. The Bible doesn't teach it and that is that. It's difficult to take this seriously, except that a majority of the American people seem to agree, Ralph Reed makes the cover of *Time*, and the State School Board of Kansas succeeds in demoting evolution from science to myth. This is 1999, not 1925. The Creation Science Institute of San Diego actually teaches that the Grand Canyon was formed in a matter of weeks—at the outside, months. Not from scientific evidence, of course, but from Genesis. What carved the world's greatest fossil record? The great flood. And the fossils of course came straight out of the ark—two million species carried about for six months, without a single excrement problem. I still wonder why Noah didn't slap one of the mosquitoes.

Who can resist calling Creation Science the ultimate oxymoron? But the fundamentalist endures (or ignores) such snide remarks simply because other books just don't provide the orgasm of the absolute. A Jewish college student commented on this exegetical glow:

I studied history in college. It's disillusioning because you discover history is what each author determines it is. But if you're studying the Torah and you believe strongly that the Torah is all truth from God—well, then you get a lot more pleasure out of it. [133]

W. A. Criswell's Baptist College in Dallas must specialize in exegetical ecstasy. Its faculty teaches that the earth is 6000 years old, the date chronicled backwards through the ages of the Biblical characters. We don't *need* geology when we have theology. One of Bryan's most famous line at the Scopes trial was exactly this: "I am not so interested in the Age of Rock as I am in the Rock of Ages."

I like this counting backwards idea. It can lead to exciting solutions for social problems. Take the problem of the aged. If we are generating the graying of America, think of the age of the patriarchs. Seven hundred, eight hundred years they were living—and more. Methuselah, the oldest man on biblical record, made it to nine hundred and sixty nine.

Now here is the interesting part of the backwards count strategy. Methuselah was Noah's grandfather. If we add up all those years and match them against Noah's age when the great flood hit, we see that he died in the exact year of the deluge. Yet his grandson, the captain of Operation Rescue, did not take the old man with the rest of the family. Why should he? The Ark was a youth movement—needing strong seed for replanting the earth. No use for ancient, desiccated relatives—who doubtless would have lobbied the new world for universal health care and insisted on ramps for the disabled (physically challenged) on the big boat itself. Solve the problem of the aged by the rising tide of republican maturity. Grandpa, go build your own boat. In the next flood, perhaps we can leave Criswell behind.

Fundamentalists often speak of reason, but the Bible is "Beyond Reason" (the title incidentally of a Pat Robertson book). Reason is the tool of faith, not its critic. And if scholarship gets in the way of certainty it is the scholarship which must be sacrificed. To some this is a step forward. In the old days, the scholars themselves got sacrificed. I remember biblical scholar John Trevor's reaction to the burning of the RSV in North Carolina in 1951, when some faithful fundamentalists discovered that his fellow scholars had translated *almah* as "young woman" instead of "virgin." "Well, we'd made some progress," he mused. "Now we burn the translation. We used to burn the translator."

Of course it must be said these days that Christian fundamentalism is rather benign compared to the Islamic version. The Muslims have carried allegiance to sacred text to the ultimate: the Qur'an is so literally the Word of Allah—who apparently speaks definitively only in Arabic—that it cannot be translated, much less be satirized. Salman Rushdie knew exactly what he was risking in having his Persian scribe—named Salman, for heaven's sake—play tricks on Muhammad by miswriting what the prophet dictated. Islamic attitudes towards the Qur'an are deadly serious—true believers having no sense of irony. In 1990, Sheikh Ahmed Ibrahim was released from 18 months in an Israeli prison. Married, with a four month old child, he had been jailed for terrorism—and was unrepentant:

> I am ready to kill and be killed myself in fighting the jihad—the holy war—because it is Allah's wish. Allah is a vengeful God. Jihad is a struggle between Right and Wrong, Justice and Injustice. Readiness to fight for God is a sacred matter. Killing for the jihad is a holy deed.
> The Koran says that there are only two ways: Allah's way or Satan's way. I chose Allah's way.[134]

Fundamentalism—east and west—is an exact science: you must get it right.

For my own part, I think the only book God ever wrote was the natural world. And I am quite prepared to treat that divine script reverently and stamp it "Holy." DNA may not be infallible, but reading its messages is miracle enough for me. In the beginning was the double helix.

Fundamentalists Want Traditional Values and Don't Mind Telling You So

Fundamentalists never liked the word "modern" applied to their doctrine. Falwell called his television program "The Old Time Gospel Hour," reminiscent of the Fuller Seminary program out of Pasadena in the early 1940's, "The Old Fashioned Revival Hour." The great enemy is called the "modernist," or, in the later phrase, "the secular humanist" (the liberal, the progressive, the socialist—they even seem to think Democrats are suspect). There is always this litany of referral to the founding fathers—two hundred years of godly history and that America is a Christian nation. Never mind that neither Franklin nor Jefferson were Christians: Franklin was suspicious of preachers—all except the Methodist George Whitefield, for whom he sponsored a tabernacle, which became the first building of the University of Pennsylvania [a statue of myopic Whitefield stands to this day in the entrance yard]. Jefferson took scissors and literally cut every miracle out of the gospels, from the Virgin Birth to the Resurrection, pasting the deistic digest remains together as *The Life and Morals of Jesus of Nazareth.* The publication of *The Five Gospels* in 1993 by the Jesus Seminar, seriously challenging any hope of literalism for biblical devotion, is dedicated to Jefferson.[135]

Burl Ives died just a few years ago. Forty years ago, I heard him in concert sing a folk hymn called "Forty Years Ago." The plaintive words wished for a return to childhood in "old camp meeting times"—when "old-fashioned people" sang Hallelujah rimes, calling the "mourners" to the wooden bench at the front of the brush arbor arena, calling for the Holy Ghost "to show the savior found." And when the choruses rose up to the throne of God, the pilgrims shouted out their thanks as they fell to their knees and the words poured out like the day of Pentecost itself:

> Oh praise the Lord I'm glad to see we're coming back again—
> The Holy Ghost is here tonight—so let us say Amen!
> New-fashioned ways we don't approve—though some may call us slow:
> We like the good old-fashioned ways of Forty Years Ago.

And we don't want any neurotic Greek revising the old, old story, retelling the last temptations in modernist sociology either.

For All Their Talk of Freedom, Fundamentalists Want Uniformity

Fundamentalists don't trust differences. We ought to remember Procrustes. The old outlaw tied all his victims on a bed and those that were too long were cut to size, those too short got stretched out to fit. Procrustes must have been a TV evangelist. All must have the Same Truth, the Same Morals. This is—let's name it directly—Fascist. *Fasces* was literally a bundle of rods with an axe bound into the middle, a symbol of tribal authority. So fascists have always worshiped central control and uniforms: uniform clothes, uniform creeds, uniform racial markings. It was no accident that the Moral Majority supported heavy military spending and lifted up Ollie North as an American hero. Tolerance has the smell of treason on it.

And intolerance has the smell of blood on it. We have a vivid reminder in Niebuhr's newspaper of the lust for procrustean atonement by the fascist mentality. Singapore judgment decreed that an eighteen-year old American citizen named Michael Fay living there must be flogged for spray painting a car. The flogging was to be carried out by a martial arts expert, wielding a yard-long rattan cane, for six strokes—dipped in a chemical that would ensure absolute pain, split skin, profuse loss of blood, and scarring for life if used with appropriate vengeance on Fay's bare buttocks.

What was America's popular response to this sentence? By letters and polls, our citizens favored the flogging by two to one. In San Francisco, a phone-in poll of nearly four thousand registered 74 % in favor of flaying out Michael Fay's blood. A man in Fay's home-town of Dayton, Ohio, said that he'd be glad to administer the whipping himself. Cane the lawbreakers here, the taggers, the looters, the druggies, the litterers, the insolent. Whip asses and watch Beavis and Butthead flush right down the drain.

Stephie Salter wrote a wrenching piece about all this law and order mania in America. She called this "It's a Grand Old Flog" – a vicious pun lashing

America's blood lust "in the name of a cleaner, safer, nicer U. S," and satirizing this mania by calling for the television networks to carry the caning in prime time. Think of the deterrent effect, she says, as permissive America swells the ratings with macabre curiosity. We could actually watch Fay being stripped and buckled into the leather belt which mercifully would protect him from real bodily harm [those internal organs and that lower back]. And the sight of arms and legs fixed to the cross-frame stand should hold us for the discipline we applaud:

> With screams as soundtrack, we can watch each lash land, his flesh open and his red American blood flow to atone for a nation's sins. [136]

I've been to Singapore. The streets are safe and the city immaculate. Its economy makes it one of the four tigers of Asia and the buses run on schedule. That's what uniformity is all about. Fascists always make the trains run on time, and the factories hum, and the chips calculate. Disorder is evil. Why did the Romans crucify people? They ran an empire safe from pirates, with wonderful roads, and an efficient mail service. What more could anyone want? Deviation brought instant deterrence: the wheels of authority ran smoothly on the blood of dissidents.

Should religious dissidents be encouraged? The blood atonement fundamentalists don't think so. The fight to mandate school prayer is not designed to please the Muslims, not designed so that Nichiren Shoshu Buddhists may chant *Namu Myoho Renge Kyo* in the classroom. Fundamentalists are *not* primarily interested in freedom of religion, but in *correct* belief. But beware. Censorship may be only another word for uniformity.

They Openly Advocate Patriarchy

Fundamentalists pick up lots of sympathy because they support the family, but this family support translated into being anti-ERA, anti-abortion, and proudly patriarchal. The key text on the family is Ephesians 5:21-33, where is it plain that the husband is the head of the wife, just as Christ is the head of the church. The family structure, as Pat Robertson explained it during his campaign, is like a corporation: a hierarchy moving down from God as owner of the company, to husband as chairman of the Board, to wife as executive assistant to the chair, to children as workers in the plant.

The conservative antidote to feminism was Marabel Morgan's *The Total Woman*, where she outlined several strategies with which women can assume their rightful place in life as wives, mothers, and lovers—all based on the testosteronic Biblical principle that women are servants of men in the same way that men are servants of God. Any woman wondering what her purpose in life is need not worry another second: your job as a woman is to keep your man happy, whatever that takes—including imaginative sexual favors. Don't be ordinary, Marabel tells you. Spice up his life. Next time he comes home from work, greet him at the door dressed only in Saran Wrap. He'll heat up faster than the microwave.

It must work. Marabel's first seminar group of women were wives of the Miami Dolphin football team. That next season the Dolphins went 17 and zero, and, through 1999, the only perfect record in the history of the NFL. The patriarchal moral: if women treat men right, the men can—and will—perform.

Feminist Karen Brown suggests that the varieties of fundamentalism world-wide are "extreme responses to the failed promise of Enlightenment rationalism."[137] It is "the religion of the stressed and the disoriented." Brown thinks that fundamentalism is the retreat of those who were "seduced and betrayed" by the rationalistic promise: we can actually comprehend and therefore control our world. The failure of the modern world (bureaucratic politics, scientism, industrialized imprisonment) is seen as reason enough to reject it, though the habits of mind that world spawned ("clarity, certitude, and control") are continued in the return to "forty years ago."

Brown grasps the central issue: what has to be controlled above all else is the flesh. The body contains energies inaccessible to consciousness, impervious to commandments, inhospitable to uniformity. The body, as Murphy put it, is the locus of extraordinary powers, which lie below choice, and which, if released, can produce altered states and "miraculous" human moments. Brown narrows this sensibility: the agenda in rejecting modernism *must* include the subjugation of women, because they remind us unrelentingly of the mysteries of the organism: "This characteristic ensures that fundamentalism will always involve the control of women...."[138]

This sheds new light on the anti-abortion campaign of the New Right and the fundamentalists. This campaign really has nothing to do with belief in the authority of the Bible. The Bible *nowhere* specifically forbids either abortion or birth control. To do this, we must think of the fetus as a person, so that abortion becomes murder—and that *is* against the decalogue [See note on Exodus 21]. This interpretation—this effort to conceive of conception as personhood—is, to many,... inconceivable. The fetus is potentially a person, but so are the egg and sperm, and no one, to my knowledge, has suggested that masturbation is murder. Bad for the complexion, the eyes [my glasses need changing], the lungs, the back of the hands, and fairly messy, but not infinitely foul. You don't want pregnancy, so where do you draw the line? Mt. Athos? The nunnery? Oral sex? Outercourse? Incantations? Crocodile dung? Six weeks? Twelve weeks? Abortion is clearly a form of birth control, a retroactive condom, a rhythm system for the off-beat, a way of saying "no" after you have said "yes"—and saying **no** after you have screamed **NO**.

What is at stake is power, as Wilhelm Reich pointed out in *The Mass Psychology of Fascism.* Rush Limbaugh borrowed the catchy word "feminazi" to caricature certain women's movement leaders. Camille Paglia applauds, and, probably, so do most men. As the old saying goes, no man with four aces wants a re-deal. For many women, playing the game, that meant a full house.

Fundamentalists Think Power Has Been Granted to Them by God

Bakker and Swaggart and an endless line of Elmer Gantrys got caught with their pants down, but their real lust was not for Jessica or Debbie or a nubile church choir director. What such men seem to want is power. They find that in some way they are attractive to people, from the saccharine confidence of Pat Robertson, to the good old boy organizational ability of Falwell, to the cuddly adolescence of Bakker, to the virile country Western demagoguery of Swaggart.[139] And once they taste their power over those people there is no turning back. Why should anyone be surprised when evangelists and public figures of power—including priests and presidents and speakers of the house—are caught in sexual exploitation? Every speaking occasion is either a seduction or a rape: to take a crowd and mold them to your will, to manipulate them into a state where they will surrender all.[140] Of course Jimmy Swaggart didn't want to pay Debbie the going price for prostitution. His whole career was based on the proposition that the people should pay *him* for the privilege of being brought to ecstasy. Surrender is the name of the game. Give me your life, your belief system, your will, your reason, your bank account. And why not throw in your body while you're at it?

Power spills over everywhere. Look how it works. God is all powerful. He is the Father of Jesus, his only Son our Savior, who gives to us the Power in the Blood. We are called to put on the whole armor of God and fight against the powers of this world. Christians can't be pacifists and peace mongers: when a strong man is armed, his goods are in peace, says Jesus. "Stand Up, Stand Up for Jesus," for God and for God's Country. We alone stand against the forces of darkness, the godless Communists [still over a billion left!], the Middle East terrorists, the secular humanists, the liberals, and the impotent men who have no sexual power with women.

It translates so easily: God's power becomes military power, strong defense budget, no nuclear freeze, no pacifism (never mind the admonitions about killing in the scripture—just don't kill your own people). This is Chuck Norris theology, Rambo redemption, and America loves it, as any member of the Michigan Militia will tell you.

It translates perfectly into capitalism. Make no mistake about this: fundamentalism is financial power. They even have a theology for it, called the "word of reciprocity." On channel 37—the local Christian Broadcasting Station—I listen to the 700 Club hosts and their ilk [Rev. John Hagee, etc.] equate God and mammon: despite what Jesus said to the rich young ruler, the windows of heaven will open and pour wealth upon us. You can't outgive

God, says Criswell, and he follows it with the capitalistic clincher: there is nothing particularly Christian about being poor. As Bakker told Fletcher: God wants us to enjoy heaven right here on earth—which, ironically, is Bakker coming close to the truth.[141]

It translates perfectly into Numbers. Even Acts in the New Testament is full of numbers. The book of early Christian evangelism is punctuated by the passages that read: "And the Lord added to their number day by day" (Acts 2:47b). Power over a *few* isn't power. We must reach everyone or Jesus can't come back. This need is made to order in our time for politics and media, mass evangelism, radio TV, computers, and satellites dishing out the gospel world wide. This is the new style of missionary journey, and every convert is a vote of confidence in the evangelists' method and message.[142]

The final depth of the scandal created by our evangelical friends was not greed, not lust for power, or sexual indiscretion. It was the failure to be fundamental enough. The full gospel is simply not being preached by the fundamentalists: the gospel of freedom, love, and justice. By *freedom* I mean enhancement of human choice. Let's be clear about this once for all: to be born again means to multiply our possibilities—not paralyze them. Jesus did not say, "I am the Darkness of the world." He *opened* eyes, healed the blind, widened out the choices for using our talents. *Love* means non-exploitive affection, where we use things instead of each other. Love means vulnerability and tentative empathy with natural life: love for the world, not escape from it. *Justice* means the social incarnation of freedom and love—the distribution of fair and equal possibilities for human fulfillment, not manipulation for selfish privilege.

What is so fundamentally wrong with fundamentalism is that it is so fundamentally wrong. The gospel is richer, deeper, more inclusive, and so much more beyond our grasp, than the tele-evangelists would have us believe. How ironic that even the best of the evangelicals use the future's technology to harness us to the past, to suppress our imagination, to repress our possibilities, to restrict our spiritual growth, with a excluding gospel that repeats the words but denies the spiritual power. The real scandal of TV evangelism is not moral indiscretion, or even shameless greed, but bad theology.

What the tele-prophets would take from us is not our money, or our virtue, but our Lord—who had no wealth, no power in government, no army, not even a place to lay his head (much less a mansion on the bayou), who trudged a tiny, dusty corner of the earth with a few friends, saying softly, "Blessed are the poor," and "By this shall all men know that you are my disciples, if you have love one for another."

And just in case anyone should think that the grace of God could be bought or exploited, he also said: "It is my Father's good pleasure to *give* you the Kingdom." Print that in **red.**

THE GOSPEL ACCORDING TO KAZANTZAKIS: TEMPTATION

I first read Kazantzakis' novel *The Last Temptation of Christ* in graduate school in the early sixties—it was published in English translation in 1960. We all knew of three temptations, which Jesus has succeeded in sloughing off with a combination of superior wit and knowledge of Scripture—unfair I thought, for the gospels to call these *temptations*, since it was clear that he couldn't have fallen (being God) and therefore wasn't really tempted. The whole gospel story always suffered from this problem: if everything was pre-ordained to be the way it was, then where was the story—the real conflict and resolution? A divine Jesus could have no genuinely human personality: no anxieties, no hostilities, no strange bodily functions, no surprises. *That* was the problem: no *surprises.* The greatest story ever told came out the same way every time. The good news had nothing new. No wonder the church bathrobe dramas were so dull, not to mention the films on the life of Christ. The passion play had no passion in it.

Kazantzakis' novel about Jesus carried a stunning theological theme: Jesus was a *man,* struggling with great faults, a paranoid, guilt ridden dreamer, a man who lusted after Mary Magdalene, who resisted the vocation of Messiah so desperately that he left Jerusalem before the Jews and the Romans could kill him, married and live happily almost ever after in Bethany—with darling little Jesuses all around him. Mary of course has tempted more than one author.[143] Edward Wagenknecht calls our attention to the "fascination which the courtesan exercises over the imagination of men," but adds that there is nothing in the gospels to indicate that she was ever a woman of bad character.

> Tradition identifies her, quite unbiblically, with the woman who was a sinner and who anointed the feet of Jesus as He sat at meat in the house of Simon the Leper, and sometimes also with Mary the sister of Martha and Lazarus. The error is universal, and it is probably much too late in the day to do anything about it. [144]

The same applies, I think, to any efforts to "correct" the life of Jesus as presented in the gospels. Biblical scholars may color-code and demythologize the historical Jesus, but they will succeed at the price of closing down the church itself. The moment the people cease believing Jesus is divine in a miraculous sense, the moment the story they have come to accept as the greatest is fundamentally retold as a human tale, in that moment we shall see the death of the Christian community. Christianity did not take over the planet because Jesus said nice things about little children and gamboled among the lilies of the field. Paul Cho's Church in Seoul does not fill with two hundred thousand people every Sunday to hear that the cross was another heart-rending example of how a good man can bear pain. Catholics go to mass because the priests can put God in their mouths, and nobody in Virginia Beach would read Leviticus if they suspected that the Lord God Himself had not inspired every word. Kazantzakis has it nailed—so to speak—in Paul's encounter with the aging Jesus, where Paul's version of the crucified Savior renders the real Jesus not only unknowable, but unimpressive. The common people would not believe even the man from Nazareth himself if he does not conform to the image of the Christ of faith conjured up by the story, now fixed forever between the covers of the sacred book. They need the **Christ**, not the **man**; the Speaker, not the speech; the Idea, not the reality; the Comfort, not the demand; the Word, not the words; the Savior, not the challenge.[145]

Of course, the married Christ turned out to be a dream, an occurrence at Owl Creek Golgotha. But at the very least Kazantzakis made the old story fresh. Everyone's Christ has Sunday love, companions, and a modulated voice rolling over the multitudes, but Kazantzakis' Christ had sweat, mistakes, sexuality, and surprise.

Kazantzakis' Jesus was also divine, but not as a kind of cosmic cheap shot. In the novel there was no parthenogenesis (Matthew, constantly scribbling notes of the life of his master, invents this), no walking on the water (Peter dreams the famous miracle), and no risen Lord appearing to anybody (Jesus' last word on the cross is the last word in the book). Jesus heals, but seems surprised at his own power, and when his power is focused on the supreme miracle of the raising of Lazarus, the resurrection is frightening and incomplete. Lazarus is still covered with earth, smells of decay, with worms crawling over his body, his legs and arms swollen and green, and grass in his hair.[146] The miracle is an ambiguous affirmation of power, Lazarus an awful specter, which Barabbas attempts to slaughter in the name of the Zealot cause against the Romans. His knife slices and finds no blood, and in macabre hysteria he seizes the rotting man and snaps him in two like a fallen branch. It is for this murder that Barabbas is imprisoned, awaiting the word of release at the Passover paroxysm.

Jesus becomes Lazarus. In the famous dream sequence, he lives at the home of Mary and Martha as their "brother" husband, takes his name—even begins to look like him.[147] As Jesus grows old, he is more and more precisely described as the "earth-man," as the second Adam, as the humus one: made of earth. As hum-an. Lazarus is raised from the grave only to die again, as all nature dies and is reborn to die. The whole world, Kazantzakis tells us, is the rotting Lazarus.[148]

Is this our final destiny? Kazantzakis' answers with a resurrection of his own: a work of art. The novel itself is a kind of Lazarus, created out of human sensuous experience, given transitory life by human imagination: one life while it is being written, another while it is being read. But words are not fixed. They are all translations of the spirit, incarnations of the spirit, which blows where it will to give life and death.

Anguish in Galilee

"A cool, heavenly breeze took possession of him." This is the way Kazantzakis opens his drama of the messianic hope in all of us. He then creates thirty three chapters as symbolic of the life of Christ, shaping the work as a circle by opening and closing the drama with dream sequences, dividing the entire work into three parts of eleven chapters, each melded together by the *winds* of the Holy Land. The wind, biblically, is metaphor: the Spirit blows where it will, and we are born again.

The strange tale is told: the claws of nightmare as Jesus resists his destiny, the cross-making carpentry, the prophetic crucifixion of the Zealot, the visit to Magdala. Jesus spends the night in Magdalene's house, moves toward her in the morning light and whispers her name, only to be alarmed by the sound of his own voice and rising desire, then moving off toward the monastery in the desert. We experience the death of old Simeon in the desert monastery, the bonding with Judas, and birth of Jesus' mission to speak to the world.

The Early Ministry

As Jesus begins to find his destiny, there is "a warm, damp wind today which lifted large waves on the lake of Gennesaret." The ministry is inaugurated by the apocryphal defense of the adulterous Magdalene. There follows the halting story-telling that grows imperceptibly into an infuriating sermon on the mount, the multiplication of followers, the discussion of the nature of freedom and the aims of discipleship between Judas and Jesus, and the wedding feast, where Jesus and his disciples dance—and the Magdalene feels virginal again.[149]

Jesus' nausea in the Temple at Jerusalem precipitates a bizarre encounter with John the Baptist.[150] The three temptations in the wilderness are presented just outside the circle Jesus draws to host the tempting visions: the serpent woman [who completely suggests the last temptation on the cross], the lion of power, and the dazzling light of divinity. [151]

Afterwards, an exhausted Jesus is refreshed by Mary and Martha in Bethany, foreshadowing his dream life with them after Magdalene's murder. The news of John's death shifts Jesus' message from love to the axe, and leads to the riot at Nazareth—with the consequent decision to preach fire, rather than love.

The Journey to Jerusalem

"The north wind had blown and pushed it toward the south," as the disciples gather in Capernaum just before they push south to Judea. The important (and inevitable) raising of Lazarus[152] sets the context for the explanation to Judas that Jesus must die. Holy Week unfolds: the triumphal entry, the cleansing of the temple, the killing of Lazarus, the Passover Supper, the night in Gethsemane, the betrayal Peter's denial, the appearance before Pilate.

So we are brought to the *Via Dolorosa* and the crucifixion, [153] where Kazantzakis does not allow this moment of heroic agony to be shared by other condemned men. Then at last the famous dream sequence marriage to Mary Magdalene, the return to the reality and final victory of the cross.

The blasphemous suggestion that Jesus might have been a family man—and performed acts appropriate to impregnating a wife—is not new. The non-canonical *Gospel of Philip* clearly portrays the Savior as a sexual being.

> And the companion of the [Saviour was] Mary Magdalene. He loved her more than all the disciples [and used to] kiss her often on her [mouth]. The rest of the disciples [were offended and] said to him: "Why do you love her more than all of us?" [154]

D. H. Lawrence's sensuous handed resurrection whimsy in *The Man Who Died* gives us a Jesus "swooning" on the cross, and, after staggering out of the tomb, is massaged back into manly condition by an "Egyptian" priestess—who announces triumphantly that "He is Risen." Barbara Thiering's reconstruction of the gospels (*Jesus the Man*) tells us rather matter-of-factly that the "account of the marriage of Jesus with Mary Magdalene lies very close to the surface of the gospel narratives." [155] The Magdalene is apparently the nameless woman who pours ointment from an alabaster flask over his feet and erotically caresses him with her hair. Thiering further comments that this is obviously a reference to the Song of Solomon where the maiden pours out her fragrance on the king—a wedding liturgy in the Davidic tradition.[156] Joseph Lewis in 1925 wrote a indictment of this sacred "pornography" entitled *The Bible Unmasked,* in which he sketched in the woman's lascivious motions, and told all mothers of young children to hide the Bible from their innocent eyes.

So the idea that Jesus was married to Mary Magdalene was no pure invention by Kazantzakis, though he safely encases it in hallucination. In reading the novel it is no problem to understand Jesus' marriage to Mary Magdalene and subsequent relationship to Mary and Martha as a dream. Jesus faints in the midst of his agonizing memory of Psalm 22: "Eli...Eli...," and, after the vision, returns to consciousness long enough to complete the cry, "...Lama Sabacthani!" The vision is introduced by a guardian angel with green wings, who seems quite capable of whisking Jesus through the air, folding him in a wing, and even transforming himself into a little servant boy who will unobtrusively look after Jesus during his tenure as a family man. In the transition from crucifixion to earthly paradise, the cross simply becomes a blossoming tree stretching from earth to heaven, with thirty-three birds in its branches singing out their joy at the son of Mary's thirty-three years.

The novel ends with Jesus' "wild, indomitable joy" as he realizes that he has not betrayed his mission of sacrifice. The central question remains: did Kazantzakis illumine the gospel of Christ?

The Newest Revised Version

What Kazantzakis discovered is that the gospels are imaginative stories, constructed out of pieces of tradition, and woven together by a series of artists called evangelists. The gospels are profound fiction, attempting to evoke something of the power of the actual historic presence of one Jesus of Nazareth. This does *not* mean that the writings are untrue, only that they are not true as literal historical records.

What the Gospel proclaims as true is this: Jesus is not primarily a teacher, but an event, an experience. The event is that Jesus—as his name implies—is our savior. But salvation from what? What can it possibly mean that he is a sacrifice for us? He saves us from sin, so the records say, and therefore we must decide what sin is, in order to know precisely what we are saved from. Each Gospel seems different on this crucial—quite literally *crucial*—point.

In Mark sin is the inability *to recognize* the meaning of the event. In Matthew sin is the inability *to love* the community in which the event takes place. In Luke it is the inability *to include* the very world that made the event possible. In John sin is the inability *to receive* the event as that power which made the world.

In the gospel according to Kazantzakis, sin is the inability *to choose* the very freedom which *is* the event. In the gospel according to Scorsese, sin is the inability *to imagine* the divine-human event as struggle.

In each Gospel, the central theme is Duality: symbolized by the words Divine and Human. Each holds somehow that Jesus was both, but they hold this in slightly different ways. In Mark, Jesus is the Son of Man, an apocalyptic figure of great wonder (*wunder*). He is more divine than human—for here his humanity is a mystery mask for his divine status. In Matthew, Jesus is the King of the Jews, a new Moses, giving out a new law of love and care for the despised. He is more evenly human and divine, with the emphasis falling slightly on the human, by virtue of his lineage in the Hebraic heritage. In Luke, Jesus is the Savior of the World, attractive to Jews and Gentiles, men and women, powerful and poor. He is evenly human and divine, with the emphasis falling rather winsomely on his divinity, since he must, after all, ascend into the heavens to influence all the earth. In John, Jesus is the Son of God, the blasphemous enemy of the Jews. He is theologically human—but only to make the point that he is the cosmic lamb of God through whom all things were made. The hallmark of John's Jesus is his divinity. His humanity is a metaphor for his divine power.

In *The Last Temptation of Christ*, Jesus is the Son of Mary, the tortured Nazarene dreamer, whose Oedipal struggle focuses the divine—human duality as the battle between flesh and spirit, body and soul, pleasure and martyrdom, woman and man. Human life is the conflict between earth and heaven, where woman calls us to remain earth bound and God calls us to pure immateriality—to pure spirit—to our destiny as human beings. This is our curse: to be condemned to ascend from matter to consciousness. God is therefore the crucifier of the flesh. To be truly human is to transcend our animal ancestry, our mud, and take the wings of imagination—that is to choose freedom. The body calls us to necessity. The spirit calls us to unlimited possibility. We must be like the flying fish painted at Knossos, leaping out of necessity into freedom. The great temptations seduce us into seeding the earth rather than transforming into God himself.

But the last temptation is the most seductive of all, and the most tragic. It is the temptation to deny our animal ancestry and allow our bodies to be sacrificed in the name of immortality: a bodiless, unearthly life that is totally spirit—and therefore dissolves the tension between imagination and sensuous life. In our Christian culture, it is the yielding to this temptation that we often ironically label Virtue.

Jesus, then, is all of us: human *and* divine. He is not Zorba the Christ, as Andrew Greeley suggests.[157] Zorba was the life force, pure unbridled sensual energy, but he was not in the least in anguish over the conflict of the sensual life with the creative imagination. Our lives are the struggle of being both and want-ing desperately to be one and not the other. The ironic heart of our human lives is death, which we must embrace as part of our humanness—and not as an escape from it. And if there is no Messiah to relieve us of the terrible burden of living out this struggle, we will create one.

The Scandal of the Saviors of God

For Kazantzakis, human life is an evolutionary struggle in which matter gives birth to God, not the other way round.[158] The center of our spiritual lives is this struggle, this search, this ascent from the primordial to the spiritual. The Eucharist is Evolution: the transubstantiation of the body. It is not Jesus who saves us; it is Jesus who saves God by becoming free of the body. The body is not evil, as in Gnosticism, but it is transitory, and Kazantzakis locates the experience of salvation in the midst of that transitory struggle. The "bloody tracks" of the Christ are the tracks of all men who embody the "élan vital," men who are the "Bodyguards of the Odyssey":[159] Moses, Buddha, Alexander the Great, Muhammad, Dante, Don Quixote, El Greco, Lenin, Odysseus, Zorba, and Jesus of Nazareth.

If there is only one woman with different faces, as the guardian angel in the last temptation dream tells Jesus, there is only one man—one Hero, who feels authority on a mountain, who finds the still point under the Bo-Tree, who hears the voice of the Archangel in a cave, who drops through the Devil's anus into hell, who decides for Knighthood out of caste, who burnishes light on Toledo, who galvanizes the Proletariat, who is bored by a peaceful Ithaca, who unbuckles his belt and goes looking for trouble. He is the One who mounts his cross as the final fiction of accomplishment.

That, of course, is what is finished: the idea that life can be fixed, ideologies set in stone, Christ photographed for all eternity. Kazantzakis has not given us an orthodox Christ, and by this much, both the Greek Orthodox Church and the American religious right are correct.

But what on earth do any of us need with an orthodox Jesus? As I recall, the Jesus of the Gospels was crucified for sedition, blasphemy, and heresy. Yesterday in churches across the world, Jesus lived and died, but tomorrow he will be resurrected in a fresh aesthetic moment. In the beginning was the imagination.

The Last Temptation of Christ is a sustained attack on the Gnostic reading of the gospels, and has stimulated a redemptive rethinking of Christology in America. The flesh of Jesus is taken seriously, and, for a moment, we really do behold a kind of glory.

THE HERESY OF BELIEF: SPONTANEITY

Why doesn't the good news seem new? Why does the Church forever seem intent on being old? I know God is supposed to be the Ancient of Days, but wasn't she ever young and restless? At least Joseph Smith showed a little imagination by inventing another testament, telling us that "God" was actually a man who made love to a real woman—who was also a god.

One attends rituals that conspire against surprise, as if spontaneity might somehow hint that the universe is not predictable. I always liked the Hindu idea that when the gods created the world, they were just playing. An imaginative historian suggested that the difference between the two great adversaries in the sixteenth century Protestant reformation was that the Pope was a hedgehog and Luther was a fox. Authority vs. Innovation—and innovation won.

Now a new fox is on the loose, moving from Roman Catholic to Protestant, and ironically bearing the name of an ancient sacred authority. The setting for this "loosening" was San Francisco, the sacred city for creative deviance: "Matthew Fox, avant-garde priest defrocked by the Vatican for his free-spirited theology, will become an Episcopal priest and begin a high-tech, high decibel 'Rave Mass' this year in the basement of Grace Cathedral." As Don Lattin reported it, Fox had visited a group of "unorthodox" Anglicans in England and was inspired to create a rock and roll liturgy [in the same spirit as culture Christian experiments with jazz masses of yesteryear]. These new inflections of worship—hot gospel for libidinous youth—were called "Rave in the Nave," with all the "rites" and privileges thereof: "ear-shattering sounds" from the bands, "mouth-opening women" dancing about in bikinis, "eye-opening message" pulsating on monitors enjoining the faithful to "Eat God." Said the Rev. Alan Jones, dean of Grace Cathedral, the seat of the Episcopal Diocese of California: "I'm grateful it's in the basement."[160]

Orthodoxy is a right wing noun. Quite literally. *Ortho* means "right" and *doceo* to "teach." Every religious institution is stamped at its base TC—theologically correct: made in the center of authority. The body must have some standards of health, some limits of behavior, some frontiers it must not cross.

Heresy is a left wing verb. *Herein* means to walk in the direction of chaos, copulating with disorder and breeding off the center. Heresy lives at the limits of the civilized, tempts responsibility toward license, suggests novelty to tradition. Heresy makes a vocation out of trespassing.

But heresy and orthodoxy are mirror twins. They reflect each other in precise irony: limits are always invented, borders convenient fiction, and order the greatest fantasy of them all. The heretical Jacob succeeds the orthodox Esau, and is transformed from deceiver into patriarch. History is the frame we build around the twins' mirror dance with each other. My opposite is myself.

Luther never intended to become a heretic. But he did want to be free from his father in Saxony and *ipso facto* in Rome.[161] Calvin never intended to found a Church. He was only restoring the original righteousness of an institution fallen into the ruins of original sin. The revolting peasants in Germany found out how quickly new orthodox fences could be erected by their heroic heretic, and Calvinism now conjures up self-righteousness, witch hunts, and emotional rigor mortis. Henry the VIII was lauded by the Pope as *Defender of the Faith* in 1536, and ten years later was the self appointed head of a whole new arm of Christendom—which now embraces the newest heretic on the block.

So it was with considerable caution that I read about the defrocking of Matthew Fox. As a priest of the Dominican order, Fox developed an international reputation for living on the edge of orthodoxy. He wrote a manifesto against the doctrine of original sin, entitled *Original Blessing,* and mined the church tradition for sensuous spirituality in *The Coming of the Cosmic Christ.* He founded the Institute for Culture and Creation Spirituality, housed in Oakland's Holy Names College, and publishes a bimonthly magazine blending Christian doctrine, eco-mysticism, arts therapy, radical politics, goddess worship, and that peculiar ambiance of corporeal Catholicism which exudes from the cathedral.

Fox was being tutored as an Anglican and scheduled to be ordained in the fall of 1994. Episcopal Bishop William Swing wanted to set everyone's conservative mind at ease over this event, saying that Fox's "understanding of Jesus Christ is both orthodox and biblical." Fox, sagely observed the Bishop, was just attempting to translate the Christian revelation into a language not spoken much in traditional circles. Familiar with the controversial career of John Spong, Fox was sure that there would be "elbow room" in the historic middle way.

Look what they've done about ordaining women, about maintaining a balance of lay and clerical decision-making. On issues of birth control or married priests, they have not hid their heads in the sand. [162]

Fox wants to appeal to the young, who live inside the rhythms of rock, and whose drive for *experience* leads them to designer drugs such as "Ecstasy." "You can go drugs, or you can go religion, go transcendence, go for spiritual power of community and ritual." On a countdown to 2000, the road from Rome winds safely through the middle way, and this latest flight to contemporaneity has received—how shall I say it?—rave reviews.[163]

The echoes of this appeal reaches far back of the nineties right into the Great Anglican Awakening of the sixties: to John Robinson's *Honest to God,* Malcolm Boyd's *Are You Running With Me, Jesus?*, and James Pike. Pike, most of us remember, was the Episcopal Bishop of San Francisco, who systematically denied every orthodox doctrine he could find, shed his wife of many years for a secretary of many days, communicated with the dead, played with poltergeist, got himself actually tried for heresy, and was certain that the real Jesus was in a jar in a Qumran cave. Perhaps in that December ordination for Matthew Fox, James Pike hovered near the holy hill, if the shade of the Grace Cathedral heretic ever found its way back from the wilderness at the Dead Sea, where Pike disappeared forever looking for the truth.

Bishop Pike is not the only Anglican who suspected that Qumran was sacred space. Barbara Thiering, the Australian scholar and teacher at the University of Sydney, absolutely knows it is. And not only did she not disappear in that wilderness, she has brought it to the attention of the world in the most bizarre interpretation ever written about Jesus, published as *Jesus the Man: A New Interpretation from the Dead Sea Scrolls.*[164] A consequent television documentary displayed her convoluted angle of vision, entitled *The Riddle of the Dead Sea Scrolls* (James Mitchell producing and Rowan Ayers writing the script). The film was shown in Australia, Great Britain, and the United States, and the intense reaction it evoked was recorded by Dr. Leonie Star, under the title *The Dead Sea Scrolls: The Riddle Debated* (ABC Books, 1991). [165]

Thiering's *Jesus* is not just heretical—but on the verge of hysterical. The riddle at the Dead Sea was created to solve a problem: the authors of the Scrolls thought that all the prophecies of the Hebrew scriptures were being fulfilled, but that their community (which was supposed to be *the* fulfillment) didn't seem to fit the prophecy. The answer: the people were taking the scriptures too literally. It seems that the prophets had been given a *secret* revelation in *code,* and the words of scripture must be interpreted by the key to the code—which was in the exclusive possession of the Qumran community.

Now the Hebrew word for *interpretation* is *pesher,* [166] and Thiering quickly lets us know how the pesher technique works. A scroll writer begins with an Old Testament book, for example Habakkuk—dealing with events around 600 B.C. [the Babylonian armies invading Judea, spreading terror in their path], and works through it verse by verse. After each passage the writer adds: "Its pesher is…," explaining that the passage is really a scriptural flash forward, not about 600 at all. The Babylonians aren't Babylonians but stand for "Kittim"—meaning Romans! The passage is referring to the Roman army *now* marching across the land, "inspiring fear and terror." The word *pesher* is also used in the Old Testament to mean "interpretation of dreams"—as gifted men such as Joseph or Daniel "discover the hidden meaning" of that Rorschach sleep of old.

> In simpler terms, the pesher is like a solution to a puzzle. A rough anal-
> ogy might be the solution to a cryptic crossword. The clues do not look as if
> they make sense, but anyone who knows the technique and has the neces-
> sary knowledge can solve the puzzle.[167]

Her solution makes Kazantzakis look like Cardinal Ratzinger. Among other special readings, Jesus was married to Mary Magdalene, had two daughters and a son, divorced her, and married a lady named Lydia. Acts (Chapter 16) tell us that she was a seller of purple and that the Lord opened her heart to listen to Paul, after which she became a female bishop. Thiering interprets "opened her heart" to mean that she fell in love with Jesus, ended her virginal status, and became his second wife. He was not crucified in Jerusalem, but at Qumran—which was a kind of Dead Sea imaginary model of the Holy City. And Jesus actually did not die but [Passover Plot-like] was drugged and "buried" in a cave along with the two "thieves"—who turn out to be Judas Iscariot and Simon Magus. Simon (the very one who later showed up in Samaria in the book of Acts and was converted by Philip) apparently had some magical/medical knowledge, and gave the antidote (cleverly mixed together from the spices left in the tomb by the women) to the drug Jesus had taken on the cross. Energized by this medicinal resurrection, Jesus made his way to Rome, where he died just short of his seventieth birthday.

Now that—possessors of the pesher secret decoder—is *really* a crossword puzzle. There must be something in the blue lifts around the Salt Sea that inspires novelty, although the river that slices the great trench from Galilee runs downhill past Jericho and stops dead.

CHAPTER THREE

THE RIVER THAT RUNS UPHILL:
THE BODY AS SPIRIT

EINSTEIN HELD A LONG-TERM VISION: THERE IS NOTHING IN THE WORLD EXCEPT
CURVED EMPTY SPACE. GEOMETRY BENT ONE WAY HERE DESCRIBES GRAVITA-
TION. RIPPLED ANOTHER WAY SOMEWHERE ELSE IT MANIFESTS ALL THE QUALI-
TIES OF AN ELECTROMAGNETIC WAVE. EXCITED AT STILL ANOTHER PLACE, THE
MAGIC MATERIAL THAT IS SPACE SHOWS ITSELF TO BE A PARTICLE. THERE IS
NOTHING THAT IS FOREIGN AND "PHYSICAL" IMMERSED IN SPACE.

JOHN A. WHEELER

I WILL TELL YOU SOMETHING. YOU KNOW WHAT SPACE IS. THERE IS SPACE IN
THIS ROOM. THE DISTANCE BETWEEN HERE AND YOUR HOSTEL, BETWEEN THE
BRIDGE AND YOUR HOME, BETWEEN THE BANK OF THE RIVER AND THE OTHER—
ALL THAT IS SPACE. NOW, IS THERE ALSO SPACE IN YOUR MIND? OR IS IT SO
CROWDED THAT THERE IS NO SPACE AT ALL? IF YOUR MIND HAS SPACE, THEN IN
THAT SPACE THERE IS SILENCE—AND FROM THAT SILENCE EVERYTHING ELSE
COMES, FOR THEN YOU CAN LISTEN, YOU CAN PAY ATTENTION WITHOUT RESIS-
TANCE. THAT IS WHY IT IS VERY IMPORTANT TO HAVE SPACE IN YOUR MIND. IF
THE MIND IS NOT OVERCROWDED, NOT CEASELESSLY OCCUPIED, THEN IT CAN LIS-
TEN TO THAT DOG BARKING, TO THE SOUND OF A TRAIN CROSSING THE DISTANT
BRIDGE, AND ALSO BE FULLY AWARE OF WHAT IS BEING SAID BY A PERSON TALK-
ING HERE. THEN THE MIND IS A LIVING THING, IT IS NOT DEAD.

J. KRISHNAMURTI

POETS CANNOT KILL; THEY DIE. METAPHYSICS CANNOT DIE; IT KILLS.

JAMES CARSE

In 1893, Frederick Jackson Turner read a paper to the American Historical Association at Washington, D. C. called "The Significance of the Frontier
in American History." His thesis was simply that the character of our people
was essentially formed by that advancing frontier. Americans were spacious
in spirit like the sky, curious, possessed of a grasp of material things, restless
and rugged like the land, loyally individual, fiercely free. Now the frontier
had been pushed to its geographic limits, and perhaps, with it, our character
was also fixed.[168]

Of course, both our frontier and our character have changed, even though Turner's thesis has been immortalized for non-historians in the mythic movies of John Ford and John Wayne. The twentieth century, exhausted by a thirty-year world war, transformed by the insidious new martial arts—chemistry in World War I and physics in World War II—brought us unimagined new worlds. Freudian psychology sent us into subterranean psychic adventures of feeling and volition. Einsteinian physics sent us into cosmic atomic adventures to explore four-dimensional worlds of light and relativity. John Kennedy announced our full commitment to send an American to the moon—and proudly called his political vision "the new frontier."

But new frontier was too bucolic, too flat a phrase. It was as if we were enacting Edwin Abbot's romance of many dimensions: 1776 was *lineland* (one basic thrust of political independence); 1893 was the last full charting of *flatland* (wide on industrial development and long on manifest destiny); 1969 was *spaceland* (intersecting planes of privileged power pierced by ethnic and aesthetic revolution).

In 1971, William Irwin Thompson wrote a manifesto for the new age containing speculations on the transformation of American individualism into a radically planetary culture. A century ago, we were at the edge of California. Now we were at the edge of history itself. New dimensions were everywhere breaking through: "The painting has spilled over its edges to involve the whole environment. Music has spilled out of the orchestra to involve the body in configurations of light and color."[169]

And now we have begun to "involve the body" in virtual reality: from close encounters and star treks to "new Expanses" of intellects ''Creating space." Those intellects are legion enough: Newton and absolute space, Kant and Euclidean space, Einstein and curved space, Berger and brain space. Pure space has expanded: phase space. linear space, Banach space, vector space, Riemannian space, sample space, flight space, psychedelic space, oriented space—and cyberspace. The universe is much larger than we thought.

Martin Heidegger sensed what was coming. He is famous as the philosopher who connected being with time and therefore saw that both thought and reality must change. As Being intersects Time, it becomes an Is—a "Being-There" in existential space.[170]

In existential space, the body *must* be affirmed as *body*—not as symbol, or shell, or disposable instrument of personality. Lawrence Durrell in *Spirit of Place* has a lethal indictment of his namesake in Arabia: "But…what a disgusting little thing he was….What a little neuter, ripping and goring his body because he loathed it so."[171]

But, in the same passage, he praises Henry Miller to the clear Grecian sky, commenting that Miller may "shake you a bit on the physical side" if you do not know "every inch of physical passion" and if "your experience in the world of the body" is too limited. Experience explodes in Miller's *Black Spring*: celebratory, outrageous prose about the physical space of the body—

including the famous panegyric for European toilets and the invocation for a purity of literature, "where dung is dung" and cunts are not all "prettied up."[172]

Where does Miller finds such purity in literature? Steinbeck? Joyce? The unexpurgated Mark Twain or some underground porno classic? Look no further than the sacred volume of forgotten lore anchoring the family table:

> The Bible a la King James for example. The King James version was created by a race of bone-crushers. It revives the primitive mysteries, revives rape, murder, incest, revives epilepsy, sadism, megalomania, revives demons, angels, dragons, leviathans, revives magic, exorcism, contagion, incantation, revives fratricide, regicide, patricide, suicide, revives hypnotism, anarchism, somnambulism, revives the song, the dance, the act, revives the mantic, the chthonian, the arcane, the mysterious, revives the power, the evil, and the glory that is God. [173]

This writing itself has a physicality about it—something uncompromisingly corporeal—as if to say, take your human space seriously, ecstatically, and leave nothing out. Miller's writing has armpits and buttocks. His whole life was dedicated to awakening us from the "air-conditioned nightmare"— that civilizing insulation from ourselves.

The truth is that *all* writing has a physicality about it—the word is not only made flesh, but makes flesh different. Maya Angelou tells us that language invades her body, digs under her skin, registers in her bones and organs. One could almost monitor metaphors in her system—take linguistic blood pressure. And bad language, I think, would be more dangerous to her *physically* than high cholesterol.

Edmond Jabès has given this point *gender*: "Words are bodies whose members are letters. Their sex is always a vowel." [174] Authors know that writing and articulation create a "violent, rebellious, sexual, analogical" world, in which the words themselves search for fulfillment in a kingdom of truth: "The changing nuances, the fine and shaded colorations of the feminine vowels are married to the consonants which outline the masculine structure of the vocable." [175]

Gaston Bachelard, in analytic reverie, will later confess that he even sexualizes concept and image, claiming masculine for the first and feminine for the second—and adds the strange statement that between the two there can be no synthesis. One would have thought, Bachelard being French, that at the very least copulative verbs might provide an embrace. But no. Concepts generate in the mind; images in the soul. They are on different planes in the spiritual life. He even goes so far as to suggest that it would be a good idea to stir up "a rivalry between conceptual and imaginative activity."

Even so, writing is an adventure in discovery of the hidden sensuousness, the interior sonority, sometimes muffled by audibility—where diphthongs are heard differently underneath the pen:

> One hears them with their sounds divorced. Is this suffering? Is it a new voluptuousness? Who will tell us the painful delights which the poet finds by slipping a hiatus into the very heart of the word? Listen to the sufferings of a line by Mallarmé where each hemistich has its conflict between vowels: *"Pour ouir dans la chair pleurer le diamant"* (To hear in its flesh the diamond crying). The diamond breaks into three pieces revealing the fragility of its name. [176]

THE CHILDHOOD OF PERSONAL SPACE: LIMITS

Our text breaks apart into that most existential of all spaces, what William Blake called the "Visions In new Expanses," and, according to "wondrous human imagination," tracks the "Three Regions immense/ of Childhood, Manhood & Old Age."[177] Who can guess what Blake meant? I mean *psychological* space: the development of personal integrity, sexual identity, and final commitment.

The concept of personal space is recognized by two different groups in America. One is the behavioral scientists, who owe a large debt to Edward Hall and Robert Sommer. Hall, building on the work of H. Hediger with territorial behavior in animals, analyzes the "personal distance" in human behavior that acts as "an invisible bubble" around the personality. Proxemics (Hall's name for this kind of research) purports to study this distance cross-culturally, and the last third of *The Human Dimension* is concerned with questions such as why Arabs like to converse at a closer range than do Americans, or why the French feel insulted when people do not look at them directly.[178]

Sommer, at the University of California at Davis, published a book entitled *Personal Space: The Behavioral Basis of Design*. It was the record of his experiments with behavioral modification through the arrangements of rooms—the placement of chairs around a table in the college library, for example, to observe just how close one student could sit to another and still be ignored. Sommer's phrase for studies of this kind was "the axiology of space."[179] "Personal Space," wrote Sommer, refers to an area with invisible boundaries surrounding a person's body into which intruders may not come."[180] The way to locate these boundaries is to keep moving until someone complains [which every Texas man on the make already knew].

One of the most invasive in this series of space reports was *Too Close for Comfort: The Psychology of Crowding Behavior* by Paul A. Insel and Henry Clay Lindgren.[181] It proves at least one thing: social scientists are certainly ingenious in rooting out the primal facts of behavior. Insel and Lindgren recall an inventive researcher named Dennis Middlemist who set up his observation in a men's lavatory in order to analyze men's behavior at the urinal.

There were three urinals in the washroom, which made it possible for them to observe the behavior of unsuspecting subjects under the conditions of crowdedness: alone, in the company of urinal-user two spaces away, and in the company of a user at the adjacent urinal. The investigators manipulated the degree to which a subject's personal space was invaded by employing a confederate to stand at the appropriate urinal and at the same time placing washing equipment in the basin of the other urinal and hanging an "Out of order" sign on it.[182]

Middlemist and company could have worked for "Candid Camera." But this is science.

An observer concealed in a toilet stall, using a periscope that permitted him to observe the subject's lower torso, employed a stop watch to time the unzipping of each subject's fly, the initiation of the stream of urine, and the cessation of the process. [183]

The results of this breathless research were compiled in what I can only call a peeping tome. Middlemist—I'm not making this up—found that the closer someone stood to a given subject, the longer the subject took to start urinating. Elimination, apparently, creates an autonomic private space on this crowded planet. The toilet is a sanctuary of sorts. Think of that tower in Saxony.[184] The imagination moves from urination to defecation. If only the pope had not put a spiritual periscope on Luther, and crowded him in the Wittenberg tower privy, we might have been spared the Protestant Reformation and the Wars of Religion.

The second group to recognize and in fact celebrate personal space is the new consciousness experiments that Tom Wolfe terms "The Third Great Awakening." When the decade of the revolutionary sixties died at the Yale University non-riot, the movement—as it was cryptically known—was resurrected bodily with multiple appearances all over our promised land as the new consciousness. Kennedy's new frontier was dreary stuff compared to this psycho-theological explosion: ESP, ECK (Eckankar), TSK (Time, Space, and Knowledge with Tarthang Tulku), psychic cults, the Church of Satan (Anton LaVey), psychokinesis, UFOs, Noetic Sciences, Jesus People, Moonies, the charismatic movement, pentecostalism, Esalen, Lindisfarne (William Thompson), Arica, Scientology, New World Family, the Harrad experiments, Walden III, Don Juan and the separate reality, Maharishi Mahesh Yogi and transcendental meditation, polarity therapy and message, TA, primal scream therapy, Guru Maharaj Ji and the Divine Light Mission, Rinpoche and Vipassana West. The real journey to Ixtlan was from social consciousness to inner peace and your personal power spot. Wolfe, with bemused anger, also dubbed it the "Me Decade."[185]

By far the slickest personal space marketing in this explosion was EST (Erhard Seminar Training), and Wolfe, incidentally, used an EST training experience as the key to the very character of present American life. The object, clearly stated, was to allow the awareness that your decisional life cannot be granted to you from the outside, but must be assumed by you from the inside. Werner Erhard, nee Jack Rosenfield, called this "transformation."

> To explain it (and it can't really be explained), you could say that transformation is a shift in the definition of locus of the self from content to context, from identifying one's self as point of view, story, personality, body, and so on, to recognize one's self as the context in which all things occur. It's not an event; it's a context for events to occur in a space.[186]

EST's purpose was "to create the space in which you can understand your self in context." Erhard wanted us to create the story of our lives rather than be the story. Personal space—by this training—is what we see when we get clear.

So, let us assume that we are awake, latter-day Millerites, Werner clear, and therefore unashamedly physical. How do we know ourselves to be spatial? We think we are bodies, but *where* are the thoughts of our being physical?

In our Western culture, the historical answer has been that mental events occur in an imaginary space we have created for their residence. As B. L. Whorf suggests, thoughts must exist in some kind of space if we assume that everything resides within a "four-dimensional space."[187] This assumption is the basis of the so-called mind-body problem that has mystified us since Plato and Aristotle. Many thinkers, deeply suspicious of Plato's essences—or their own misreading of Plato's "essences"—that define human ultimateness (yet are unwilling to acknowledge the somatic life as absolute), have offered special distinctions to assuage their ambivalence about spirit and flesh, thought and matter. H. Richard Niebuhr, for example, has distinguished inner and outer history in *The Meaning of Revelation*, and Kant has distinguished phenomenal and noumenal worlds in *Critique of Pure Reason*. Popular recognition of this ambivalence was offered by the entire inner game industry: inner tennis (Gallwey), inner skiing (Kriegel), inner exercise (Miller), inner running (Rohe). Endless inners. All the world is still waiting for the book on *Zen and the Art of Behavioral Modification*: Inner Skinner.

The irony is that mind-versus-body is a self-inflicted problem, since it only arises by conceiving of mind as existing in space and searching for a spatial relation between matter and mind. Jean Paul Sartre understood this a generation ago as another way to state the Cartesian problem. If we consider the body as a neurological-chemical-physiological complex limned out by certain laws—a thing among other things, and consciousness as some kind of interiority, then connection between the two becomes impossible. The reason is clear: it becomes an effort to unite consciousness with the "body-of-the-Other" rather than with my body. As Richard Zaner sums up Sartre's position:

My own body as it is for me cannot be apprehended in sensuous perception like other physical things, including the body of the Other. I do not sense my skeleton, my brain, my nerve-endings, and the like; and even coenesthetic, proprioceptive, and kinaesthetic data are not apprehended by me as *objects*. [188]

What is clear is that we do not experience our own bodies as things among other things in the midst of the world. J. H. Van Den Berg, in an article entitled "The Human Body and the Significance of Human Movement,"[189] refers to the telling experiment which showed that only one out of ten persons—even after being told that his hands would appear—recognizes his *own* hands in a series of photographs of hands.[190] Our objectified body seems strange to us, as if it is not really us—which of course it isn't. We cannot see ourselves seeing or touch ourselves touching. As Sartre puts it:

Can I not see and touch my hand while it is touching? But then I shall be assuming the point of view of the Other with regard to my senses...[and] seeing eyes-as-objects....[191]

Gabriel Marcel labels this the problem of the "outside."[192] Whatever do we mean by saying that something is "outside" of us—truly external? Obviously, we construct such an object, and yet, we also "think" it independent of our perception. The link between the inside (me) and the outside (it) is my "consciousness," and the "datum common to my consciousness, and to other possible consciousnesses, is my body."[193] Sartre's "Other" and Marcel's "Outside" are both outlined by sensuous perception—objective and "real." Sartre's "Interiority" and Marcel's "body qua mine" point to a mysterious separation between different kinds of spaces, which somehow is supposed to be bridged by this "consciousness." My body is not merely a larder of chemicals— though it *is* that. It is also—and principally—*mine*.

Is this the best we can do?

Ralph Berger, a University of California biologist, has reminded us that there are other ways of thinking about thoughts—without either lapsing into mysticism or reducing mind to an epiphenomenon of the body. He calls his approach "psyclosis," which is defined as the fundamental "circularity of experience." [194]

The experience of space, writes Berger, is primarily dependent upon visual perception. "The visually experienced boundary of the body is correlated with much but not all of the somatosensorily experienced field of the body."[195]

Much, not all. There is an area in the body that is "devoid of sensation," and that is the brain itself. In fact, "direct stimulation of the brain" produces no experience of the brain. Brain space, despite intruding electrodes, trauma, or disease, is not itself directly experienced. It is our study of *other* human and animal brains that lead us to suspect that we might have one of our own. As far as experience goes, the concept of empty heads is absolutely literal; we have "a lacuna within our spatial world."

Our mind-body confusion arises, says Berger, when we attempt to localize an individual's thoughts spatially within his body or brain. The brain may be necessary for thinking, but thoughts themselves are not in our brain space. It is rather like a battery and electricity. The battery, we think, stores electricity, but this is only a metaphor. There literally is no electricity in a disconnected battery. Only when there is a conducting medium between the terminals of the battery does electricity, if you like, *become* present; then it "pervades the entire system," including the connectors, and is "not located solely in the battery."

Metaphorically, the brain is the source of consciousness (mind, thought), but consciousness is manifest only when the brain is connected—that is, existing in an interrelated physical environment. "Thoughts originate from perceptions, and there is no possibility they can be localized in any space other than that which is the perceptual experience itself—which is to say they have no *locus* at all."[196] The ghost of Descartes still haunts the physiological psychologist and needs to be exorcised by a visit to Dharamsala, Australia,— or especially Arizona.

The Hopi, in Arizona's Monument Valley, are instructively "non-Western." They apparently do not distinguish between thought and matter in our dualistic way. Thought, they say, touches everything: like light, it pervades the universe. For the Hopi, thought of a tree engages the tree, encounters the tree itself and not merely a mental image of the tree. *We* deal in surrogates. Our whole created imaginary space is filled with thoughts of actually existing trees and people. We are voyeurs peeping into our own lives, as Miller knew. But the Hopi thought-world has no imaginary space, and must therefore locate thought about space in real space—which is to say, in existential space. Space and thought pervade each other precisely the way battery and electricity do.

Berger's thesis, then, is quite clear. Brain space is the "portal of consciousness," not its "container." It is this environmental view of physical space—call it ecological space—that allows us to come to terms with time. Time is the name we give to the achievement of difference, and ecological space is simply room in which to be different.

We can see time and difference *both* in the Grand Canyon, and a grand metaphor flows out of the canyon by looking carefully at what the river does to rock. A group of neuroscientists did just this, rafting down the Colorado with naturalists, anthropologists, and professional boatmen over a period of years—from 1975 to 1982, all the while observing, reacting, and talking about every subject in the cosmos.

William Calvin, neurobiologist at the University of Washington, then spent three years writing and rewriting a five hundred page account of those trips—condensing it into a single two-week journey through space and time. At Day 5/ Mile 82, while rethinking the classical laws of thermodynamics spiced with a dash of Chuang Tzu Taoism, Calvin noticed that the river channel narrowed significantly due to the rise of harder rock—granite intruding up through the metamorphic schist. Since the same amount of water must pass each second, the river is deeper and faster, with swirls created in the current. Professional skill is required to keep the boat going forward, since the swirls turn into back eddies—and would, in fact, carry it back upriver.

Calvin tells us that, in theory, at least, there might not be any path at all down river if the current drove deep enough below the surface, leaving only eddies going backward. The river then would appear to run against gravity. Thus the title of this incredible piece of writing: *The River That Flows Uphill*. The double entendre is intellectually erotic: the evolutionary river has carried its passengers from big bang to big brain.

> Ever seen a river flow uphill? Go down to the bottom of the Grand Canyon and stand on the shore, downstream of one of those big rapids on the Colorado River. A grand sweep of water flows back upstream.
>
> Evolution, too, seems like a river that flows uphill, hoisting itself by it own bootstraps to ever-fancier innovations. The attainment of DNA, of cell, of sex, of brains—they're the waterfalls of the uphill river, ascent amid turbulence.

Language and consciousness are the most recent and mysterious of these "uphill waterfalls," and may be the brain circuits' spare-time innovations for such specialized skills as throwing and musical ability. Idle hands may please the devil, but our sequencing brain cells are "God's" workshop.

> New uses for old things—that means that some skills are unearned gifts. They arrive without instruction manuals. We're still trying to figure out our storytelling consciousness, perhaps bootstrapping ourselves up to yet another serendipitous surprise as we explore the beneficent bonus. I've always liked the way that Tom Robbins phrased it: "Our great human adventure is the evolution of consciousness. We are in this life to enlarge the soul and light up the brain." [197]

So the result, if not the purpose, of evolution is the human brain, the most complicated organ in the universe—*naturally* as far as we know. And yet, studies of just how that brain works have only just begun. Concerning the phenomenon of vision, Francis Crick—who has browsed in the library of DNA as much as any living being—has this to say on the current readings of the brain:

Another thing I discovered was that although much is known about the behavior of neurons in many parts of the visual system (at least in monkeys), nobody has any clear idea how we actually see anything at all. This unhappy state of affairs is usually never mentioned to students of the subject. [198]

Of course neuroscientists know something about our cerebral cortex processing motion, shape, position in space, color, etc., but not how the brain puts this together. And this isn't the only area not talked about to the students.

I also discovered that there was another aspect of the subject one was not supposed to mention. This was consciousness. Indeed an interest in the subject was usually taken as a sign of approaching senility. This taboo surprised me very much. [199]

It was not just the neurophysiologists who "disliked" the subject—it was also true, Crick tells us, of psychophysicists and cognitive scientists. In fact seminars meeting at UCSD psychology department in the late eighties could scarcely come up with a consensus as to what the problem was, much less solve it. With his Nobel Prize safely guarding his reputation for un-senile behavior, Crick says straight out that he thinks that consciousness is likely to "involve a special neural mechanism," most likely distributed over the hippocampus and many areas of the cortex, and thus open to experiment.

In some ways, the brain is a computer, an organic neural net that stores memory of the firing patterns of its neurons—and can replicate an entire pattern with a small part of any one pattern. So much work is being done in artificial intelligence and it seems a good candidate for the leading edge in psychology.[200]

Two problems face neural net models of the brain. The first is designing parallel computers with modifiable connections acting with anything like the speed of the human brain. And the second is what Crick terms "a mechanism of attention." Attention, he writes, is "likely to be a *serial* process working on top of the highly parallel PDP processes."[201] These problems are also made more difficult by the fact that neuroscience lies in the existential space between science (researchers working directly on the brain), engineering (researchers working with artificial intelligence), and mathematics (modern Platonists who grow intoxicated developing relationships between abstract entities). The difficulty is essential. As the neuroscientists like to say: if the brain were simpler, we couldn't understand it.

This, I would guess, is the field of the future, and the center of it is molecular psychology: the delicate interference with the consciousness system and exquisitely recorded alteration effects. Crick asks us to consider the meaning of the word "recently." In classical studies "recently" means within the last generation. In neurobiology and psychology it means within a couple of years ago. In molecular biology it means last week.

Recently—a couple of years ago—Harvard University gathered scholars from their own ranks for a Mind, Brain, and Behavior Interfaculty Initiative, including such diverse participants as Gerald Fischbach [professor of neurobiology at Harvard Medical School], Michael Jensen [professor of business administration], and Lawrence Sullivan [director of the Center for the Study of World Religions].[202] The MBB (the inevitable Initiative Initials) developed as part of President Rudenstine's "crisis themes" for university research—the other four being children's education, ethics, the environment, and health care. Just as neuroanatomists have mapped the cortex, so this group would map "the human mind"—and unscrew this inscrutable: "Can love and hate, ecstasy and despair, really be the result of nerve cells passing molecules back and forth?"

Recently—a generation ago—Lewis Thomas wrote the devotional text for this incredible adventure:

> You start out as a single cell derived from the coupling of a sperm and an egg, this divides into two, then four, then eight, and so on, and at a certain stage there emerges a single cell which will have as all its progeny the human brain. The mere existence of that cell should be one of the great astonishments of the earth.[203]

Rudolph Otto would have understood. This is the astonishment—the *wunder*, the wonder, the mysterium tremendum—we feel in the midst of the space where God is. To say it anatomically, the heart of a religion of the body is the brain. And Richard Restak (*The Brain)* assures us that we have three separate, intimately interconnected "brains": Reptilian, Paleomammalian, and Neomammalian.[204] Not exactly theological, but trinitarian to the cortex.

Think Digital

Heidegger named it, Thompson timed it, Crick identified it, Harvard discusses it, but Steve Williams animates it—or generates it. Williams is, at forty or so, the chief computer-graphics animator for George Lucas' company, Industrial Light and Magic in Mill Valley. He is the genius who resurrected the dinosaurs in *Jurassic Park* after sixty five million years, a considerable challenge to Lazarus for miracle status. [205] The aside about Lazarus is no joke. Williams' brain—interfaced with other digital prophets—has now given birth to a radical and frightening possibility for bringing people back to life. Forget Terminator 2 or Indiana Jones. In the cradle of the twenty-first century, it will be possible to re-create any human being for which we have images. Humphrey Bogart could be digitally duplicated and made to move, speak, and act exactly as Bogart would were he alive and in his prime. Only he isn't limited to doing what he did—he could be given new lines to say, and actually star in a new film. Already, Marlon Brando is on database in three-dimensional form, and one can only hope that it is the *Waterfront* Brando and not the Graf Zeppelin of *Apocalypse Now*.

Williams, who built a Tyrannosaurus Rex and T-1000, says we have the technology to make the skin and hair right now—and it's just a matter of money and will to do the rest. Soon, governments will be able to create "live" television coverage of "actual" acts of war—an American president, for example, shown on Iraqi television:

> He could be shown beating a digital Saddam Hussein, lured into meeting, a voice over might say, by hopes of a peaceful settlement. The rage of the Iraqis can be imagined. Or write your own scenario. [206]

It's difficult enough right now telling truth from fiction in the media—incidentally the timely premise of the 1997 satire on presidential misdirection, *Wag the Dog*. In the future it will be impossible.

And while we are bringing other bodies back to life, we are losing our own. Already, Williams tells us, kids are coming into the company who have never cut wood, or thrown a football. They've grown up staring into a computer window and now create a reality which robs them of their own, including carpal tunnel syndrome from working on keyboards. *Where* is Mary Shelley when you need her?

Williams' work is the stuff of popular culture studies, but if we want to get a grasp on the philosophical dimensions of cyberspace, then we might turn to Michael Heim's *Metaphysics of Virtual Reality*. The connections are embedded in the opening epigraph, a quotation from John Dewey's preface to F. M. Alexander's *The Resurrection of the Body*:

> In the present state of the world, the control we have of physical energies, heat, light, electricity, etc., without control over the use of ourselves is a perilous affair. Without control of ourselves, our use of other things is blind.[207]

And Myron Krueger's *Foreword*—he's an inventor of virtual reality systems—carries the warning much deeper. Virtual reality—defined as an electronic reality with which one can *interact*—is not just another technology. Since we become completely absorbed in this new world, "virtual reality constitutes a new form of human experience"—which may be *more* important than film, theater, or literature. The Gutenberg Galaxy has given way to the Electronic Universe: the sacred texts are now the hyper texts—"nonlinear, free-association format" incorporated into multi-media.

Krueger poses the most interesting of questions for this study. The new information society does not disassociate the mind from the environment in contemplation—one thinks of Augustine seated before a blank sheet of paper or Heidegger bent over a wooden desk in his mountain retreat—and then re-enter with insight ready for the printing press. Virtual reality changes—in the most fundamental way—our relationship to information

> It is the first intellectual technology that permits active use of the body in the search for knowledge. Does this imply the death of abstract symbols and with it the demise of the sedentary intellect? Or will we invent new three-dimensional, colored, animated symbols that will interact with us rather than wait passively for us to read them? Will this rejoining of the mind and the body create a new breed of intellectual? [208]

The point is plain. Canonical philosophical questions are simply no longer academic. Thompson is correct: the future of the planet depends on a melding of mysticism with technology. Michael Murphy's work is interesting, not just because he loves the 49ers or lusts to run a six minute mile at the age of fifty something, and itches to hear athletes describe their extraordinary experiences—such as jumping out of the solar system. The "future of the body" *is* the future. What is reality? What is existence? Who am I? Says Krueger: "These are aesthetic issues with engineering consequences." [209]

Heim is concerned about the transformation of the human body into digital omnipotence. As our attention is more and more focused on our cognitive and invented worlds, we become trapped in our cybersystems—seduced by the telepresence of the transmitted scene, pulling the user away from "the internal bioenergies that run our primary body." The interface which we control—even when interacting with a world out of control—may "warp our visual imagination." [210]

Gibson, in fact, calls cyberspace "an infinite cage."[211] In *this* cage, apparently, the bird sings gladly—more than content to stay in the prison he has constructed for himself. We learn to think of ourselves as if we were appearing on some kind of television, our lives a video game in which we have entered the screen—rather like going through the looking glass into a playful world invented by a gentle mathematician, whose work world was filled with people he couldn't control.

Heim thinks that, involved as we are in these images, we are finding it difficult to become aware of our own internal states. The "attention"—so prized in Zen and Murphy's extraordinary athletes—is carrying us away from the body that is born for attention. The interface created subsumes the minds of those who have created it: we have fallen in love with ourselves, while our love alienates us from that which loves. **Narcissus in cyberspace.**

There must be an answer to this increasing danger of losing touch with ourselves as our brains play with space. Heim finds it among the wise men from the East. He is both practitioner and a teacher of Tai Chi Chuan, and points to Taoism as a way of holding on to the human side of the hypertext heaven:

> The Taoists urge us to contact our inner physical organs, to "see our liver," "smell" our lungs, and "taste" our heart. By this they mean something

quite simple. They mean not to lose the acute sensitivity to our bodies, the simplest kinds of awareness like kinesthetic body movement, organic discomfort, and propriosensory activities like breathing, balance, and shifting weight. The loss of such simple inner states may seem trivial. Taken as a whole, however, this awareness constitutes the background of the psychic life of the individual. "The body is the temple of the spirit."[212]

Taoists—and anybody who has read a line of the literature of health and wholeness rolling off the press since Alan Watts discovered God in a waterfall—know that the outer body houses a subtle body which can be energized through meditation, uniting the autonomic nervous system to conscious life, bringing outer and inner into harmony. Heim is now a metaphysician of Virtual Reality, a Tai Chi master of cyberspace. His son calls him a Techno-Taoist. [213]

THE ADULTHOOD OF SEXUAL SPACE: DIFFERENCE

The second psychological region is "manhood," that stark recognition of who I am as a sexual being. But it is not of men so much that I want to write just now. It is the shape of women.

That subject read differently to my mother than it does to Germaine Greer. My mother lived to be ninety-three and, well past ninety, still maintained her weight and figure from the time she married. She exercised yogi-like every day, touched no fried foods, rose early in the morning to challenge the birds for figs in our back yard, and mixed together a delicious diet of brewer's yeast, blackstrap molasses, wheat germ, and yogurt. She had to be the inspiration for Groucho Marx's diet doggerel:

> Blackstrap molasses and the wheat germ bread,
> Makes you feel so good that you wish you were dead;
> You add a little yogurt and you feel well fed
> On the blackstrap molasses and the wheat germ bread.

Greer is another case. She, too, is interested in breasts and buttocks, bones, hair, and the "wicked womb," and she echoes Merleau-Ponty when she says that "whatever else we are or may pretend to be we are certainly our bodies."[214] And when she and Jim Haynes published a newspaper in London named *Suck*—the progenitor of the *Screw* genre—full of pictures of voracious thighs, moist lips, and tremulous tumescence, one was sorely tempted to think that bodies were all we were.

But Greer's manifesto *The Female Eunuch* sought to enlarge and reform woman's sexual space and marshal ultimate sales resistance to what she called "the psychological sell." The traditional-marriage sales pitch was, like all successful evangelism, the strategy of a simple idea: Women are designed for *Kinder*, *Küche*, and *Kirche*.[215]

Much of Western tradition supports this view, from God's ability to create without a female partner in Genesis to Marabel Morgan's saran-wrapped submission in Florida to the charming and subtle patronization of William F. Buckley, Jr. But Greer wanted to skewer another intellectual who should know better: "Erik Erikson invented the lunatic concept of an *inner space* in a woman's somatic design, a hole in the head, as it were, which harbors the commitment to take care of children." [216]

Erikson, fresh from diagnosing Luther's constipation and Gandhi's truth, was unrepentant. From the original *Daedalus* article, "Inner and Outer Space, Reflections and Womanhood," to its rewrite in *Identity, Youth, and Crisis,* [217] he softly insisted that the female psychosocial role was fundamentally oriented by her reproductive cavity, the "productive inner-bodily space set in the center of female form."[218] He defended Freud's correction of Napoleon. Anatomy *is* destiny. And his famous study supporting this defense was of three hundred boys and girls in Berkeley, observed over a two-year period constructing toy sets and scenes for make-believe motion pictures. Once Erikson was able to get them involved, "certain properties" guided them. and he concluded that "among these properties the spatial one was dominant." The girls' dominant configuration in the constructions was interior (people or animals enclosed while the boys built walls with protrusions and high towers (people and cars moving outside enclosures). "The differences themselves were so simple that at first they seemed a matter of course. History in the meantime has offered a slogan for it: the girls emphasized inner and the boys outer space." [219]

Is this lunatic? Greer is not the only feminist who thought so. Betty Friedan practically frothed at the mouth when Ashley Montagu chirped about "the natural superiority of women" or when some intellectual patronizingly suggested that women ought to have an orgasm while mopping the kitchen floor. Francine du Plessix Gray, author of *Lovers and Tyrants*, married and mother of two, describes women as "the only exploited group who are always being flattered into powerlessness." [220]

But the question stands. Is this inner-space interpretation lunatic? Erikson, I think, made too much of sexual differences, but he at least was unafraid to take the actual body seriously as a clue to cultural values—not what they are, but what they ought to be. Human beings, he reminds us, not only have bodies, they are somebody. That somebody is not an abstraction to be defined in a vacuum, but must be seen ecologically. If there are new insights to be gained without a body, Erikson has come to that space. He died May 12, 1994.

Are women "cunts"? Yes, that is part of what they are. Is that vagina a wound where evolution atrophied a penis into a clitoris and dwarfed the female's potential as a person, so that she must forever envy men, and by her hostility earn immortality as that "pernicious rib"? That *is* lunacy, and Erikson said so. Sexual space has to be emptied of gender politics (ERA was a given, not an agenda item) and researched with all the organs of perceptions-existential. This would include Berger's "brain space" as sexually differentiated—which in *Cyclosis* seems almost clinically unisexual. Dr. Jere Levy, professor of psychology at the University of Chicago, has done considerable research on the gender difference in human brains. She reports, for example, that more men than women take jobs as architects and engineers—not because of social discrimination, but because of the ways in which the brains are organized.[221] Ken Wilbur, transpersonal psychologist, accepts the different structures and biological functions of the male and female body—even to the innate wiring that actually produces the stereotypical behavior we associate with gender specificity (male: aggressive, unemotional; female non-aggressive, emotional). Wilbur also thinks we can transcend the body *and* these differences.[222]

These and many other "findings" based on serious study of the actual body have to take the place of the diatribes of both the sexists and the feminists. Existential space is that corporeal moment when we experience the mutuality of our differences. It is also that moment in which we experience our differences as identity.

Journey to Anamnesis

One woman's existential journey is both sensitive to tradition, and deeply suggestive to one who likes to make connections. It is Jean Shinoda Bolen's *Crossing to Avalon*.[223] Well known for her mythic-Jungian approach to psychiatry (*The Tao of Psychology, Goddesses in Everywoman*), Bolen's book is an account of her pilgrimage to various European "sacred" spaces—a trip offered to her by a friend at a time of deep personal stress in her marriage, at the crisis age of fifty. The geographical journey took her to a Dutch castle in the Netherlands [to meet the Dalai Lama], to Chartres Cathedral in France [to walk the labyrinth and sense the Earth-oriented Goddess tradition underneath the Christian tradition], to Wearyall Hill near Glastonberry in England [the legendary site where Joseph of Arimathea and entourage came ashore after sailing from the Holy Land—"weary all"], to Findhorn and Iona and Lindisfarne in Scotland [vortexes of spiritual power—the latter two literal islands of "holiness"].

Avalon is that mythic isle which is the home of the Priestesses of the Goddess—for Bolen the "archetypal otherworld and a mother realm."[224] Crossing over to that "island" recapitulates the story of the quest for the Holy Grail: King Arthur's Round Table, a mystic vision of the Grail, the knight Perceval, the Fisher King, and the "errand into the wilderness" to find the healing cup.

But the familiar Arthurian Grail stories were written by men [Chretien de Troyes (1180), Robert de Barron (1190), and Wolfram von Eschenback

(1207)]. Writes non-male Bolen: "The legends came out of a masculine, patriarchal, and Christian time and culture."[225] The three main knights (the ones that actually find the Grail) at the Table represent the three ways of approaching the mystery: Galahad (the way of the Spirit—direct communion with the godhead), Perceval (the way of the Heart—the hard road to self-realization), and Bors (the way of the Mind—contemplating from a distance). There are other versions of the stories, variations which are filled with Celtic and Greek mythology, Tibetan and Egyptian ideas—hundreds of pagan influences. And King Arthur tales are told differently when these pagan ideas are feminine.

The Cup now is obviously a female symbol: a concave vessel holding the blood of life. The Quest becomes the male search for union with female regenerative power—which is the primal communion. The Grail appears at Camelot at Pentecost [the power of the Spirit is earthly harvest], and vanishes—inspiring the Knights to their quest. The Grail appears at Camelot, and is clearly the cup of the Goddess—who acts through Arthur's half-sister: "Morgaine...lifted the cup between her hands, seeing it glow like a great sparkling jewel, a ruby, a living, beating heart pulsing between her hands...."[226] What was left out of the three masculine approaches is now entered in: the experience of spiritual mystery through the body. Bolen's therapeutic journey has taken her to the shrine of Woman:

> That the sacred can be experienced through the body is everywhere denied by patriarchal religions. For the body to be considered holy once again, the Goddess (the feminine aspect of Deity) must return, for it is only through a Goddess consciousness that matter can be perceived as having a sacred dimension.[227]

The Christian Sacrament has been taken from the desiccated, authoritarian Priest and been returned to the green, moist Priestess—the Earth-Mother. *Hoc est corpus meum* no longer is the mantra of exclusive masculinity, the *hocus-pocus* of magicians of the sacred. "This is my body," means the fecund body of the Goddess in re-union with Herself and in redemptive union with the God. The Father, Son, and Holy Spirit now have been transformed into Maiden, Mother, and Crone: menstruation as the portal of the New Birth. This is the **Old**, old-time religion!

Bolen describes her initial encounter with the Dalai Lama in the Netherlands in the context of the Grail Quest, remembering that Perceval failed in putting the right questions to the Fisher King—whose wound in the groin has rendered the King impotent and laid waste the land of his kingdom. Her carefully convoluted question only elicits silence from the Tibetan Buddhist spiritual leader, and she realizes that any true quest is interior—that her questions can only be asked of herself:

> If we ask the right questions, the answers will come. If we seek the Grail, we may find it, for, as I keep learning, the mysterious healing Grail is

hidden in people, in places and in experiences.[228]

The male version of her own quest was written years ago by Bernard Malamud, the story of a mid-life crisis for an athlete named Roy Hobbs—whom all Robert Redford fans now know as *The Natural*. In Malamud's American culture version, the grail becomes the pennant, the Knights are a New York baseball team, the Fisher King is the manager of the Knights, the sacred spaces are the fields of kairos dreams—set in the midst of chronos cities, where true heroes stop time with a swing of Excalibur.

The questioning in *The Natural* illustrates this perfectly. Malamud—with Levinson's cinematic help—has Perceval (Hobbs) questioned by two Goddesses. In the *Warm Up* section, the dark Goddess, Harriet Bird, asks him why he plays baseball. His answer: To have people say when he walks down the street, "There goes Roy Hobbs, the best there ever was in the game." It is the answer of Everyman. Steroid Man. Man's Man. Man.

"Is that all?" the disappointed goddess interrogator says. "Have you ever heard of Homer?" Like all male athletes, who never had either the time or the inclination to read the classics, and attempt to cover that emptiness with arrogant crudity and deflecting jokes, Roy manages: "The only Homer I know has four bases." He fails that test—and the wound she inflicts with a silver bullet marks his failure forever.

In the "Batter Up" section, the earth Goddess, Iris Lemon, in the crucial matching scene in the hospital—a maternity ward where Roy is stricken by the effects of his encounter with darkness—asks the same question: "Why do you want to continue to play?" Roy repeats his answer of so long ago: "I could have been the best that ever was." But the gaze of the Goddess lights his face—and another answer at last lights his eyes. "God, I love baseball!"

That is the right answer. The greatest Knight of them all rises from the maternity ward and gives birth to victory, and Pop Fisher, whose own wound was deepened by defeat, is healed at last—artificial light, exploding from the power of a man who realized who he was, cascading over the bodies of jubilation. And when Roy and Iris return to the field of vegetation in rural America, playing ball with their son, it is difficult to avoid calling this drama, the World Ceres.[229]

In her own drama of "inner destination," Bolen visits Chartres Cathedral, where she becomes both the dynamo *and* the virgin, "a tuning fork moment," like a pregnant woman who first feels the child move—an "in-the-body spiritual experience." This new birth of feeling seems to be induced by the deep sense of place that resides where pilgrims have paused over the centuries. In Glastonbury, she finds a symbol for this "overlapping" of the ordinary and the extraordinary: the *vesica piscis*—the vessel of the fish, "an almond shape created by the intersection of two circles." Carolyn Foster describes this Bolen epiphany beautifully:

> Viewing it at this sacred site leads Bolen to experience the union of God

and Goddess within her, which aids the healing of an inner conflict mirrored by the rupture of her marriage. She opens to forgiveness for herself and others.[230]

The journey to wholeness in this fractured world is not at all sure—does not always luxuriate in the romantic endings depicted by Iris and the cinematic Roy, is not always funded by a friend to touch the still point of stained glass.

Often, disenfranchised minorities think that they must separate themselves from their oppressors in order to achieve enough ego strength to offer solutions instead of resentment. Witness the Black Muslim movement in the sixties, the inflammatory ministry of Louis Farrakhan, the xenophobic rhetoric of assistant Khallid Muhammad [note the 1994 assassination attempt on Khallid]. Farrakhan fired his assistant, and in 1999, to bring healing to the Nation of Islam, publicly apologized for any hatred his own words fomented.

Ms. Gray suggested celibacy as a political program for women in the seventies, the eighties brought political correctness, and there has been this baleful rush to tribalism after red fascism in the nineties. But in healthy mergers variants must share something beyond their similarities. Blue and blue make more blue—endless, boring, bland blue. But a marriage between blue and yellow yields a new color—refreshing green.

The time for tirades, manifestos, and encyclopedic reports of sexism is past. Everybody knows now that women can fly, that they have childhoods among ghosts, that they wear red shoes on Sunset Boulevard, that they rise up phenomenally, run with wolves, hold the chalice rather than the blade, transcend PMS and laugh at DSB, carry the Virgin of Guadalupe proudly, that they labor in Eden weep in Amherst, don gowns of judgment, wield power over capital and kings, that they descend as Goddesses, stir the loins of the Saviors, and give birth to the world.

But cowboys also get the blues.

The Men's Liberation movement has a massive new bibliography, workshops, organizations, and male identity gurus. Robert Bly is now famous for his manifesto of maleness, *Iron John,* [231] as well as his PBS special with Bill Moyers, entitled *A Gathering of Men.* Shepherd Bliss of Berkeley joins him, with his Sons of Orpheus support group—men only (mostly gay)—going off into the woods, playing drums, beating old dinner pails, hugging trees and each other, dancing off into the underbrush, singing expressive songs, and pouring out their innermost thoughts in a protected torrent of disclosure. We had Shepherd and his Sons at the University of the Pacific for an evening of gender definition, complete with most of the above behavior. The chair of our Philosophy Department, Dr. Gwenneth Brown, gave an excruciating response—blistering the men for running around, acting like two-year-olds. Dr. Brown is a stiletto feminist, who thinks that men fondling each other in the forest and beating pie plates because they are oppressed by women is just about the silliest thing she ever heard. Mr. Sensitive may be better than the

Terminator, but what we really need is Mr. Equal Rights.

But it is Bly's contention that men *must* separate themselves from women periodically, in order to understand their maleness. Women cannot help them do this—only a male guide, a warrior archetype, a wild man who can delineate himself as the kind of wolf a wild woman could run with.

THE MATURITY OF SACRED SPACE: SECURITY

Inexorably, the journey leads to the region of age, the *eschaton*, the end. This odyssey originally carried the title "A Religion of the Body." Enough references force their way into the entire text to justify that phrase, but there *is* a genuine theology of space, a sacred space. Mircea Eliade wrote an entire book about it, *The Sacred and the Profane.* What emerges is his conviction that every religious cult establishes an *axis mundi* for its followers. The pole of the world, the center of all that really is, runs through the heart of our land and puts us in touch with the divine. And the fact that the Cheyenne in Wyoming, the Catholics in Jerusalem, and the Tenrikyo in Nara, Japan, all can take us physically to the center of the world raises no difficulty for religious thought. Writes Eliade: "…it is not a matter of geometrical space, but of an existential and sacred space that has an entirely different structure, that admits of an infinite number of breaks and hence is capable of an infinite number of communications with the transcendent." [232]

Eliade, however, does not mention the richest and most powerful example of sacred space: the resurrection of the body. That traditional, creedal phrase is the title of the modern publication of the writing of F. Matthias Alexander. The director of the American Physical Fitness Institute, Edward Maisel, selected it as conveying the profound implications of the work of Alexander, the father of the sensory awareness movement in the West.[233]

The Alexander Technique

Alexander is familiar to us as the curious, uncompromising prophet of the kinesthetic sense. From the 1890s, in his native Australia, when he discovered what came to be called the "Alexander technique," till his death in 1955 in England, he carried on an international practice of physical re-education based on the dynamic relativity of the head, neck, and torso. He influenced the minds and bodies of such diverse and famous men as H.G. Wells, Aldous Huxley, William Temple, and John Dewey.

Alexander's technique was original and deceptively simple. He translated everything "physical, mental. and spiritual" into muscular tension.[234] Civilization has thrown our natural organic apparatus out of balance, and the delicate instrument of the body no longer registers correctly. Hence we must give up any deliberate effort to change our set reactions to stimuli. What we must do is…nothing. That is, we must refuse to do what we have been doing. We must inhibit each subtle muscle program until the correct tension is allowed to be. Not felt. Not forced. *Allowed.*

In his teaching, Alexander covered breathing, stuttering, mind-wandering, child training, physical exercise—even golf. Golf, as we all know, is the acid test of muscular tension since, next to making love in a hammock, it has to be the most unnatural sport on earth. Alexander diagnosed golf problems as the effort to "end-gain." Golfers want to hit the ball straight down the fairway, instead of *allowing* the club, eyes, hands, and the ball to become one thing in process. End-gaining makes us continue to react to sensory stimulus we thought produced the proper stroke but, in fact, slice the ball. The wrong stroke, in other words, has come to *feel* right, and the teacher must unfix the golfer's aim and teach him to swing without "swinging." Here was a natural high priest for the California mysteries: Shivas Irons and true gravity—golf in the Kingdom meets Alexander the Great. [235]

The kinesthetic secret to the teaching of golf, the act of writing, or anything else was, according to Alexander, posture. When the neck muscles freed the head to go up, the spine almost literally lengthened (some of Alexander's patients actually grew taller). One is sorely tempted by Alexander to read posture almost metaphysically.

And, in fact, a German philosopher named Erwin Strauss in 1948 wrote a paper entitled "The Upright Posture."[236] Invoking Milton's description of Adam and Eve in *Paradise Lost* ("Two of far nobler shape, erect and tall, Godlike erect, with native honour clad"), Strauss builds his case that our upright position is utterly unique in the animal world and characterizes us as human. Our posture, Strauss thinks, is virtually theological. "Language has expressed this through terms like 'upright' and 'upstanding' and antonyms like 'fall,' 'stumble,' and collapse.' In denoting the freedom and jeopardy of human existence, language links the human world with the human figure."[237]

The Strauss article is, at least, an ingenious look at the old Greek epithet that man is the only animal that walks upright. Telling someone to straighten up captures body and soul together. Zen masters probably do not read Strauss, but they insist that meditation posture should include an absolutely straight back with the head riding nervelessly high. Perhaps sacred space is, after all, not a sanctuary outside of our own bodies, but *is* our vertical body. Maisel, inspired by Strauss, could have then conveyed the religious meaning of Alexander with the more obviously physical title, "Erection of the Body."

If Alexander sounds more acceptable today—rather like an Esalen inner guru or some new purveyor of Zen and the art of fill-in-the-blank—or at least seems less strange than he did in the early part of this century, it is because his work has reached us through men like Hans Selye, Paul Schilder, Alexander Lowen, and Wilhelm Reich.[238]

The Very Strange Case of Wilhelm Reich

Wilhelm Reich is a particularly interesting resurrectionist. He is notorious for his worship of the orgasm and his bizarre experiments for re-energizing our sexual powers with "orgones"—palpable energy radiation from our bodies, collected in a large confessional-like box, literally constructed to capture this sacred space! Unbelievable as it may sound, and revealing America's continuing terror of open sexuality, Reich was arrested for advertising his orgone boxes for sale, died in a Maine prison, and had his books burned in New York City in 1960. Not 1860—*1960*.

What Alexander pointed to as a malfunction of the kinesthetic sense, Reich names ominously "the trap." The trap is the human character structure that does not allow us to experience fully our bodies. But Reichian therapy does not dwell on the nature of the trap, which we may compare to Freud's term *repression*. Reich is interested in the *exit*, nothing else. He constantly exposed examples of our grief as willful ignorance, as when we decorate a trap with literature (even Shakespeare!), with science ("the Pasteurs, the Flemings"), with art as a mask:

> The crucial point...remains: to find the exit out of the trap. *WHERE IS THE EXIT INTO THE ENDLESS OPEN SPACE?* [239]

The way out is to follow Christ. Not through the Church, which has murdered Christ by asceticism and other worldly piety. Not through communism, which has murdered Christ by impersonality and collective prudery. The way out is a Christ who was loved by women, who was crucified by men who hated body energy, and who is constantly being raised from the dead by all who finally realize that they carry Christ—which is bodily, genital life—within them.

> Your belief in the resurrection of Christ is true: Living life remained unthwarted and walked on this earth clean, without sin, without dirt of the soul, for thirty-three years until it ended on the cross. But, being Life, it did not really die. Life cannot be killed, ever. It hung from the cross bleeding in agony from many wounds, but it is truly invincible. Having expired in one body, it will certainly return in another body. It will bleed again and again for ages at the hands of thwarted, hardened, armoured life which cannot feel sweetness in the limbs or bear the look in the eyes of a deer on a sunlit meadow, without shooting or knifing or choking to death the reminder of its lost paradise. Still, in the end, Life will resurrect and conquer the evil, sinful devil which is the Life force gone stale in the body. [240]

Some thought Reich insane; many thought him dangerous; everyone thought him odd. He seemed the epitome of the mad scientist: arguing with

Einstein in a Princeton basement over the mysterious rise in temperature generated by his orgone collector, telling Freud to his face that the father of psychoanalysis was sexually repressed, announcing that involuntary celibacy caused cancer, defying the U.S. government to judge him as a scientist, peering into the Norwegian biosphere searching for the secret of life—and coloring it blue, erecting a laboratory in the wilds of western Maine, like some deranged white-coat inventor streaking back to the future, or a modern Dr. Frankenstein. Yet he took the body as the only genuine locus of religion and flung the metaphor of resurrection floridly across the endless, open, sacred space.

Is there anyone who does not need this resurrection of the body? Sometimes the Alexandrian teachers find a natural-born saint. One kinesthetic instructor said of the young Muhammad Ali, "He drifted about the ring like a piece of blown thistledown, always in balance and always ready to move or strike."[241] Leon Spinks should have fought the champion when his *feet* were made of Clay. That puffy, weary, bleeding dethroned Ali we saw reminds us that sacred space has always been marked off by the old ones. And no one could miss the pathos of the tremulous, ravaged Ali holding the Olympic torch at the Atlanta games in 1996—the fire vaulting up from then to now.

Even Alexander could not live forever. Strokes marred his face at seventy-six and took his life ten years later. Resurrection cannot mean immortality. For all our love of the mysteries of the organism, we must face pain, disintegration, and death—what Unamuno called "the tragic sense of life."

Our companions through existential space are not only Blake's *Apocalypse* and Reich's *Function of the Orgasm,* but also Agee's *A Death in the Family* and Kosinski's *The Painted Bird.* And with an exquisite aesthetic sense, Francine du Plessix Gray's *Lovers and Tyrants* carries us through the ancient polarity between physical and personal, between flesh and spirit. Her heroine, Stephanie, has tried to become a woman by coming to terms with her father's death, by marriage and motherhood, and, when threatened by disease and death, by finding temporary refuge in a relationship with a bisexual called Elijah. The novel climaxes with their journey through the southwestern desert, through Utah and Arizona to Las Vegas, through John Ford's mythic American frontier West.

Just before they conclude their pilgrimage looking for genital America—from anal Utah, phallic Monument Valley, to oral Las Vegas—Elijah asks Stephanie to tell him one more time the story of her enlightenment in the mountains with her family. Stephanie invokes poetry as her past becomes present: "Once out of nature I shall never take my shape from any natural thing." Elijah whispers, "Yeats, right?" She is suspended inside the glass of total awareness: of wind, the smell of thyme, the great sculpted ridges that became extensions of her body.

> And I'm overwhelmed with the sense that I'm surrounded with all that I have loved best in life—the white heat of that particular landscape, my children, the man I've loved the most in my life....the man who taught me to love, who exorcised me from my mother's world, who gave me the shelter that eventually enabled me to be a writer. You see, it was the same landscape which I'd crossed

with him some ten years before on a day in which I'd felt only his dourness, his oppressiveness—that's the point, we've always got to be ready for the total transformation, the transfiguration of the other, perhaps the transfiguration of all reality. Oh God, Elijah, I think that may be one meaning of the word resurrection." [242]

So, at last, by a ''commodious vicus of recirculation," as Joyce puts it in *Finnegans Wake*, we come back to where we began—all regions explored—hoping to know the place for the first time. To know these co-ordinate associations and their interconnection, these sinews and "Human Nerves of Sensation," this matrix of our organic unity, this astonishing self which *is* a body.

PART TWO

IMAGINATION

CHAPTER FOUR

AROUND THE WORLD IN 80 RELIGIONS:
THE BODY AS DANCE

WE ARE ALL MAGNETS AND WHAT IS LOCKED IN OUR FIELDS OF CONSCIOUSNESS
IS MERELY THE "FACTS" WE ATTRACT.

WILLIAM IRWIN THOMPSON

IT NO LONGER MATTERS WHICH COMES FIRST, THE REALITY OR THE IMAGINING
OF REALITY. AS JEAN HOUSTON WRITES IN *THE POSSIBLE HUMAN,* "I HAVE
ALWAYS THOUGHT OF A MYTH AS SOMETHING THAT NEVER WAS BUT IS ALWAYS
HAPPENING."

GLORIA STEINEM

WHO IS GOD? WE ASKED THAT STRAIGHTFORWARD QUESTION, BELIEVING THAT
PEOPLE EVERYWHERE HOLD IN THEIR HEARTS VIVID IMPRESSIONS OF THE
SUPREME BEING, THAT THESE VISIONS REVEAL THE GRANDEST EXTENT OF THE
HUMAN IMAGINATION AND SHOW US AS MUCH ABOUT OURSELVES AS ABOUT THE
ULTIMATE REALITY.

LIFE, DECEMBER, 1990

Where am I? In front of a computer in my office, surrounded by thousands of books and bromides urging me to print out wisdom; in my house, surrounded by eucalyptus, fruitless mulberry, rye grass, and fecund vines that trellis this corner of North Stockton; in California, edging old America, sliding into the fiery rim of promise and apocalypse; spinning on a bluish ball, through the infinite galaxies, expanding past place in this brief history of time. The Buddhists tell me that I am nowhere; the Hindus say I am everywhere.

I have often asked my students to tell me where they live in their bodies and they look at me strangely, as if the question made no sense. *Sense* is exactly what I do want made. As Thomas Moore reminds us, the human body is an incredible source of imagination: "The body is the soul presented in its richest and most expressive form."[243]

Back in the fabled psychedelic decade—the stoned age, as Herb Caen might have said—when the sixties were making opiate the religion of the people, we played a game called "Group Therapy." One rolled the dice and moved a personal icon to a new space where one was directed to pick up a card. On the card was written a question of self-perception, which had to be answered to the satisfaction of the entire group: each participant required to judge your answer as either "With It" or "Cop Out." To continue on the board toward psychic health (naturally the space in the center), the player must receive unanimous "With It" signals. If some "Cop Outs" came up, even though you were being completely honest—and still had a majority of affirmatives—you could explain yourself, and ask for a re-vote. The questions were actually designed to make one thoughtful, and what began as a game, soon took on the ambiance of the therapeutic. It started silly and ended serious, rather like life itself. In fact, on the box holding the set was written this question: "Is it really a game?"[244] The first time I played it with a group, I turned up this question: "What do you think would make you a better lover?" I remember answering: "It doesn't really seem possible." I got laughs and unanimous "Cop Outs."

One night, we played it with several friends from the athletic department—one of whom has since become the President of the NCAA—and I picked up this question: "Of what part of your body are you the most proud?" I thought a moment—just long enough to elicit smiles all around—and said: "My right arm." The coach types let it go: a round of "With It." Except for one woman, the wife of the athletic director, who flashed a huge "Cop Out," explaining that, given my background and vocation as an intellectual, I wasn't being honest. It was, she urged, my *mind* of which I *must* be most proud. Athletes may fly around a track, but thought is quicker than the wind.

It was a contest of sorts: Man vs. Woman, Host vs. Guest, Humanities vs. Aerobics, Clergy vs. Laity, Attorney vs. Jury. So I pleaded my case. I certainly had a useful brain, had made some genuine, if minimal, use of it, but my ability to throw a football, shoot a basketball, pitch a softball—flex power into being—gave me more pleasure, and made me much more proud than anything my mind had achieved. I began my case staring off into space, gradually moving my focus directly to her, and, fixed with hesitant, but calculated resoluteness, invited her to change her vote.

But she had won. The part of my body of which I was the most proud was my pride. My ability to sway an audience, to mesmerize a crowd, to understand a subject in school while pretending I knew nothing, to play above a sport, to resurrect a text, allow bones to live with the flesh of metaphor, to help people laugh. She had guessed where I lived.

Where am I? Some students tell me they live just behind their eyes. Some say in their lips or their skin. A student once turned the question on me: And you, Dr. Meredith, where do you live? I *had* learned from Group Therapy, but I do not know who I am without my body. "I live in my reflexes," I said. My ability to reflect. To react. To make connections—as James Burke would have it, to associate, to imagine.[245]

Where am I? In my imagination. All of us are.

Mark Johnson has given us powerful support for just such a claim.[246] In *The Body in the Mind; The Bodily Basis of Meaning, Imagination, and Reason,* he writes convincingly that all structures and patterns of meaning are matters of imagination. Imagination, he tells us, is not limited to artistic creation, fantasy, discovery, and novelty, nor is it some kind of outdated artifact of a former psychology—a rather awkward transition from pure sensation to intellection, now made unnecessary by the neuroscience of cognition.

> Imagination is our capacity to organize mental representations (especially percepts, images, and image schemata) into meaningful, coherent unities. It thus includes our ability to generate novel order. [247]

It is important to "enrich our notion of imagination" if we are to get rid of the dichotomies that have dominated—and stifled—Western philosophy: mind and body, reason and imagination, science and art, etc. And the most promising approach for this "enriching," thinks Johnson, is Immanuel Kant's theory of judgment.

Kant had inherited a problem: how can "structures of imagination" be constitutive of objective experience? How, indeed, can imagination be creative? Kant's answer is that a "transcendental unity of apperception" accounts for the fact that we can share experiences, even though we *alone* have the particular experience that we have. This synthesizing activity, this pure reason, is not derived from our empirical experience, though it happens in the midst of it. As Johnson puts it, this ultimate unifying structure of consciousness is the operation of imagination:

> We are thus brought to a momentous conclusion about the importance of human imagination, namely, there can be no meaningful experience without imagination, either in its productive or reproductive functions. As productive, imagination gives us the very structure of functions. As reproductive, it supplies all of the connections by means of which we achieve coherent, unified, and meaningful experience and understanding.[248]

Kant held, Johnson agrees—and I have no mind to disagree—that creativity takes place neither in the productive, nor the reproductive operations, but in a third mode he calls the capacity for determinate judgment. It is the act of reflection.

Reflection is that activity that allows the mind to shuffle and sift representations, looking at possible ways for all these to be organized beyond the control of understanding (the reservoir of concepts). If we use concepts already available to us to determine what a thing is [clawed creature with fur that meows and purrs is recognized as cat], we are not being creative. Only associative. If we reflect on cats as qualitative images of human beings, and cause them to tyrannize their house mates in fat arrogance, and torpid disdain of the work ethic and mindless insouciance, that *is* creative. And Jim Davis has mined solvency drawing it. Garfield is beyond the control of understanding.

What kinds of reflections are possible? Kant gives us four: the immediate pleasure we derive from contemplating an object or idea, the purpose of the object, the way the object is replicated, and the formal "rightness" of the object.[249] We commonly call this fourth dimension by the simple word "taste." But it is not solipsistic aesthetics as announced from a narrow angle of vision: *De gustibus non est disputandum.* "Taste" can be discussed and even judged:

> Such a reflective judgment might give me pleasure as I sense a certain "rightness" in its formal features. Its form is not "right" (or beautiful) merely because it fits some concept (some purpose the object can serve) but rather because there is a certain harmony and grace in the relation of its formal features.[250]

These judgments of taste are guided not by rules of rationality, but by the "free play of imagination." Something is beautiful not because it matches a pre-conception of "beautiful," but because our minds are sensing a harmony between what we are experiencing, and our ability to think about what we are experiencing. Imagination has become our rationality: rationality without rules.[251]

Now the same kind of free activity required to judge something "beautiful" also is required to create something "beautiful." There are certain techniques which must be mastered in producing art, a trained will shaping randomness by reason (Aristotle). It would be quite impossible to write a sonnet that had only thirteen lines, or a triolet with double rhymes. But fourteen lines of verse is merely formal and minimal. The genius is in the "beauty"—and that is indefinable in advance, admits to no rules, and lives only in imagination. So at last Johnson's Kant defines genius:

> We might say that genius is the capacity to initiate a free harmonious play of imagination that issues in a new ordering of representations that makes sense to us without the use of concepts.[252]

Does this mean that the direction of nature is toward the unnatural? That is, from embodied animality, through brain-located rationality, to disembodied creativity? That there are two worlds after all: the material and the formal, sensuous and intellectual, phenomenal and noumenal, capricious and ordered, the flesh and the spirit? Or perhaps even three worlds: body, mind, and soul; sensation, understanding, imagination?

A religion of the body denies any such split, and suggests—or rather insists—that these "worlds" are joined by the incarnation: the Word made flesh is embodied imagination. That is, the way we invent the world—that new ordering of representations—is already potential in the organism and has no existence without that organism. The schema of a triangle may exist nowhere but in the imagination, but the imagination exists nowhere without a body.

SENSUOUS SALVATION: POSSESSION

I would only believe in a God who dances, wrote Nietzsche.[253] Philosophy, he said, is not a "science," but something almost "spiritual"—something aesthetic.

> It is not fat but the greatest possible suppleness and strength that a good dancer desires from his nourishment—and I would not know what the spirit of a philosopher might wish more to be than a good dancer. For the dance is his ideal, also his art, and finally his only piety, his "service of God." [254]

Sam Keen, conservative presbyter consumed by fire in his man's belly, read Nietzsche and turned out a lyrical, creative—and sometimes excruciating—celebration addressed *To A Dancing God.* Alan Watts, Anglican turned Bay Area houseboatsattva, told us that Buddhism is like a dance: no special place on the floor where one is supposed to go, just moving to your own special rhythm. What do men need? Only four fundamental things, says Zorba the Greek: food, drink, women, and dance.[255] The history of modern physics can be—and has been—symbolized by *The Dancing Wu-Li Masters.* And Baba Ram Dass, nee Richard Alpert, decided that life itself constitutes *The Only Dance There Is.*

George Leonard calls his trenchant meditation on the unity of body and mind, *The Inner Pulse: A Search for the Perfect Rhythm That Exists in Each of Us,* [256] because he sees the entire universe as centering in a rhythm to which we must respond. Nowhere on this planet, he writes, can we find a people that does not make music and dance.

> In New Guinea, a tribal chieftain coaxes hypnotic overtones from a Jew's harp made of a living, buzzing beetle. Half a world away, a band of Bambuti Pygmies awakens the jungle with happy singing and clapping. High in the Himalayas, temple musicians shake the valleys with the awesome wail of twenty-foot-long horns, while priests in meditation produce three tones simultaneously (a lifetime's devotion from a single voice). In Trinidad and in Central Park, West Indian musicians strike Calypso tunes out of the cut-off tops of used oil drums. There is no end to this global feast of sounds, old and new....[257]

The human animal is a born dancer, not in spite of the inert environment—hostile to art, forcing men and women to become fortresses of civilized permanence against entropy—but as part of it: "… at the burning center of existence itself, there is music and rhythm, the play of patterned frequencies against the matrix of time." [258]

So dance invites us to a family of words circling about the body: rhythm, harmony, music, vibration, vibrato, pulse, movement, grace. These words are not synonymous, but they are related. And they are fundamental. Twenty-five hundred years before Leonard, Confucius wrote that a nation's character is typified by its dancers, and that one may judge a king by the state of dancing during his reign. The stage—what Peter Brook called "the empty space"—by its "stationary center and fixed proportions," hosts the cumulative presence which is "imaginative reality" of theatrical arts.

The "stage" is quite different for a native American, and the dance seems to conjure up not weightlessness but rootedness. Jamake Highwater (*The Primal Mind*), who has written extensively on classic dance and Indian culture, points out the telling distinction between European ballet and Navajo Eagle dance. The ballet depends aesthetically on its ability to overcome gravity: dancing on point, great leaps and lifts done with illusory ease. The Navajo is grounded, even as an eagle, and rises into the dance *without* leaving the earth—becomes the eagle without soaring away into the sky. Dance is the way primal people idealize action as a magical force, a magic which connects them with nature, rather than conquering nature. Our senses include the sense of balance and of rotation, what sport science now calls a kinesthetic sense, enabling us to *feel* the environment.

> The relationship between sentience and movement affects everything from the expression in our eyes to the flow of adrenaline in our bloodstream. In its most fundamental form this spontaneous link between sentience and movement is called dance—a direct, nonverbal, unreasoned assertion of ideas and sentience expressed in motion. [259]

Raoul Trujillo begins his narration on the PBS special "Lord of the Dance" by drawing out the connection between spirit and body in African celebration:

> To some people nothing is more spiritual than the dancing body. Among the Yoruba of West Africa, worshipers call the gods through the dance and the gods come. By possessing the bodies of the dancers, the gods literally join in the dance. According to the Hindu story, the world was created not by a Divine Word, but by a Divine dance.

In the traditional Christian heaven, where bodies are no problem, angels dance to glorify God. Even away from the Church in the secular art form of the ballet, the dance reaches up—away from earth. The feet are elevated—not flat on the ground, as in medieval carvings of Salome's dancing before Herod. In the dances of death sequences, in the paintings of Botticelli and the carvings of Donatello, we go "back to the division between soul and matter: our goal as Christians is to free ourselves of our heavy, weighted bodies." [260] We aspire upward—as in the styles of architecture.

Highwater makes the point that Native Americans, in building their Sky City at Acoma in New Mexico, constructed all of their buildings close to the ground, seeming to rise right out of the rock. Only the Jesuit cathedral soars above the people and the land. The European cathedrals drew your eyes upward with the vaulted ceilings, and darker glass in the lower windows and lighter glass in the clerestory—again to draw one's vision to heaven (God, of course, is equated with light). Observing the procession at Seville during Semana Santa in Spain, one sees the penitents moving to a definite rhythm—devotion through movement. They sway back and forth—transmitting their energy upwards to the images, which now dance with human pulse. As the tableau of the crucifixion is carried along, the swaying causes "Jesus" himself to dance: the rhythm of both reverence and joy. As Thomas Kane puts it: "The body can't be totally denied—even in the most conservative of Christian worship."

In India, the dance can construct a physical location for the mystic ladder: procession, performance, possession, purification. "The minds of human beings and snakes are identical," says P. S. Ramachandran, serpent ritual Guru.[261] Devotees draw a mandala in the earth, using ground spices as pigments, and the *pulvalas* (dancing virgins) transform the ground into sacred space. It takes hours to create, and represents the ancestral home of the snake gods in the forest. A table is set for the gods and the procession begins. The performance can last for twenty-one days sometimes, depending on the depth of need brought to the ceremony. The guru describes the divine energy as beginning with a feeling in the girl's left thumb, or left toe, that rises through the body, and, then—completely possessed by the snake gods—the girls (virgins) erase the mandala. The devotees, we are told, consider the sacred space a kind of theater, and the ceremony, properly performed, as revealing divine mysteries.

What is the central element in this Indian dance? Kapila Vatsyayan, from the Indira Gandhi National Centre for Arts, tells us that all bodily exercises depend upon control of the breath. The main difference, she says, between Indian and European forms of dance is the control of breath: which aerates the nervous system, activates the brain—and becomes mind. India has a martial art named Kalari Piack which is *directed* to the deities. Kapila is direct and clear about meaning of Kalari Piack. There can be no mental discipline without physical discipline: the body beautiful, the body disciplined, the body controlled—these are the essential tools. The goal is to get to that sense of release, joy, union—the two have become one. "Worship," she says, "can certainly be an art form."[262]

Essentially worship must be done with the body—paint, words, design, are all ancillary. In dance, we can *see* the yearning for salvation. A young woman falls in love with a young man—who is actually the Lord Krishna. So temple dance and secular dance meld, the way body and spirit meld. This is the Bharata Natyam Dance—performed by Malavika Sarukkai. She is supposed to dance as if she is walking into the street of love, but, overcome by the moment, she improvises movements that show Krishna walking into the street toward her—comes into her and *becomes* her. The sexual union of the lovers represents the longed for union of all creation with God. As Kapila tells it, sex is divine or vulgar not in being part of human life, but in how we *think* about it: "The body is not the main thing—but the soul." Yet Malavika dances as if the soul has no great desire to be rid of the body: "Krishna is something magical, intoxicating, and fills me with great longing"—as her fingers plunge into each other, imitating intercourse. Then she adds softly:

Dance…changes you inside. You feel a deep sense of harmony. Mostly we are fragmented—dance is a way to harmony.

The thesis leaps out at us: it is the body that expresses the inner feelings of the worshipper. The title of this survey of religious dance styles from three continents brings us back to America, where the hymn, "The Lord of the Dance," was written. It was composed here by Sydney Carter, with a tune adopted from the American Shaker Hymn, "Simple Gifts." No matter what the circumstances, joy or sorrow, life or death, we dance. We dance in the midst of all the ambiguity of life, on any continent, wherever we may be:

I am the Lord of the Dance, said he.

I would not believe in a worshipper that did not dance.

The Year of Living Strangely

Dance, as myth in motion, is also inflected by culture. There is more than one Lord of the Dance, and there is no more exotic place to see this diversity than in an archipelago known to the West as the East Indies.

Five hundred years ago, Columbus sailed west and discovered America. In 1992 the Merediths sailed west and discovered Indonesia. Now while the second journey may seem only marginally connected to the first, there is a relationship. We found what Columbus was looking for—he, after all, was attempting to find those spice rich islands of the Indies when he ran into the grand impediment. The fair wind under the Northwest airliner took us to Java—the real garden east of Eden—and the year of living very strangely.

The occasion was a Fulbright lectureship to Gadjah Mada University in

Yogyakarta in central Java, the principal island in an archipelago of almost eighteen thousand islands, stretching three thousand miles across the Indian Ocean and the Java Sea. The town sits in the shadow of Mt. Merapi, the most active volcano in Asia, and is the site of the world's largest Buddhist monument, Borobudur. Forty miles away, along the banks of the Solo river, archeologists found the remains of one the most primitive forms of human life—surely the remains of a religious studies professor—labeled in the paleontologist texts *pithecanthropus erectus* ("Java Man"). Java man turned out to be very healthy, not to mention prolific. Central Java is one of the most populous areas in the world—ninety million in a swath of land two hundred by seventy-five miles: an unbelievable five thousand per square mile in the fertile crescent around Yogya. Jakarta, on the western tip of Java, showcases fertility with seven and a half million and counting. *Pithecanthropus*, it seems, was really *erectus*.

The main street in Yogya, Malioboro, ran directly north and south between the Sultan's palace (the *kraton*) and the Tugu monument, marking the founding of the city. Extending straight south, the line intersects the Sultan's shrine at the Indian Ocean—and, extending straight north, intersects the sacred mountain of fire itself. Malioboro is the horizontal *axis mundi* around which the Yogya world turns: the unstill point of Javanese culture.

We had a surprising number of visitors. Pat's sister, Shirley Miller, came from Richland, Washington—just in time for the great spring festival at that incredible Buddhist monument at Borobudur. This stone sanctuary (1,300,232 blocks cut by 30,000 sculptors), was designed to be an architectural mandala. One circles inside the huge walls where 1460 exquisite stone reliefs of the life of Buddha are joined in long rectangles of silent myth, gradually ascending past the bell-like stupas, until emerging at the center height—looking out over the sacred volcanoes, smoking in the distance.[263]

I also took Shirley to see the *Ramayana* ballet at the Trimurti [the Hindu godhead: Brahma, Vishnu, and Shiva] theater, performed slightly northeast of Yogya at a place called Prambanan, just in the shadow of the largest Hindu temple in Indonesia—and one of the finest anywhere. That Indian epic is the defining myth of Javanese life, anomalous as that sounds for a country that is ninety per cent Muslim. Rama and Sita [the ideal man and woman] images, puppets, dolls, and batiks, are everywhere—and so are the dances from the story. From late May through September, during the full moon, the story is enacted on an open stage at Prambanan by two hundred dancers and gamelan musicians, presenting all four parts of the drama in each lunar cycle.

Shirley saw the one night "summary ballet," from the abduction of Sita by the demon king Rhawana, to the reunion with Rama—after miraculous adventures aided by magic arrows, maidens turning into golden deer, mythical birds, and imaginative monkeys. At the end, Sita has to prove her purity—as all really "genuine" women do. She submits to a test by fire, and, of course, is not burned—protected by an innocence designed to appease the most male of egos. Men do love virgins so, except in bed. Shirley—an ardent feminist—had a lot of questions about that story. I explained the Indonesian gender imagination as best I could, which is incarnated in the way the story is danced.

Dancing for the Gods

Javanese dance, Yogyakarta style,[264] is divided into three major types of characters: female, refined male, and strong male. Each is based on the use of space (levels of their limbs). The female, as you would guess, uses a very narrow space, in which the limbs are closed and low. She almost never lifts her feet from the floor, stepping only slightly up in a kind of subtle and graceful slide. The emphasis is on the lower part of the arms, with hand and head movements. She will always be in a kind of crouch, what the Indonesians specify as a *demi-plié* position, which, along with these other constraints, give the aesthetic impression of "femininity." This is the reflection of the ideal Javanese woman: short, slender (with a lovely face), restrained, shy, moving slowly to avoid confrontation and anxiety, never saying yes quickly, no matter how much her desires move her toward her lover.

The refined male also moves slowly, very low (but wider than the woman), with a *demi-plié* stance, and feet restricted from being lifted over seven inches above the floor. The aesthetic projection is one of delicate manner and unobtrusive style, only slightly taller than the ideal female. The strong male type opens up to space at a horizontal level, lifts his legs and arms very high horizontally, moves quickly sometimes, and always strongly. He must be danced by a tall man (5'7" by Javanese standards), and conveys not only competence, but power. All male virtues are projected by the patterns in space of the arms: symmetry as humbleness and stability, asymmetry as pride and energy. There is no such dancer as a "strong female." Thus doth art imitate life. [265]

Rabindranath Tagore, one of the first modern Indians to visit the islands, said that Lord Shiva gave his dance to Indonesia, and left India with his ashes.[266] Bali, even now after virulent tourism and all night Australian pub crawls, is still a pristine sanctuary of religious life. Since the Tibetan "incursion" by the Chinese, Bali may be the only completely "religious" culture in the world. There are more temples on Bali than homes—and even the rice fields are regulated by religious ritual and the lunar calendar. I think it would be almost impossible to visit Bali and not see an exotic and genuine sacred celebration. The richness and originality of this religious consciousness is directly displayed in the dance.

It is well known that the Balinese have no word for art: they "do everything as well as they can." What they do best of all is dance, and the religion of Bali lends itself quite naturally to the dramatic possibilities of the dance. If the defining myth of Java is the *Ramayana*, then the central myth of Bali is the Rangda/Barong dualism. Rangda may have her origin in the Hindu Durga (Shiva's wife in her ugly aspect—Parvati is the nice one), but, whatever her origin, she is one grotesque lady in Bali: great bulbous eyes, fangs, stringy hair, incredibly long tongue—red with the blood of children she has eaten, and spotted with tiny mirrors so we can anticipate her next victim. Barong is the righteous one, but somebody has to tell you that. He has the body of a hairy yellow lion or dragon, like something out of a bizarre Chinese New Year's parade. His face also has protruding eyes, and long, lethal teeth— mouth sprung open in horrid bicuspid pose.

This is the ancient struggle between good and evil, between the wicked witch and the benevolent beast. Rangda attacks and Barong restores. It is the Balinese concept of reality and balance: both sides are present and powerful, but neither side ever wins. And the Balinese are in no hurry to mount this contest in tourist time—even though they do present a short version in an artificial theater in Babalua for the Nusa Dua and Kuta busloads, who are just passing through with their capital showing. The real show lasts all night, much like the shadow plays [*Wayang Kulit*] done all through Indonesia. We were taken to a genuine performance by the director of the College Study Abroad Program, Rucina Ballinger—who had been a student at Callison, and now was married to a Balinese prince.

We arrived at the dance drama late, it was already in progress at 7:30 P.M., and packed with entire Balinese families—babies included. When Barong was laid waste at about 11:00, I guessed it was over. But the hairy old beast roused himself, only to fall again about 12:30 in the morning. Rangda seemed the worse for wear at 1:00, but managed to muster the energy for another round or two. At 2:00 A.M., we found the driver who would take us back to Mandala, and left the great battle still raging, every Balinese family still enraptured—cheering and laughing—as an endless stream of dance types choreographed the balance of birth and death.

Chokorda Rahi, a Balinese authority on dance, tells us that foreigners have great difficulty learning these dances. They do not work like us, he says, and since they don't work as we do, they cannot walk like we do. The dancing comes from the walking.[267] The men carry loads on the end of a bamboo pole, balanced over one shoulder. The pole bounces with each step and the man then develops a light, bouncing walk—recreated in the dancing style. One shoulder inclines upward, arms up. He walks along the ridges of the rice fields, up and down as the terraces rise and fall, until his feet articulate the balance, seen in the dance as lateral poise, and by the gods, I would guess, as harmony of spirit.

The women transport their goods and gifts to the gods on their heads. This weight develops a spine almost rigid, a core for straightness, and the hips, like shocks, absorb the excess movement to keep the line of the back and the load still. Then the eyes move independently of the rotation of the head, left and right, and they must lower the eyes without moving the head in order to balance the load without tripping. Balinese women still greet the passer-by with a flick of the eyebrows and eyes, which in the dance translates into the familiar fast-arching eyebrow—eyeballs flashing back and forth in swivel sockets. The gods are grateful, I learned, that ecstasy is contained, while the supplicant experiences the world.

A VALENTINE TO OLD SOLOMON: PASSION

Smiles I saw. What I *never* saw in Indonesia was a kiss. And with all that multitude around, I suspected some erotic activity somewhere. A religion of the body must have its rituals, and at the very least should include a holy kiss. If the Muslim world can produce a work like *The Perfumed Garden*,[268] it ought not take offense at the Song of Solomon.

Indonesians do send valentines, but they are exceedingly decorous and prim. One would never think that bodies ever touched other bodies anywhere romantically. Perhaps their libidos are just too sensitive and tactile involvement volcanic—like Java itself. Freud would have understood.

> In order to keep the social disasters of self-gratification at bay, while still getting some id-heat by association, the good citizen turns to the artist, who, it is assumed, will court Eros with enough discretion to convert the process of sublimation into something pleasurable and socially productive.[269]

A Muslim Imam did explain to me the reason that women *always* sit behind the men in the mosque. Not patriarchal preference, but hair-trigger eros. Think about it, he said. The faithful must prostrate themselves, kneeling and bowing—head to the ground. Women, in such a position in *front* of the men, would be irresistible—provoking unspiritual thoughts, a tremulous distraction from Allah's beneficence. It is an occasion for religious reflection—and imaginative chemistry.

The Chemistry of Love

A kiss is a decision of the imagination. The body worships with its mouth. A person may copulate quite impersonally, flailing away in generic sex, as John Wesley used to put it (in a somewhat different context), having the form but denying the power. When Debbie Murphree, the prostitute who serviced Jimmy Swaggart, was asked if she ever kissed the preacher, she replied with incredulous emphasis: "Oh, no! I never *kiss* any of my clients!" Right. Intercourse, yes. But kissing?…That is *too* personal.

In an inventory of the so-called sexual organs, the mouth is said to be the closest to the brain, but, of course, sexual pleasure isn't in the mouth or the brain. It's in the entire body, activated by the imagination, and completed by chemical and hydraulic action.[270] Lip lust has a structure and a long history of literature attempting to describe it.

John Atkins traces this erotic impulse in *Sex and Literature*—a book, he says, not intended for puritans. The Romans apparently had three words for the kiss: *oscula* (touching the cheek in friendship), *basia* (touching the mouth in affection), and *sauvia* (touching the lips in passion). [271] The Celts seemed to have no word for it, the Irish and Welsh *pog* and *poc* adapted from the Latin *pax*—referring I suppose to the kiss of peace. The mouth kiss in India seems probably introduced during the Mahabharatic period [*sic*], following the ancient sniff kiss—spreading a little *prana* along with Vedic teachings. We are told that the Chinese thought the European kiss was vulgar and rather suggested cannibalism, an idea, incidentally, not far removed from the invitation to kiss in the play, *On Golden Pond:* "Would you like to suck face?"

Remy de Gourmont in *The Natural Philosophy of Love*[272] suggested that the practice originated with the birds. Our avian friends, it turns out, don't have any erectile tissue, so coition takes place by "simple contact"—a slight pressure or rubbing:

> Displeasing as the comparison may be, it is a play analogous to the mouth to mouth kiss, or, if one prefer, to the pressure of two sapphists clasped vulva to vulva. [273]

Not having any erectile tissue seems exclusion enough to me—particularly as an older heterosexual, without the added implication that kissing was born on the isle of Lesbos.

C. M Beadnell in *The Origin of the Kiss* took us even further back, all the way to the protozoa. At this truly primal level, the organisms come in contact and during "surface apposition" exchange material so that, after separation, there remains the interchange of two different environments in both "partners." Anyone who has ever been treated to a Bangkok bath—a slithering, erotic, full body kiss performed by young flesh—will understand this miracle of primal life.

An "exchange of environments" applied to human beings translates as deep kissing. If *The Clan of the Cave Bear* is any indication, this kind of behavior doesn't go back very far, coition consisting of quick grunts from the rear. But the ancient Greeks—no strangers to rear action themselves—knew and appreciated the art form bequeathed by the winged ones. In the *Greek Anthology*, Rufinus writes:

> Europa's kiss is sweet though it reach only to the lips, though it but lightly touch the mouth. But she touches not with the edge of the lips; with her mouth cleaving close she drains the soul from the fingertips.[274]

Further in the *Anthology,* Paulus Silentarius ("Cycle of Agathias") compares the kisses of three ladies. Galatea's kisses are lengthy and strong; Demo's are very soft; Doris—doubtless an ancestor of the famous count—bites.[275] Paulus likes Demo best because "her mouth is sweet as honey." [It's really difficult not to say that he had good taste.]

Europe liked its progenetrix and her "closely cleaving" exorcism, especially in France. In the Pays de Mont area of Vendée, these exploratory tongue kisses were said to last for hours, the custom becoming famous as *maraichinage*—and giving us the popular expression "French kissing."

The French practiced it, enjoyed it, and gave it a name, but it takes a journey eight thousand miles to the east to find it systematized. The *Kama Sutra* remains the most orderly sex manual ever written as a religious tract—*kama* meaning pleasure and *sutra* meaning scripture. Vatsyayana subtitles it *The Hindu Art of Love,* and draws out the varieties of eroticism with such incredible mechanical detail that it might better be called *An Engineer's Guide to Orgasm Maintenance.* Atkins suggests it is worship of the "God that Will not Fail."

The section on the lip-kiss is file cabinet neat. Three forms are described: *Limited* (the woman touches the lover's lips but does not suck on them); *Trembling* (the man takes the lower lip of the woman between his own—and since she is uncertain whether or not to withdraw or respond, her lips quiver with ambiguous passion; and *Exploratory* (the woman places her hands over the eyes of her lover while closing her own, and taking the his lower lip between her own, gently massages the captive with "a rotary movement of her tongue."

The man may also take complete charge—real men don't allow ambiguity—and practice the Straight kiss, the Oblique kiss, the Revolving kiss, the Pressed kiss (also called Drinking the Lip—when you've got enough suction going), the Cupping Kiss, the Responsive kiss, and the Super-Pressed kiss—a super turn-on where you grab her lower lip between your thumb and forefinger, squeeze it into the shape of a ball, touch it with your tongue, then suck away without biting. One could even engage in what the Hindus call "the battle of the tongues"—a most sensuous form of martial action. And if one's imagination needs prompting, Atkins invites us to remedial kama by describing the four types of kiss on other parts of the body: the Balanced on the pelvis, navel, and chest; the Forcible on the breasts, cheek, and vagina, the Affectionate on the forehead or the eyes, and the Worshipful—on the breasts, slowly down to the waist, and holding.... Who needs MacPlaymate when you have this programmed sex waiting for you?

Lenore Kandel would understand the word "worship" here. And Matthew Fox, Thomas Altizer, George Leonard, Kat Sunlove, and perhaps even Bishop Spong. In a playful way we all do. But what causes us to respond to each other and prompts us to these odd "exchanges of environment"?

One Valentine season, *Time* magazine featured on its cover a huge heart poured out of a test-tube, all in red and black. The heart contained a man and a woman in silhouette overlooking a lake—with shadowy mountains at sunset. The title of the issue: "The Chemistry of Love"—scientists investigating romance as a *biological* affair, with an article by Anastasia Touflexis putting "love under a microscope." Observing what? Apparently, there are three stages to this chemistry: *imprinting* [evolution, genetics, psychological and sensual experiences stimulate "romantic" reactions]; *attraction* [the brain produces phenylethylamine (PEA) as well as dopamine and norepinephrine—natural amphetamines that provide euphoria (ecstasy only warranted for two or three years); and *attachment*, [endorphins (natural morphine) in the brain producing lover's serenity]. Meanwhile, the pituitary gland secretes oxytocin, which stimulates prolonged feelings of fulfilled attachment. Oxytocin is affectionately known as "the cuddle chemical." Writes psycho-biologist Anthony Walsh, author of *The Science of Love: Understanding Love and Its Effects on Mind and Body:* "Love is a natural high."

And that's not all. An article in the city paper brought the news that all this chemistry of love can also prevent cavities. That's right. A kiss a day can keep your dentist away. The Academy of General Dentistry reported that smooching can fight tooth decay. I knew it could fight stress, boredom, depression, racial prejudice, and metaphysical anxiety. But tooth decay?

Howard Glazer, spokesman for the dentists, is reported to say that when you anticipate a kiss, your mouth waters, and when you land a kiss, the peck triggers more saliva, which washes debris off the teeth and leaves enamel-building calcium. So scientific kissing is more than just lip service to hygiene. Apparently, passion can control tartar, if very little else.

Now, the author of the Song of Solomon was no dentist, but he (she?) knew about mouth to mouth resuscitation, even if the King James translators didn't. "Let him kiss me with the kisses of his mouth: for thy love is better than wine," they have Solomon's maiden say. This is not only a poor translation of the Hebrew,[276]but bad aesthetics—and even worse dentistry. How else, I ask you, could anybody kiss except with the kisses of his or her mouth? An elbow to the mouth delivers a message of sorts in a basketball game—and has an element of passion—but it is scarcely designed to communicate affection, and certainly will not help your partner's teeth. And we'll leave foot-in-the-mouth to social bumblers and karate experts.

As the translation stands, it looks just plain redundant—or stupid. Were the old Hebrews so unimaginative as to drain love poetry completely dry in the very first line of erotic invocation? What does the following line mean as translated? "For love is better than wine." What does wine have to do with the "kisses of his mouth"? Obviously this is some kind of metaphor. But pointing to what?

Enter the infinite scientific wisdom of the Academy of General Dentistry. Of course. When one anticipates the handsome king puckering up and slavering over the quivering female, her glands respond to the sweet mystery of life, and flood her mouth with good old fashioned saliva. *Now* the metaphor makes sense: "Let him put his mouth on mine and let us exchange saliva, for this love liquid is better than wine." We all understand this not just as graphic poetry, but as deep kissing. Apparently, the French could have learned this from the Hebrews, who most certainly could have been inspired by those earthy Canaanites, who might have been looking at too many camels in the desert.[277]

In The Song of Solomon, whatever the biblical critics or Toni Morrison wrote about it, kissing is a molar melody: osculation retards gum disease, obviates the need for root canals—insertion halts extraction. Who knows? Perhaps the tongues of Pentecost had more to do with salivation than salvation.

Look at the record. Solomon's teeth were perfect: "Thy teeth are as a flock of sheep that go up from the washing, whereof every one beareth twins, and there is not one barren among them." The handsome devil hadn't lost a bicuspid. Now I understand why he had a thousand wives. It wasn't oriental lust; it was an early form of dental insurance.

Well, Candide was right. It is the best of all possible worlds. The wine of love stimulates us to ecstasy, induces a sense of deep security, and leaves our smiles of satisfaction untainted by the ravages of decay. No wonder the Hebrews believed in God.

Feeling Space

Isn't "feeling" the penetrative power of space what we really mean when we describe something as *spiritual* ? The king is handsome, the maiden is beautiful, the landscape is lovely. The sensory world has been translated by the neurotransmitters into the imagination of categories. The spirit of place and person, indeed the chemistry of love, is an aesthetic space: an embrace of the body of God. When the embrace is truly ecstatic, we reach for "spiritual" language: it was out of this world.

When we move out of this world, from physical to aesthetic space, we are simply seeing more clearly what we have already experienced. Aesthetics I would define as the study of feeling space.

Martin and Jacobus understand this perfectly. The study of art "penetrates beyond facts to the values that evoke our feelings." Aesthetics gets beyond consideration of the work of art and goes to the work itself—becomes part of it, smells it, vanishes and tumbles through its perspectives, licks and listens until it *is* the work. Creative education is finally kinesthetic: there is no education *but* physical education. It is the work of aesthetics to make us excruciatingly aware of physical space. ''Space is the power of the positioned interrelationships of things."[278] Yet we treat it almost as an object: "We *know* space, but because of the anesthesia of practicality, we fail to *feel* space."[279]

Edward T. Hall, who along with Edmund Carpenter and Marshall

McLuhan, spent years studying art for what it can tell us about sense, communication, and perception, has reported on his studies in *The Silent Language* and *The Hidden Dimension.* As we have already noted, his word for the systematic study of cultural space is *proxemics.* Hall thinks of art as "the history of perception,"[280] and insists that it is the artist's task to help audiences enrich their own perceptions by removing obstacles that hinder their entry into another world.

We do not see distance, any more than we *see* nature. We see a perspective that we learn to associate with a certain distance. This is why 3-D movies were a fad and not a find. The eye provides its own depth through education, not stereoptics. Rembrandt, Hall discovered, was a three-dimensional painter. While viewing one of Rembrandt's self-portraits, he found himself caught by Rembrandt's own eye. "The rendition of the eye in relation to the rest of the face was such that the whole head was perceived as three-dimensional and became alive if viewed from a proper distance."[281]

It is this dominance of distance that is challenged by what was called modern art—the impressionists (Cézanne, van Gogh), the cubists (Picasso, Mondrian), the surrealists (Dali), the nonobjectivists (Kandinsky). Abstract art would never have developed in Asia because the Indian and Chinese thought-world—exactly analogous to the Hopi's—was not disconnected from space. In Taoist tradition, for example, there is no such thing as inner and outer, up and down, spirit and flesh, as discrete dimensions, directions, or entities. The valley is valley precisely because the mountain is mountain. One does not have lowness, the other highness. They are one and they flow together. [282] When the Tao dances, as in Tai Chi, this flowing is embodied—"felt"— by the hands reaching out and gathering in space. What is space? My two hands. Encircling emptiness, embracing tiger, returning to mountain.

India's Vedanta art in particular offers no support for separate inner and outer spaces. The Indians give us only convexity, never convexity against concavity, which would be realistic perspective. They, like the dancers, are interested in depicting *prana* (breath) as the energy source of human life, and so their aesthetic space is puffy—full of curves and convexities. Their statues look bloated, as if the stone had been pumped up with air.[283]

The art historian Alexander Dorner recognized as early as 1950 that the three-dimensional aesthetic perspective was shattered forever by the philosophy of modern physics, that space was not so much *there* as *alive.* Space was "love," as Einstein had suggested, in the sense that the option of a static, objective space existing outside of human perspective was no longer open to us. "The wound of three-dimensional spirit-body polarity is no longer open: it has been covered with a new tissue of pure energism."[284]

Hearing Space

No one has to be reminded that music is uniquely important to human life. Perhaps birds do sing—though I doubt that hyenas laugh—and we have now recorded the songs of the whales. There are those who would argue that the hills are not alive with the sound of music—not unless Julie Andrews spins and smiles melodies in Austria's Alps. But no one who has ever heard the haunting night lyrics of the Gibbon monkeys in the Mentawi Islands could support that argument. Music is God's gift to us, wrote Luther—and Satan, he added, is its enemy: "The devil does not stay where music is." [285] "Music," said Baudelaire, "excavates heaven." [286]

Baudelaire must have been a closet physicist. George Leonard could teach the subject—and *does* in a work like *The Silent Pulse*. Music, he writes, works by vibration, which is how every object in the universe works. [287] The dry molecules in the retinas of our eyes would vibrate five hundred trillion times looking at the yellow wing of a butterfly—more than all the waves generated by all the oceans for ten million years. With a blue wing, the number of vibrations would increase. With X-rays, the increase would be a thousand times, with gamma rays a million. These rates of energy can be arranged into an electromagnetic spectrum, having more than seventy octaves—with the light we see being only one of these octaves. The "tones" of this spectrum have their overtones, color harmonies, similarities that appear at octave intervals.

> Many of the basic discoveries of the scientific world, in fact, have simply confirmed the musical nature of the world. For instance, the Periodic Table of Elements, in which all the chemical elements are listed in order of atomic weight, breaks down into seven octaves, with properties that tend to repeat, as in musical octaves. No wonder so many scientists and mathematicians are also musicians.[288]

Johannes Kepler, the astronomer who worked out the laws of planetary motion, and who said he was "thinking God's thought after Him," had a high old time measuring God's body. He thought each of the planets was not only in motion, but alive, and inhabited by a guardian angel—who alone could hear the music generated by that planet as it played its "song" orbiting around the earth. Shades of Fritz Capra and the *Tao of Physics:* new age non-sense in the seventeenth century? Bizarre bath water?

But two Yale professors, Willie Ruff, an assistant professor of music, and John Rodgers, a professor of geology, applied Kepler's laws and musical notations to a projected one hundred year period beginning on December 31, 1976. According to Leonard's account, they put the information into a computer linked to a music synthesizer, generating a thirty minute sound tape, simulating one hundred years of motion. The result? An actual piece of "music," with Mercury singing like the slide of a piccolo (it moves the fastest in the sky), and Jupiter (moving slowly—still waiting no doubt for Kubrick's spacecraft) rumbling out the bass. Rodgers was amazed: "Venus changes from a minor sixth, and earth makes a marvelous minor second. In fact, it's just like Kepler said."[289]

Even so, music space is somewhat different from visual space. Music is somehow "transcendent" when compared to the space in which bodies have locations. Music forces us to be aware of transcendence because, when we hear a tone, we become aware of space itself, not objects in space. The tones are there, but also here and over there. And they are divisible into rhythm and accents and harmonies. Says Zukerkandl, "The space we hear is a space with places." [290] Color, images, buildings, words all catch the eye, the hand, and the sense of smell. But sounds intrude on us and seduce us (in the case of the Robert Shaw Chorale) or shock us (in the case of Smashing Pumpkins) into recognizing that space is outside of us as well as inside. William Sadler notes, "…seeing and hearing are two distinct modes of existence revealing to us two distinct characteristics of space, not two different spaces." The visual is an *experience of distance*; while the "space" of audition is a *participatory experience.* [291]

So musical space is primarily characterized by interpenetration, again analogous to the Hopi teaching about thought and object. Music enfolds us and we become part of it—as anyone knows who has ever had his home wired wall to wall with quadraphonic ambient guitars, or been kidnapped to a rock concert by one of his children. Transcendent music? In days of old, Yes, Genesis and The Who *were* eschatological. Today? U-2, with its brush arbor end-of-the-world cacophony? Perhaps the Phish-heads are the enfolding tribal heirs of the Grateful Dead, or a cultish ingestion of the String Cheese Incident.

The Tibetan Buddhists knew this centuries before any German philosophers thought about it. It was not enough to paint mandalas, waft incense, spin prayer wheels, or make finger rhythms. The monks sat in long rows also meditating with their voices—chanting in deep, sonorous tones; chanting with such ecstatic relaxation that a single monk could sing an entire chord of three notes. Huston Smith has fixed this phenomenon for us in his magnificent film, *Requiem for a Faith.* Listen, he begs us, to a low Ommmmmmm of D, then F sharp, and finally one monk simultaneously intoning three distinct notes—D, F sharp, and B. [292]

It is not a vocal trick, Smith reminds us. It is a theology of space. By striking just those notes, overtones are formed that ease the ear past the normal scale of sound and suggest other inaudible, ethereal, and eternal sounds. Baudelaire and Kepler would have been welcome in the Himalayas. Music does excavate heaven.

O Taste and See

Animals feed; human beings dine, at least according to one of the most delightful texts in Western culture. Our cabaret universe would not be nearly as much fun without space for preparing and ingesting food—and for the reading of Brillat-Savarin's *The Physiology of Taste*, with its delicious subtitle: *Meditations on Transcendental Gastronomy.* The crown of creation is the gourmet, he tells us. Gastronomy is one of the principal bonds of society. It draws out the spirit of fellowship, molds singles into groups, and "rounds off the angle of conventional inequality." And fie on those who think they are physically educated and do not know how to eat: "And this is the place to cry eternal shame on those doltish eaters who swallow down the choicest dainties with criminal indifference or carelessly and sacrilegiously absorb the limpid fragrance of the rarest nectar." [293]

Brillat-Savarin's model was a certain M. de Borose, born in 1780, killed in March of 1825 by a lightning bolt, underneath a poplar tree. (Brillat-Savarin would have no doubt been offended to find his body overdone.) In his tribute to M. de Borose, Brillat-Savarin describes the proper way to dine: "They savored each dish with right philosophical attention, and gave to the work all the time that it demands, yet never forgot that a moment comes when reason says to appetite: *Non procedes amplius* (Thou shalt go no further)."[294]

And "transcendent gastronomy" need not be limited to men. Such sensitivity is "by no means unbecoming in women," since it is appropriate to the "delicacy of their organs," and somehow makes amends for the pleasures they must forego, and the "ills" with which nature has shackled them.

> There is no more charming spectacle than a fair gourmand under arms: her napkin is prettily tucked in; one hand rests on the table; the other conveys to her mouth delicately cut morsels, or a wing of partridge for her teeth to savor; her eyes are bright, her lips like cherries, and all her movements full of grace; nor does she lack the grain of coquetry which women show in everything they do. With such advantages she is irresistible....[295]

We are dealing here with what Hall terms "olfactory space," for taste, as we know, depends on smell. Without proper adjustment between the nose and the palate, the experience of eating is only essential, not existential. I have always been deeply suspicious of Christian communion services, the partaking of the Lord's Supper. To me, the smell has always been missing. Instead of fresh bread, with its succulent aroma and soft texture, we are given antiseptic wafers or symbolic crumbs—or worse yet, mashed soda crackers. Instead of aged wine, with its caressing odor and rich surface, we are given thimbles of thin liquid or sips of acrid cheapness—or worse yet, Welch's grape juice. When Jesus is celebrated by solemnly reciting "This is my body," the very least we could do is stop pretending we do not have one.

Aromatherapy makes no such pretension. An ancient sensual science, aromatherapy uses oils, massage, fragrances, and meditative rituals to aid the body's natural curative powers. Pioneered by Judith Jackson [*Scentual Touch: A Personal Guide to Aromatherapy*] in this country as part of the new consciousness movement, it has become a—shall we say—healthy business. Judy [it's all right to be familiar: she's my first cousin] illustrates this olfactory space beautifully in her 1997 book, *The Magic of Well-Being*. Looking every bit the gorgeous woman she was when she appeared on the cover of *Life* magazine in 1947, her picture graces this introductory text: "Well-being should be more than just staying alive; it should be living more fully in every moment, while looking and feeling great."[296] I'm glad the laying on of hands is a revered Christian ritual.

The Taoist tradition, in fact, directly connects our sexuality with our appreciation of food and olfactory space. "The world the aspiring Taoist Immortal inhabited offered him many concrete things, which he could absorb to build up his inner complex of energies. Sights, sounds, smells and especially foods, contain the yin and yang in different proportions, and so need to be taken at the right times in the right amounts. The environment itself can be, so to speak, sexually milked of its essences." [297]

A milking of the environment's essences with no specific concentration, such as sexuality, is precisely what happens in the Japanese tea ceremony. The tea ceremony is the Taoist communion service. It judges our worship of suffering, our cluttered lives, our fear of silence, our sensory anesthesia, and our final lack of humor. Kazuko Okakura in *The Book of Tea* suggests these judgments unmistakably. Tea, he says, is so subtle to the taste, not like "the arrogance of wine, the self-consciousness of coffee, nor the simpering innocence of cocoa."[298] The setting for the ceremony is also subtle, deliberately simple, as if things in space were no more important than the space itself.

Taoist aesthetics teaches us how to be present to the mundane, how to be ultimately accessible as human beings. Chinese historians have always characterized Taoism as the "art of being-in-the-world."[299] The art of tea is the art of rekindling our sense of joy in the present moment by removing the obstacles that prevent our experiencing it. Taoists have always found the followers of Confucius too practical and the followers of Buddha too gloomy, immortalizing these impressions in the story of the jar of vinegar.

Tom Robbins, the scruffy Taoist masquerading as a novelist in the Skagit Valley of Washington, has amended the ancient parable and made it available as scripture for this religion of the body. The story is usually told with Confucius, Buddha, and Lao Tzu all tasting a jar of vinegar (symbol for life itself), and registering quite different reactions. Robbins begins with the traditional form. Practical Confucius finds it sour, but perhaps useful in food preparation; compassionate Gautama tastes its bitterness and wants it poured out to prevent further suffering.

Then the cast changes. Sacrificial Jesus sticks his finger in the vinegar and, even while realizing that the sour-bitter liquid is not fit to drink, offers to take it himself, that others may be spared the experience. Lao Tzu becomes a strange couple from the edge of the American search for sensuous freedom and natural life.

But now two people approach the jar, together, naked, hand in hand. The man has a beard and woolly legs like a goat. His long tongue is slightly swollen from some poetry he's been reciting. The woman wears a cowgirl hat, a necklace of feathers, a rosy complexion. Her tummy and tits bear the stretch marks of motherhood; she carries a basket of mushrooms and herbs. First the man and then the woman stick a thumb into the vinegar. She licks his thumb and he hers. Initially they make a face, but almost immediately they break into wide grins. "It's *sweet*," they chime. "Swee-eet!" [300]

SIDDHARTHA'S SPIRITUAL ODYSSEY: TRANQUILITY

The great enemy for most of us is anxiety. We are afraid we don't measure up: we aren't strong enough, rich enough, pretty enough, talented enough, sexy enough, healthy enough, smart enough. Religion has developed its many techniques of the sacred to calm us, reassure us that the universe is friendly. The entire apparatus of sacrifice is designed to persuade cosmic powers to deal kindly with us—as we saw in the case of Bali. In some sense, this is what keeps religion alive: its capacity to tranquilize us in the midst of demonic life. It cannot be aesthetics alone that lures us into the great vaulting cathedrals, that draws us to the Esalenic retreats for baths and sonorous silence, that drives us to our knees in tents of the evangels and ashrams of the holy. Jesus' first sermon was heard gladly, so we are told, by the common people, and we can see why: not a sparrow falls, but the Father sees it, and *us* too. He "who flung the stars to the most far corner of the night" knows who we are—and cares. "Fear not" is a New Testament litany. Religion that does not calm the soul is no religion at all. People go to church because it makes them feel better, looking for Mr. Good God.

Young people in the sixties went to India for the same reason. Transcendental meditation in the holy city of Rishikesh at the headwaters of the Ganges, Kundalini Yoga in the mountains above Bombay, mystic unity with Sai Baba in the streets of Bangalore or with Sri Aurobindo below Madras: all symbolized the royal teacher, whose very name means "He who has accomplished his aim."

I still teach Hesse's *Siddhartha,* and young people in the nineties continue to be inspired by his soft quest for tranquility. The young Brahmin is learning to make love with his gorgeous teacher, Kamala—Kama in Sanskrit, as we learned, means "pleasure" (an allusion to the "love pleasures" in the *Kama Sutra).* When she asks him what manly traits he has to offer her, he answers: "I can think, I can wait, I can fast." Every year, one of my guests in World Religions is a Theravada Buddhist monk from Cambodia, living in Stockton to nurture the refugees swarming all over the San Joaquin Valley. He came in 1974 to give spiritual guidance to those who had escaped the Khmer Rouge and the killing fields of Southeast Asia.

His honorific name is Bhante Mahathera ("the blessed wise elder"), and he was head of the International Buddhist Association—as well as the first Buddhist monk ever to appear on television (for the BBC). His face is unlined, his speech soft but strong, his hands totally smooth, his eyes crinkle and spark with winsome humor. He moves slowly, and his brain seems to be in Alpha almost permanently—instead of the frenetic Beta of surface life.

In January of 1989, a deranged man named Purdy dressed in army fatigues, leaving his toy soldiers in his motel room in Morada, walked over to a school ground not two blocks from my office, took aim at little Cambodian children playing on swings, and shot them to death with a AK-47 machine gun, killing five and injuring thirty—then blew himself up with a hand grenade. Bhante was called in to quiet the fears of the community. He exorcised whatever demons caused this madness by appearing at the school, and blessing the grounds with water and fresh leaves from an oleander bush, sprinkling the space where Purdy had acted out his horror—the slaughter of the innocents, without a redeemer. [301]

Bhante is one hundred and ten years old.

In the winter of 1989, I witnessed the hundredth birthday celebration of this Cambodian holy man. It was a remarkable celebration: Bhante, smooth skin reflecting the golden tapestries, eyes still twinkling above tragedy, speaking to the media out of a lucid mind and memory. The only guns going off that day were lighting and preserving on film this moment of warmth and life.

Bhante *is* Siddhartha. He left his wife and child and a promising career in law, to go into the forest for meditation and the life of a monk—a life which has taken him all over the world, including a nondescript old house on the edge of nowhere, ministering to bedraggled refugees chanting in the dark of American xenophobia.

He can think, wait, and fast. In fact, he eats only one meal a day, seems unhurried about anything, and specializes in warm clarity of thought. When one student asked him to define Nirvana, he replied, "Why? You want to go there? You want to go there now?" The answer is clear, rather like Gertrude Stein's epithet about Oakland, California: "There's no *there* there."

There is no there in Nirvana. Going is not what one does in relation to Nirvana because one never would arrive, since in fact there's nowhere to go, which means that one can't make an effort to go, which means that all anxiety about whether or not you're there is rescinded, which means that Nirvana is rather the moment when all "thereness" vanishes and the "now" is revealed as the only moment there is, which is a gift of being that we cannot earn, but only be aware of, and sometimes requires the trauma of being inside a shattering glass door to set aside all the distractions of linear life that cloud our vision of this pure, uninhibited simplicity that is Nirvana.

Or something like that.

But still, Bhante *left his wife and child.* And the original Siddhartha left his wife and child, and Hesse's Siddhartha left Kamala for a life on the river, where all things return—where "the years passed and no one counted them." Who would want to be one hundred and ten without the love of the woman you love? Who would want to be one hundred and ten without your boys playing football at the school grounds or recreating *Shane* in the shadow of the Grand Tetons, or hiking in the high Sierra? Why in God's name did Siddhartha think he had to leave Kamala's lips for the wisdom of the river? If he just had to experience the "now" in the flow of the "eternal return" he should have taken her with him and made love to her as often as the wise ones chant in the evening shadows. It seems so obvious to me that sensuous life between lovers is profoundly worshipful. I see no reason to accept the idea that somehow the flesh is the insidious distraction from holiness, or that real life is present in abstraction from the fragility and the entropy that is being human.

Sri Nisargadatta Mahraj, who taught Jnana Yoga/Advaita Vedanta by conversing with seekers, articulates beautifully this spiritualized quest for final wisdom:

> I see what you too could see, here and now, but for the wrong focus of your attention. You give no attention to your self.... The way back to your self is through refusal and rejection.... All you need to do is to get rid of the tendency to define your self. All definitions apply to your body only and to its expressions. Once this obsession with the body goes, you will revert to your natural state, spontaneously and effortlessly. [302]

But why? Why must attention to the self mean refusal of the senses—and rejection of the body. Is this the price of tranquility? Complete disassociation? This strange detachment from the miraculous process of birth, imagination, and death?

I honor Bhante and Siddhartha and the Sris of the world—and all those who have "found their aim." [303] Perhaps that is what Joseph Campbell means when he tells us to "follow our bliss." But I can't believe it means the denial of love's body, where coming and becoming translate the same sense of joy in being alive. I realize that sometimes we seek too much, and because of our seeking we cannot find. In the last chapter of Hesse's novel, he makes Siddhartha say: "When someone is seeking it happens quite easily that he sees the thing that he is seeking; that he is unable to find anything, unable to absorb anything, because he is only thinking of the thing he is seeking, because he has a goal, because he is obsessed with his goal."

Seeking therefore means to have a goal, but finding means to be free: to be receptive—to have no goal. Does it follow that sensuous pleasure is a goal, that two people in love imprison themselves in seeking each other? If being free means forfeiting the body's springtime, or experiencing autumn as a spiritual retreat, then it's highly overrated and far more dangerous than even the existentialists supposed.

I should think that being free means precisely the reverse of this. It means that we can experience each other not as conquests (Now I have you, won you, overcome your opposition—your inhibition, seduced you, mesmerized you, or even instructed you) but *as* each other (Now I am truly me in your presence and you are truly you in my presence, there is nothing that we want from each other except each other). We don't talk together in order for the other person to understand, but because the other person *already* understands. We don't try to show each other a good time: for the first time we know what good is by being with one another.

Wisdom Under Glass

Norman Cousins once wrote a piece entitled "What I Learned from a Thousand Doctors." Cousins also added that the very worst place a person could be when sick was in a hospital. It may be that the worst place a person who wants healthy religion can be is in a church. The Cousins/Meredith hyperbole, of course, is both true and false. It's true enough to be illuminating, and false enough to demand an apology.

This is what I have learned from a thousand visits to the world's religions.

In **Hinduism**, the problem of human life is overcoming the ignorance that has separated the individual soul (*atman*) from the world soul (Brahma). Salvation therefore consists of ascending by a series of rituals (the yogic discipline of sight, movement, sound, and silence) towards higher consciousness until the body is transcended and the soul is released (*moksha*) into pure spirit.

In **Buddhism**, the problem of human life is the suffering (*dukkha*) caused by the false assumption that we possess individual souls. Salvation therefore consists in the realization achieved through meditation that there is no duality between human beings—that higher and lower, light and dark, right and wrong, are only concepts that grow out of thinking that we are different from the world—and so we have nothing to transcend—all desire is now extinguished. And the enlightenment that this realization brings sweeps away the distinction between light and dark, servant and master, male and female, and leaves compassion as the only morality.

In **Sikhism**, the problem of human life is the inequality caused by worshipping many gods and the elite social positions granted without deserving them through hard work. Salvation therefore consists in allegiance to the One God of All and a strict life of honesty, sharing the fruits of our labors, and performing deeds of service to all humankind—ending both discrimination and sloth.

In **Jainism**, the problem of human life is the physical and spiritual pollution of the soul (*jiva*) caused by contact with matter (*ajiva*)—which is totally evil. Salvation therefore consists in complete individual detachment which renounces all bodily needs and seeks liberation by non-injury to all living creatures (*ahimsa*). This is not compassion, but non-participation in the matter of the world.

So, in each religion coming out of India, the essence is **release**: In **Hinduism,** we are released from thinking that our souls are bound to lower consciousness; in **Buddhism,** we are released from feeling ourselves to be individuals; in **Sikhism,** we are released from acting in selfish indiscipline; in **Jainism,** we are released from even sensing the physical world.

The Far East, I found, shifts the emphasis from release to balance.

In **Confucian** thought, the problem with human life is civilizing barbarous behavior. Salvation therefore consists in devising and inculcating a system of propriety.

In **Taoism**, the problem with human life is the illusion that we somehow are supposed to transcend nature. Salvation therefore consists in allowing harmony with the natural world to neutralize our desire for domination.

In **Shinto**, the problem of human life is impurity and infertility. Salvation therefore consists in rituals of purification and impregnation.

In **Zen**, the problem of human life is the illusion that either the past or the future has reality. Salvation therefore consists in paying attention to the present without attachment.

In each religion coming out of the Far East, the essence is context: in **Confucian** thought, we are inculcated with the community; in **Taoism,** we are made responsive to the environment; in **Shinto,** we take our place as priests of the ordinary; in **Zen,** we look through the center of the connecting circle of the world.

The Middle East, I'm convinced, takes us out of balance and context into external authority.

In **Zoroastrianism**, the problem of human life is the conflict between light and darkness, the good and evil possibilities of behavior. Salvation consists solely in accumulating good thoughts, good words, and good deeds so that they outweigh evil actions at the divine judgment day.

In **Judaism**, the problem of human life is to overcome the separation between God and the nation, created by seemingly irresistible human attempts to usurp the righteous rule of God. Salvation therefore means responding with living under God's Law—and performing covenant rituals to symbolize a special identity in history of the community of God.

In **Christianity**, the problem of human life is to transform natural instincts into holy living by use of a will fundamentally damaged by pride and selfishness. Since salvation cannot be humanly accomplished because of sin, we are saved by the divine perfection of God lived out in the life and death of Jesus of Nazareth.

In **Islam**, the problem of human life is to create unity out of the chaos of many different political, social, and religious systems. Salvation is brought about by submission to the One God, whose complete will is revealed only to Muhammad of Medina in the miracle of the Qur'an.

So in all the religions coming out of the Middle East, the essence is morality, dependent on revelation from the Holy Other: In **Zoroastrianism,** our duties are inexorable; in **Judaism,** our laws are divine; in **Christianity,** our righteousness is imputed; in **Islam,** every action is revealed.

And for **Primal Religions** everywhere (African, Native American, Southeast Asian, Australian Aboriginal) the problem is powerlessness outside of the God's pleasure. Salvation therefore is re-connection with the god through sacrifice and participation in its power.

The further away one gets from primal religion, the less one dances. This seems clear when you look carefully at a survey such as "The Lord of the Dance." As primal energies infuse primal bodies, they writhe and glisten with organismic power, invoking identity with the earth. The Indian dance slows the paroxysm while maintaining the incarnation of divine and human, Krishna's playful eroticism seducing the flesh into spirit. The Mahayana Buddhists gently twirl away the distractions of life, while Vajrayana Tibetans crash cymbals and thrash about in grotesque costumes with Himalayan ferocity. The Confucians freeze-frame their ritual rectification of names, to the measured sound of gongs and trumpets, remembering the mandate of heaven, while the Taoist mortals flow unforced in bucolic settings—exercising their yin and yang. While Japanese maidens in exquisite simplicity implore Amaterasu with fertile, swaying steps, Zen monks translate disciplined power through bursts of martial energy—and dissolve into nothingness. The Persian families inbreed their faith with fire and instruction, moving with restrained joy only in the wedding feasts. The children of Abraham in doleful submission sit silently as the rabbi reads, feet stilled while voices rise in minor key, his other sons and daughters moving across the sands in fervent declaration—the mutual ballet of prostration inspired by the vibrato recitation of the word. And the followers of the Way mute their joy with royal reverence, climbing steps of penitence to kiss authority, ingesting transubstantiating irony—the body of the Lord of the Dance.

> Zorba shook his head.
> "It's finished. I used to feel my soul rise again every Easter, at the same time as Christ, but that's all finished!" he said. "Now only my body is reborn—because when somebody stands you a meal, and then a second and a third, and they say: 'Just have this little mouthful, and just this one more'…well, you just fill yourself up with more heaps of luscious food, which doesn't all turn into dung. There's something which stays, something that's saved and turns into good humor, dancing, singing, wrangling even—that's what I call Resurrection."….
> He stood up suddenly. The wine had gone to his head.
> "Whatever are we doing here, all alone, like a pair of cuckoos? Let's go and dance!"[304]

CHAPTER FIVE

SENSUOUS SPORT: THE BODY AS PLAY

WHEN AN ARCHER IS SHOOTING FOR NOTHING
HE HAS ALL HIS SKILL.
IF HE SHOOTS FOR A BRASS BUCKLE
HE IS ALREADY NERVOUS.
IF HE SHOOTS FOR A PRIZE OF GOLD
HE GOES BLIND
OR SEES TWO TARGETS—
HE IS OUT OF HIS MIND!
HIS SKILL HAS NOT CHANGED. BUT THE PRIZE
DIVIDES HIM. HE CARES.
HE THINKS MORE OF WINNING
THAN OF SHOOTING—
AND THE NEED TO WIN
DRAINS HIM OF POWER.
> CHUANG TZU

CIVILIZATION BEGINS AT THE MOMENT SPORT BEGINS.
> NIKOS KAZANTZAKIS

DON MEREDITH PLAYED FOOTBALL BECAUSE HE WAS PRETTY GOOD AT IT AND
BECAUSE, HELL, IT WAS FUN.
AT LEAST IT WAS UNTIL HE MET HIS GRINCH WHO STOLE FOOTBALL.
> SKIP BAYLESS

Aristotle did not write a philosophy of sport. Probably few people have been devastated by this omission, but Aristotle was recognized in Greece as "the master of those who know," who did manage considerable reflection on logic, physics, biology, politics, ethics, psychology, and economics, did manage credit for establishing most of the categories of serious western thought. And his slight of sport occurred within the very culture which gave birth to the Olympic Games.

Even if he wasn't technically a Greek (Macedonian actually), the omission is at least surprising—so much so that Paul Weiss, Sterling Professor of

Philosophy at Yale, wrote a book-length inquiry into the nature of sport as a kind of amends to the master. Weiss understands the problem as simply Grecian elitism:

> Aristotle extracted a grammar from learned discourse, a logic from skilled argument, and a political theory from the practices of statesmen. But he kept away from common discourse, common argument, and common practices.[305]

Philosophy, Weiss tells us, neglects the life of ordinary men: their sweat, work, their common religious ritual—even their song and dance. In short, whatever lures and grips the uneducated. Condescension towards the unwashed started early.

Of course, as Weiss points out, the Greeks could have written a philosophy of sport, for only free men were allowed to participate in the athletic contests. But there must have been a nauseating suspicion that physical excellence was within reach of the lower castes, the slaves, and even women. Alciabides refused gymnastics not because he lacked strength and grace, but because he knew that some athletes were of low birth.

If the fact of commonality tempts the ancient intellectual to condescension, that same fact enables sport to become the spectacle of modern patriotism. John Lahr's brilliant essay in *Evergreen* carries the thesis that sports have become "America's right-wing theater."[306]

Sport as civic theater, Lahr writes, affirms the status quo by converting the very processes which dehumanize man into play. So sport in our society becomes the last stronghold of comfort and reassurance that all is well; it is the grand distraction, the tableau of affluence that keeps the populace obedient to the demands of the state by disciplining its discontent into spectacle. Sport stages thrills without essentially challenging structures of power: it asks no questions either of the viewers or the views, but simply unfolds external action.

Chuck Mills, former coach of Utah State, was a script writer for this right-wing theater. After a dismal season, anxious over increasing radicalism of students, he found a way, so he thought, to impress on his team what a privilege it was to receive an education through the sport of football: designing a red, white and blue American decal for each Aggie helmet. *Sports Illustrated* reported his locker room oration, an overkill appeal to the great athletic community that suffers, cries, laughs, and wonders together: "Football is a microform of the American Adventure.[307]

Here the phenomenon of sport as chauvinistic conjoins the phenomenon of sport as anti-intellectual. Men and women *think*. They may be skeptical in the Greek sense of "looking carefully about." God and sport become partners when G-O-D as symbol comes to mean Establishment. Satan as Anti-Christ in the New Testament means anarchy, the antithesis of G-O-D: order. Creation is always out of chaos, as the nation is always union. God and Country are synonymous in sport because *sport is an invented limit to test one's identity by gross or discrete competitive, motor movement.*

Skepticism and inquiry both are lethal to sport as a spectacle of reassurance because skepticism insists that the identity tested by bodily encounter be free to disengage from the encounter, and inquiry requires reflection on the nature and effects of the encounter. It would seem then that Aristotle was correct in his omission. And that the Athenian citizens were acting on solid sense when they asked Socrates to leave their city for corrupting the youth—which is precisely what he did. Thinking human beings—probing, inquiring, careful, free citizens—are dangerous. As governors, generals, coaches, one wants instant obedience rather than inconvenient questions. Civilization, as Freud said, must have its discontents. General Patton's staccato steps before the monstrous, mythical flag became an unnerving model of coaching in our time. Ideas must be suppressed for they may make war on war, just as thought may make sport of sport. This is the legitimate fear of every Bobby Knight stereotype in the country.

It could, without treason, be different. Sport may mean literally "to divert," but if athletes are excellence in the guise of human beings, and if they begin to see their bodies as themselves, then why would it not be possible for sport to focus rather than to divert—to point to, and be, the cultural revolution, instead of reacting adolescently against it? Why should scarcity define sport? Is sport necessarily a win-lose model of behavior?

Sport can be ecstasy, a theater of the new consciousness, a demonstration, not of our brutality, but of our imagination. Years ago, Charles Reich—for reasons not entirely aesthetic—watched Berkeley students playing touch football in bell-bottoms, and observed that it was more like ballet than a contest. A more satisfying evocation was Paul Newman as *The Hustler*, Fast Eddy. Shooting pool with ordinary players for fun money, diverting himself from the real contest with Minnesota Fats, he suddenly ran the entire table. Those ordinary men broke his hands for hustling them, but later he explained to a friend: they were *so* bad, so clumsy—he had to show them just how beautifully the game could be played, the infinite pleasure in receiving the form of beauty. Not for money. Beauty. For that moment, pool became art and the hustler a sensuous sportsman.

Why should not beauty and creativity define sport? Eleanor Metheny reminds us that competition literally means "to strive with."[308] To compete here communicates not winning, but enhancing the beauty of the bounded situation—to push out the limits of creative facility, to share excellences.

Was Aristotle wise? No doubt. Men and women do think and sweat in common. But our mind is our body given a new possibility. Our mind shapes a future, invents meaning where there is none, and brings order out of chaos. So our hands throw up the Parthenon like a fist—an aesthetic finger to the forces of decomposition. So our feet fly around the track at Olympia, transcending death in movement and grace. So our loins and lips join the other and share liquid touch and the possibility of new life. Stone into art. Track into dance. Ecstasy into birth.

This is sport into communion: this is my body offered for many. And this is the place to end this romantic invocation for a religion of sport—just before we are tempted to call Jesus the Athlete on the Cross. Günter Grass' dwarf in *The Tin Drum* does exactly that:

> Athlete most amiable, I called him, athlete of athletes, world's champion hanger on the Cross by regulation nails. And never a twitch or a quiver. The perpetual light quivered, but he displayed perfect discipline and took the highest possible number of points. The stop watches ticked. His time was computed. In the sacristy the sexton's none-too-clean fingers were already polishing his gold medal. But Jesus didn't compete for the sake of honors. Faith came to me. I knelt down as best I could, made the sign of the cross on my drum, and tried to associate words like "blessed" or "afflicted" with Jesse Owens and Rudolf Harbig and last year's Olympic Games in Berlin.[309]

Of course Grass is being ironic, not pious. The same Germany that gave birth to the radical freedom of the Reformation brought forth Hitler's refusal to shake Jesse Owens' hand. Winning, after all, isn't everything, it is—and always has been—more fun (and more lucrative) than losing. Germany's victories and right-wing theater were to last a thousand years. They invented the Blitz and the Bomb. Community became the invincible *Volk*. The students stopped rioting in the streets and law and order were restored to the nation. Hitler did indeed bring the Germans together.

THE PLEASURE OF PAIN: IMAGE

It is the most heroic cliché denying sensuous sport in the arsenal of coaches: "No pain, no gain." I heard this macho slogan—shrugging off injury and body rearrangement, over fifty years ago from my football coach in Dallas. His name—his actual name—was Fite, and he *liked* to hurt people. He never ceased being disgusted with me for allowing a mangled ankle to take me out of practice—and eventually out of football. "Of course we're going to take the hide off you," he'd snarl, "but your new hide will grow on a real man."

Coach Fite was a closet philosopher. In his own winsome madness, he was raising an important question: what is the relationship between pain and ontology? Am I a creature of pleasure—spending my energies avoiding pain? Or is there a kind of future pleasure in necessary pain? Do we become adult by inviting challenge which must test our courage? Is there no way to the resurrection except through the crucifixion?

We *will* get hurt playing this game. But is physical danger our enemy? Is comfort our friend? Why have nearly all the religious traditions insisted that the buffeting of the body is good for the soul? Coach Fite for High Priest?

In Malaysia, I saw this religious pain phenomena up close and excruciating. Early in 1992, as guests of Roger and Arlene Mueller on our way to Java, we attended a Hindu celebration, called Thaipusam, at the Sri Subranmaniam Temple in the Batu Caves near Rawang, Malaysia. We took a 5:00 A.M. train from Kuala Lumpur, arriving at a station at 5:38 A.M., where we could walk to the river and begin the journey to the cave. Temporary stalls and booths were built to serve the eight hundred thousand devotees, all crowding the two mile procession toward the great steps leading up into the cave. The cave itself was a huge stony cavern, with an opening to the sky at the far end, which allowed some brushy growth—home to a family of monkeys, who clamored in and out of the opening to watch their strange cousins' bizarre ritual. They are classified as the "lower animals," and yet there's no record of monkeys deliberately causing themselves pain—except in captivity as dysfunctional animals. Why, I wondered, do we feel so superior simply because we have the capacity to be alienated from our bodies?

The Hindu pilgrims were offering up their pain to the gods, either in gratitude for gifts in the past (a child perhaps), or in supplication for future felicity (health wouldn't be a bad idea). At the river it was dawn-dark, with braziers burning to illuminate the faithful bathing in the water, then rising into chants and trances, their faces and bodies painted with ritual marking, reds and yellows, streaks of blue. When the moment seemed right, the ritual "torture" began. A long skewer was pushed through the cheek, the mouth cavity, and out the other cheek. The tongue was completely pierced by a rod or arrow; scores of barbed hooks fastened through the skin, front and back—and pieces of fruit hung on each hook, like some kind of human display stand. Sometimes the hooks were attached to long chains held by fellow travelers, who pulled them tight—distending the skin out in rivulets of flesh. Huge chariot like structures (called *kavitys*) were placed over their heads, supported on their bodies by long spikes, embedded around the waist. There was almost no blood flowing from any of these punctures, and little scarring from previous festival paroxysms.

Devotees danced, whirling and skipping, flailing arms and legs, demonstrating—witnessing—that their burdens were light, and their pain joyous. Eyes rolled up as sweat rolled down. In the temple cave itself, lighted only by huge fires (a surreal out-take from Indiana Jones in the Temple of Doom), I saw men dance themselves into a frenzy, and, sticking out their tongues, receiving burning camphor tablets on them—letting them sizzle away. I thought of Isaiah.

> Then flew one of the seraphim unto me, having a live coal in his hand which he had taken with tongs from off the altar. And he laid it upon my mouth, and said: "Lo, this has touched thy lips; thine iniquity is taken away, and thy sin purged." [310]

Form and Substance: Having and Being

What we must consider here is the relationship between *having* and *being* a body at the same time. Paraphrasing Tillich on religion and culture, *having is the form of being, and being is the substance of having.* And extrapolating from Berger, *there is no being at all until there is having, and then the being interpenetrates the entire system—even while controlling the system from one specific space.* The most instructive way to communicate this relationship is through an understanding of pain. Any number of people have drawn out the connection between pain and imagination.

Jonathan Miller in *The Body In Question* is the clearest.[311] He begins by pointing out the particular status the body has among all the objects of the world: the person possesses it and at the same time is possessed by it, so that it is difficult to give any intelligible sense to the notion of a disembodied person.[312] So we have two images of our own body: a found self (the *Hair* inventory of toes, tits, eyes, etc), and the felt self (the body of sensations and springs of action). The felt self in not necessarily the image one sees in a mirror—it is much more important than that. It is the self we see in the mirror of our minds: the looking glass through which one must pass.

Now sensations are prompted by stimulation of the found self, but they cannot be recognized as ours until we establish a place—an existential space—where these sensations can be housed. In an infant there is pure sensation not recognized by a self, since none has yet been created. The baby has no imagination—only sensation. As we mature, we develop a brain map, a kind of neuron electoral college which selects out portions of our found self for representation:

> The electoral map is not a *picture* of the body, it is a neurological *projection* of it; that is, it is not painted on the surface of the brain, but called into existence through the nervous connection it has with the part it represents. We feel pain in the appropriate part of our felt image because there is a line of nervous connections between the sense organs in the skin and muscle and the Parliamentary representative in the brain that answers for each.
> 313

Some parts of the body seem to be absent from the map: the heart, liver, kidneys. They appear to have no representative in the parliament, and so, when threatened, depend on other parts to convey the danger. This is the phenomenon known as referred pain: a heart attack is felt on the front of the chest, or radiating down the arms—sometimes even the neck or jaw. The conclusion Miller draws is—appropriately enough—*thoughtful*:

> Pains don't happen in hands or heads or anywhere physical; they happen in the images of head or hands, and if these images are missing the sen-

sations are homeless.[314]

Under normal circumstances, the subjective image of our external body corresponds with the physical existence, but sometimes, the existence ceases and the image remains.[315] Doctors call this "the phantom limb"—where a person actually experiences pain in a missing leg or arm. The point is clear: our image of our bodies is like a translucent glove, manufactured to the dimensions of the body, but not identical with it. It is, in Mark Johnson's phrase, "the body in the mind." In the privacy of the imagination, pain occurs. In the public arena of the found and observable self, injury occurs. Every young child or athlete who has ever been told to "shake it off" knows the difference—especially tiny Kerri Shrug, who vaulted over personal pain to public glory in the 1996 Olympics in Atlanta.[316]

Elaine Scarry in *The Body in Pain* is the most graphic.[317] And she is also the most ontological. In a chapter entitled "The Structure of Torture," she takes us through "the conversion of real pain into the fiction of power," where we are led to understand that inflicting pain is also a "demonstration and magnification of the felt-experience of pain." Here physical pain is so "incontestably real" that Miller's discussion seems irrelevant and academic. Translucent glove? This is an iron fist.

Torture is the means by which a power that is contestable attempts to invest its instability with reality through the "self-conscious display of agency."

> In the very processes it uses to produce pain within the body of the prisoner, it bestows visibility on the structure and enormity of what is usually private and incommunicable, contained within the boundaries of the sufferer's body. It then goes on to deny, to falsify, the reality of the very thing it has objectified by a perceptual shift which converts the vision of suffering into the wholly illusory but, to the torturers and the regime they represent, wholly convincing spectacle of power.[318]

The torturer by interrogation, setting, and physical infliction is going to destroy the "boundary between public and private" because the distinction between inside and outside of the body has been "flayed" apart. Scarry does not think that the torturer really wants information: he wants to "unmake the victim's world" while building his own power world.[319] And the prisoner will be deprived of his agency, his power, by being made to perform part of the torture himself (standing erect, walking in squat position, etc.) until he comes to see his body as a source of the pain. He will despise himself because the lie set up by the torturer mimics something very real: that a person experiencing pain comes to feel the body as "the agent of the agony." Like a wild animal running away from its own pain, we come to feel our bodies betraying us.

The human being has been split in two. That is the final torture. As a whole human being he is a body and a voice: "my body" and "me." The body is made present by destroying it; the voice made absent by destroying it. In Miller's terms, the government has been overthrown, and left only the found self—with no discriminatory powers. The imagination is placed in "solitary confinement" outside the body in the voice of the torturer. *Having* a body has now been separated from *being* a body. Great pain mimes death, which makes the body absolutely present, while the voice vanishes so completely and alarmingly that we are prompted to construct another body—a "celestial" body—as its new home.

The two states are twins:

> The only state that is as anomalous as pain is the imagination. While pain is a state remarkable for being wholly without objects, the imagination is remarkable for being the only state that is wholly its objects. [320]

Scarry helps us see that the relationship between the two states is the story of creation. In Genesis God (through his voice—his "word") is promising that Abraham's seed shall multiply as the stars in the heaven or the sand on the seashore. God has *made* the world and will *make* a great nation. The primal pair are *told* to be fruitful and *multiply*, one of the few commandments, I think, that the world has kept to the letter. In 2050 CE the earth's population—barring statistic skewing calamity—will reach ten billion. Even today, China has twice as many people as the entire planet did in 1800.

God, apparently, *makes* mutable materiality by his immutable voice. As the fruitful ones bear fruit, they are inspired to count each little apple and log it under the *begats* of divine amplitude. A human being connects with another human being and as one becomes two, so the two become three, and the three the ten thousand things—as the Tao rewrites Genesis. Today it is still startling to watch the one grow large and split in two—the eternal miracle of replication.

But the multiplication happens because God wills it: his voice activates the birth process—"quickens the womb." After creating the original potentiality, he needs us for actuality—not merely to persist, but to re-assert the capacity to increase, to occupy more and more space, to become a greater nation, to have dominion, to be the world. As Scarry puts it: "the place of man is in the body; the place of God is in the voice."[321] Genesis, in other words, needs Numbers. The Hebraic immortality was not in some heaven or afterlife, it was in the community: a man's goods and a man's children. The reciting of genealogy was a religious triumph, a scripture of assurance that the voice was embodied.

As the voice of God recedes from human consciousness, leaving only the presence of body, the human community needs—if it is to remain human—intermediary conduits of the Voice. The nearer conduits are the prophets and patriarchs: "Thus saith the Lord…" These are still direct contacts, delivering more or less unimpeded messages—like a sound nervous system sending signals to the brain, unblocked by disassociative action. But as bodies increase and goods multiply, the voice can be muffled by material activity: "I am rich and increased with goods and have need of nothing," said the foolish farmer in Jesus' story. As Frank McConnell comments in *Storytelling and Mythmaking: Images from Film and Literature,* the narratives of Genesis and Exodus are descriptions of the "gradual disappearance of God from the scene of human action as a personal participant, and His replacement by the Law...."[322] This replacement is seen as a recognition that God acts through man, demonstrated by the double writing of the Law: once by God Himself with a fiery finger, and secondly by Moses at God's dictation. The direction is inexorable: from cult to culture, Divine King to Divine Kingship, God to man, awed supplicant to rich farmer. Whether this kind of withdrawal is correct—I'm certain Hebrew scholars don't all agree—it is suggestive, because it allows us to see the story of Jesus as the Great Reversal of this disappearance. This would give the parable of the Rich Fool even more aesthetic power. [323] The gap created by the receding voice is filled with the Law. Now God's Voice can be heard in stone. The *Torah* has never been understood in Judaism as a series of five "scrolls"—what we call the Pentateuch. Those scrolls are alive—the very voice of Yahweh Himself, as the young student in Jerusalem said.

The Problem of Parallel Universes

What is developing here are parallel universes. The world of bodies is constantly changing; the world of God's voice is everlasting. These two are completely separable, though related. There is, in Karl Barth's vocabulary, a radical discontinuity between God and Man: that "God" is not "Man" thundered at the top of our lungs. It is that peculiar notion of separation—apparently essential to Middle Eastern religions.

These "universes" need confirmation of one another. God has no body—no susceptibility to alteration—and therefore no growth and no surprises. The biblical narratives keep presenting God as omniscient, but *not* omnipotent. A great deal seems to happen that is not his will, sometimes making him so angry that he prompts a flood or two to wipe out his unruly creation. The contradiction is instructive: he knows what will happen, but can't—*or will not*—prevent it.

Why? Why isn't the Almighty *almighty*? The reason points to the parallel universes: God's body—the world—is the confirmation of the Word. Real existence is the only validation of the thought—the voice of the imagination: O taste and see that the Lord is good. Just as work is love made visible, so the world is God made visible.[324]

The Christian view of this "separation" is clearly the climax of this visibility. The torturer splits the person in two, but, in the crucifixion, the torture has inverted the process—subverted it. The pain of Jesus, which makes him completely present to his body, now invokes the voice of the Father: "My God, why have you forsaken me?" Where is your voice?

Where? In Jesus. The universes have united, instead of being split. That's what we mean when we say that God was in Jesus—Immanuel, God with us: the incarnation. So the Christian story is read backwards from the experience of torture, of unimaginable pain: the voice and the body are one. Whatever else the Jesus Seminar decides really happened to the man from Nazareth, one can print his death in bright red: he hung on nails and bled.

Who? The Word made flesh. Mary is made pregnant by the Word. The physical and the spiritual join, as the Voice reaches into her womb through the ear. It is not a displaced phallus—a bizarre fecund audiology. The story tellers are not the slightest bit interested in presenting Jesus as a biological oddity, or implying that God is some kind of spiritual sperm that can journey up the vagina and leave the guardian hymen in place. They are interested in the incredible fact that the Word *requires* flesh: that the "I am" speaking out of the burning bush at the foot of Sinai is also the "I am" speaking out of a burning heart at the foot of Calvary. The sacrifice being offered up on the cross is not made to a disembodied spirit.

It is God himself who is sacrificed.

There is no other way to know who God is but through the body, and that what Christ is, we all must be. The body is not to be diminished or denigrated, but amplified and celebrated: Spirit is another name for the potentiality of matter.

The Gnostics are wrong: matter is not evil. It *is* God. That, it seems to me, is what the Christian story is saying, and precisely what the theologians at Chalcedon were writing into creed. And, even if it's not, that's what I believe.

So one begins to understand the religious affiliation with suffering, and the possible perversion of suffering into sheer masochism. This perversion is accomplished by maintaining the split intended by the torturer. God is the voice, the world is the body. God is the "me" and human beings carry out his will. The Church is the "body of Christ." As victim, the supplicant, the monk, the missionary, the helper of the poor, the servant, the believers, must all subsume themselves under the fiction of power created by the Monarch, the King of Kings, the *One* before whom we shall have no other gods. This body must surrender to the voice—must suffer.

This *One* must offer up his only son, must pierce his pectorals and twist himself into the Wyoming sky, must skewer his cheeks and tongue, gouge out his skin, be crucified so the voice can say "this is my beloved," must confess that there is no health in him, that the poison of asps is under his tongue, that he has unclean lips, that his testicles should be crushed and sliced to guarantee subservience to the Lord of the Manse, that we should stand before the ruler of the city and affirm that we would be willing to go to hell for the glory of God, that God Himself has created a place of exquisite torture, a concentric descent into the oblivion of pain, that the howls of the damned and the wailing and screams of the transgressors of his will should go on forever and ever and ever and ever.

My God.

What I am wondering just now is this: given this seemingly inexhaustible invention of deprivations that passes for religious worship, could one make an equal case for pleasure as the ultimate "sacrifice" that unites the voice and the body? Scarry claims that pain has no "objects" but that imagination is "all objects." Why not a chapter or two on "Pleasure and Imagining"? Surely if the torturer can unmake our world and make the body completely present, then the pleasurer can do the same. Isn't pleasure without objects? The parameters of the body can be limned out by ecstasy as well as agony, and control can be established by comfort just as much as by cruelty.

Think of the peculiar phrase, "making love." Despite God's reported facility with extra somatic activity, intercourse does invite material multiplication. But what is *made* when one *makes out* ? Not just babies. *Pleasure.* This phenomenon—this sensation—has no particular end in itself, and while related to the sensory world it, like pain, is felt only in the imagination. If pain reduces the "felt self" to specifiable larder, pleasure elevates the "found self" into pure being.

Those who disperse pleasure will attract multitudes into submission, as any real lover knows. And the exact strategy of the torturer is used: the voice of interrogation now becomes seduction, the room of inevitable instrumental terror takes on the ambiance of intrigue and surprise, the sound of silence and brutality of waiting is transformed into irresistible anticipation, the victim prompted to participate in the moment as agent for the lover. All the world knows that sexual ecstasy is not just between the legs; it is between the ears. Pleasure is in the imagination. Why did Swaggart risk his entire career with Debbie Murphree? Mrs. Swaggart was more attractive than Debbie, but that was not the point. Man shall not live by wife alone, but by every fantasy of the flesh. It wasn't that Swaggart wanted power over Debbie—he had all he wanted of that on television. He wanted to be controlled by her intrigue, "tortured" in her pleasure parlor—so he could feel the spirit in his body again. When men want to be in control, they rape. When they want pleasure, they allow themselves to be controlled. Just ask President Clinton.

And now we see the relationship between denial and the love of God. If we submit to carnal love, we are worshipping the pleasurer. The corollary is clear: to be obedient to God—to worship him—is to be celibate or to allow intercourse only as instrumental in multiplication. Physical pain is to be seen as God's chastisement, like the caning in Singapore—bringing us closer to obedience and the final pleasure of pain: order instead of ardor. The history of the religious state is scarred by sado/masochistic activity masquerading as spiritual exercises.

I have seen the Church's version of sado/masochism, and decided that, if life were going to hurt, I might as well enjoy what I could before the hurt held. My high school English teacher—a wondrously demanding torturer named Agnes Taylor—once asked me in class what I lived for. She knew I was involved with the Methodists and the Calvinists—I was the original office boy for the winsomely conservative Young Life organization, which had its charter club at Dallas Theological Seminary. Miss Taylor was Captain Bligh in grammatical drag. Her words whipped, and—by God or Goddess—we sailed safely into literacy.

> "Well, Lawrence, we are waiting."
> "I live for my own pleasure," I said. [I could tell she was not pleased.]
> "I expected something better from you."

What could have been better? Something dishonest, perhaps? Something altruistic and pretentious. Some Calvinistic confession about the glory of God, or a Nixonian: "I want to make a difference in the world." Hitler was quite busy making a difference in the very moment Miss Taylor asked me that question. Something Clintonian: "I feel your pain." John Calvin was willing to burn Servetus at the stake for not stating properly the idea of the Trinity,[325] and graciously issued orders that green wood be used in order that the heretic would have more time to recant and recite. I should have quoted the Sermon on the Mount, a verse or two about loving enemies, walking a second mile, or lighting up the world. English teachers and fundamentalists love quotations.

I did live for my own pleasure—and I do—and so does everybody who has any health left in them. Deliver me from the martyrs of this world, who claim that they are living and dying for me. Mortimer Adler makes a very strong case that the greatest treatise ever written on ethics is Aristotle's *Nicomachean Ethics*. Adler insists that it *was* not simply the best among the Greek writings, but it *is* the best at this very moment. And Aristotle's major premise is that no one deliberately does harm to himself. One lives for pleasure [read "the good"], and the adventure of philosophy is the journey through alternative understandings of human essence and the consequent decision for action based upon careful observation and reason. What truly makes me happy? That action alone gives pleasure—and should be sought by all rational beings.

And one begins to understand the football coach at Crozier Technical High School. Some men, whose kingdoms are unstable, who are threatened with vulnerability and defeat, like to cause pain. They are not consciously torturers. There is a sense in which only someone else's pain will give us pleasure. [326]

SISYPHUS VS. ARMAGEDDON: CONTEST

As the Cowboys and Broncos, the 49ers and Packers renew the great

American adventure on the threshold of the twenty-first century, it seems inevitable to ask: Who cares who wins *any* contest?

Remember? In January of 1984, 105,000 sat in the historic Rose Bowl, and upwards of 120 million from around the world assembled instant images from the media's magic transmitters. Our nation stopped, vast capital flowed, while the final survivors in hard-core professional football contended for what only one might possess. The Super Bowl—a supreme moment of sport spectacle—came to Pasadena, near the city of angels where it all started eighteen years before. It seemed almost predestined that Orwell's year of the omnipresent Eye should be ushered in by America's right-wing theater in the Great Bowl, celebrating our national will to win. Soon the Great Games began, fired by Olympic dreams on the very soil where Tarzan came to Hollywood and Vine, and Lombardi elevated Rozelle's vision into an apocalypse. Every year, America pauses for civil religion's finest hour.

Why do so many seem to care? Granted that millions don't care—and some are just a trice condescending about the fact that over half the able-bodied men in America are reduced to immobilized Gullivers by the "electric Lilliputians" on their TV screens.[327] If one hundred million people suddenly fell ill on the same day each year, the news would likely make even the most haughty of medical journals. The ebola virus is global news, an infectious *Hot Zone* more lethal than the virus of viewing. Still, the end-zone invites explanation, for the phenomenon we are discussing is not limited to one occasion of mid-winter madness, but is rather a spectacular instance of international obsession.

In Money We Trust

Why all this excitement, this ritual hysteria of anticipation and imagination? Several easy answers come to mind. The most obvious (and "Jerry Maguire" correct one) is "Show me the money!" This is not your local pickup touch football for fun contest. When investors are willing to float multiple millions for a space in which to view this game, chances are good that we have moved from sport to big business. The union/management bargaining contests have demonstrated this in baseball and hockey and canceled NBA games in the fall of 1998 [for the first time in its history]. As the wealthy argue over the fine print, the average fan has difficulty conjuring up compassion for either side. Michael Jordan's paycheck for one Nike commercial probably exceeds what an Indonesian worker, producing the very shoe he hawks, would make in two hundred years. Each player for the winning team in a Super Bowl receives escalating payoffs running toward six figures in 2001, and that much again in previous play-off checks. Television advertisements during the Super Time run a million dollars per minute—an astounding $17,000 per second and the total dollars turned over at this one event is escalating toward a billion.[328] Cedric Dempsey, President of the NCAA, reports that illegal gambling on sport in America in 1998 ran between eighty and one hundred billion dollars. As Frank Lalli puts it, more than easy, the big business explanation seems inevitable and overwhelming.

Yet financial gain begs the question. Why are so many so interested that they are willing to provide backing of this amplitude? Are the behavioral engineers so God-like that they can create interest ex nihilo?

Excellence and Possibility

Attraction is there to be exploited. What is it? Perhaps the answer is the pursuit of excellence, what the Greeks called *arete*. Paul Weiss centered his inquiry into the philosophy of sport on this point.[329] With the road to Los Angeles already clogged with gladiators looking beyond Pasadena to the Coliseum, one remembered the origin of sporting contests among the Greeks. Their great warrior Patroclus dead on the field of Troy, they paused at his funeral to celebrate his life as he actually lived it. They hurled javelins and stones, raced chariots, wrestled hand to hand, and ran as fast as they could—freed for a moment from the requirements of war, from the necessity to kill with spears and rocks or to use their speed to subdue the enemy. As Eleanor Metheny points out in a paper entitled "The Symbolic Power of Sport," the Greeks created a chance for themselves to push out the limits of possibility, to see just how far they could throw, how fast they could race, by abstracting the action of battle from the confusion of warfare itself.

It is ironic in a classic Greek sense that the man whose death was celebrated by these games was himself warned to observe limits and not fight beyond the wall. Yet, dressed in the elite armor of Achilles, he overstepped his ability, flung himself at the enemy outside the wall—and was killed. His arete translated into hubris; his daring into defeat. And yet, all true athletes will understand. There are limits, but only infinite contest can define them.[330]

Thus as each man stepped up to the starting place on the rule-governed field of sport, he knew precisely what he was going to try to do; he knew how the outcomes of his efforts were to be evaluated and by whom; and he knew that he had a fair chance to perform it—a fair chance to exert his utmost effort in the performance of one human action.

> Freed of all the hampering effects of war, he was free to go all out, holding nothing back—free to focus all the energies of his being on one supreme effort to hurl his javelin at the nothingness of empty space. [331]

The "athlon" was the prize, the crown of greenery placed on the head of him who was the strongest or swiftest of all.[332] Three thousand years later—from Los Angeles and Atlanta to Sydney—the word 'athlete" still reminds us of those who hurl and race for the prize, abstracted from survival in the water or agility in the hunt. Of course, then—as now—the rewards were not always symbolic. Women's Liberation historians may refresh their outrage by record-ing that the trophy for winning the Trojan Games chariot race was a slave woman—well trained in household matters. [333] Losers no doubt received the Greek version of Linda Tripp.

Metheny goes on to suggest that team sports had their origin not with the Greeks but with the hard working peasants of feudal Europe. Noblemen rode into battle, and in tournament ritual abstraction jousted with one another amid great pageantry. But the peasants walked into battle, slugged and slogged face to face with the enemy, throwing huge rocks, gathering behind battering rams, attempting to push through the gates of cities and strongholds. Their games mirrored this team warfare: a set of peasants pushing a boulder in one direc-tion while another set strained to send it back—the goals defined by sticks set up to represent the gates of a city or any enemy's castle. Reduce the rock, change its shape slightly, substitute a more malleable substance, and we are not far from soccer, rugby,....and football itself.

So it seems at least reasonable that sport stems from paramilitary activi-ty, as an opportunity to demonstrate either individually, or as a team, just how well that activity could possibly be performed. Pursuit of excellence is a per-suasive answer.

Therapy and Control

The list of probable reasons grows. Dr. Ernest Dichter, former head of the Institute of Motivational Research (a corporate consulting firm), suggested three persuasive explanations for the popularity of American football. [334]

The first is more subtle than it appears. The illicit violence in contempo-rary society is so frustrating to the well-socialized citizen that football is both refreshing and reassuring. Football's physical struggle is performed within boundaries. There are rules which cannot be violated without penalty and the vertical principle of authority undergirds every play. The "discipline" of the game is in producing "disciples." Vince Lombardi, that apotheosis of author-ity, knew this—and it was his open secret. Everyone was calling for freedom, but he understood the submissive sub-text: "But as much as these people want to be independent, they still want to be told what to do."[335]

Total and precise obedience is the price football pays for its license to controlled mayhem. As a Michigan quarterback once put it: "There is nothing wrong with good, clean violence."

The second reason addresses our insecurity. The powerful factors of anonymity and alienation present in America are anesthetized by the "group therapy" of football spectatorship. In a stadium one feels identity with the in-group: even though surrounded by one hundred thousand nameless people, the spectators feel strangely unique. They are in and millions would like their place. Their pent-up emotions surface as they yell at others in the crowd, embrace them, urge on their team, bathe in the spectacle of color, sound and smell, in a massive encounter session: cheaper than analysis, faster than psychiatry, more comfortable than Zen, less exposed than Esalen—a primal scream with a scoreboard.

Even on television, one can partake of the euphoric in-group feeling, identifying not only with the fans and players, but now adding the sport casting expertise and color to this sporting life. Hating Howard Cosell probably kept thousands of patients off the couches. Venting one's spleen on Howard approached almost religious proportions. Frank Deford wrote: "No one has ever been a more flammable burnt offering for those who would roast him in the press than Cosell."[336] And for those whose aversion prompted them to turn off the sound on Monday Night Football, Deford had a startling pronouncement:

> Well, too bad, for them.... Don't they understand? Cosell isn't television. He's not audio. Howard Cosell is sports in our time. Feel sorry for the people who turn off the sound. The poor bastards missed the game.[337]

The therapy continues, even though Howard does not. He died in April 1995, even as Monday Night Football celebrated twenty-five years of tele-couch analysis—and Frank Gifford survived, to break Walter Cronkite's record for consecutive years in prime time. Barely. In 1998, ABC took Gifford from the booth and shunted him to a bar in Baltimore for a pre-game shill. Now it's Frank's turn for family therapy.

Finally, in the midst of national sexual confusion, biker styles, gay and feminist mysteries, same-sex marriages, Jenny Jones and Jerry Springer, new-wave rebellion, fear and loathing on Capitol Hill, sports announcers who cross-dress, a black and white pop star who's masculinity seems equally ambiguous—football provides a reassurance of masculinity. It is no accident that Marabel Morgan climaxed her antidote to Women's Liberation and the world according to Garp with that incredible sport citation. In her manifesto of machismo, she drew out the logic of Paul's imperative that women be subject to their husbands in all things:

> Gals, I wouldn't dream of taking credit for the Super Bowl.... But I can assure you... [that you] can become a super wife and a Total Woman. [338]

Charge! Faith calls! Win Winsocki—by my God I leaped over a wall! Cheer—the Lord commands it for old Notre Dame. Look yonder: that raging fullback is a flying phallus planted heroically in the quivering anxiety of what we are.

Of Myths and Meaning

The history of humankind has been celebrated in stories that reflect our deepest perceptions about the meaning of it all, and two of these myths illuminate our contemporary situation.

1. The Metaphysics of Routine

The first of these is the Myth of Sisyphus. Homer tells us that Sisyphus, the king of Corinth, was the wisest and most prudent of mortals, but came into disfavor with the gods. He stole their secrets, put Death in chains, preferred water to thunderbolts as a divine gift, and—worst of all—refused to take the gods seriously. After his death, Sisyphus persuaded Hades to allow him to return to earth in order to chastise his widow for her own indiscretions. Once on earth again, he defied Hades' order to leave—compounding his heavenly offenses. The angry gods condemned him to roll a rock to the top of a mountain forever, where it would fall to the bottom, to be rolled up again by stubborn old Sisyphus.

Albert Camus saw in Sisyphus the modern Everyman, who, in spite of all, must be imagined as happy.

> But when he had seen again the face of this world, enjoyed water and sun, warm stones and the sea, he no longer wanted to go back to the infernal darkness. Recalls, signs of anger, warnings were to no avail. Many more years he lived facing the curve of the gulf, the sparkling sea, and the smiles of earth. A decree of the gods was necessary. Hermes came and seized the impudent man by the collar and, snatching him from his joys, led him forcibly back to the underworld, where his rock was ready for him.[339]

The message seems to be clear. Nothing matters beyond the process of the act itself. As Camus puts it, we must learn to live "without appeal"—without attempting to justify what we do by some ontological climax, some permanent goal, some immortal record, some financial, social, or sexual reward.

The "longing for tomorrow" is the great enemy, for it denies our location in time. Camus cites Heidegger as witness: *anxiety*—the situation in the flow of time is the source of everything. This anxiety, for Camus, is presented as alienation—precisely what the sport experience is designed to overcome: my team membership supports my status as communal; my victory rationalizes my existence—gives me permission to be in history. My insatiable drive for more victories is the telltale sign that alienation is too deep for alleviation by surface honors.

Teshigahara's film *Woman in the Dunes*—beyond its Taoist images—also translates Sisyphus to the screen, presenting him as the entomologist hoping to make a name for himself through scientific discovery. Instead—as we have seen—the insect collector is himself collected, caught in that huge sand pit, and forced to dig sand in order to stay alive. The sand must be excavated daily—always in the same way, and with no hope of escape. The woman, who has been in the dunes so long that she identifies with the sand—*is* the sand—teaches the ambitious male to be content with digging, since all life, in and out of the dunes, is daily excavation without meaning beyond simply *being there*. Life in the sandpit is an exact metaphor for life in Tokyo, so Teshigahara suggests. Only in the city the pit is larger, the diggers more numerous, the sand more impacted.

For Tokyo write in any human community you like. We must stop pretending that life has meaning in the sense that we should *get* somewhere. The hope of finality is the ultimate frustration because our entire energy must be spent in *constructing* significances and then claiming that we have in fact *discovered* them. Houses need painting again, more money must be raised for the endowment, new students arrive—lacking the knowledge we just imparted to old students who have outgrown us.

Championships have to be won again. Tom Landry won it all in 1972, but took off his Super Bowl ring in disgust in 1973, and then, after two more championships, was still not satisfied with America's Team, bed-checking his computerized gladiators even the night before *home* games. [340] And after all those years of glory and legends in Dallas, Landry was fired, replaced by Jimmy Johnson—who, after two consecutive Super Bowl championships, was fired by owner Jerry Jones, who watches forlornly from the sidelines as his mythic Cowboys disintegrate into hubris and holiness. What is an example of defeat? It is victory. At the deepest level, they *are* each other.

Nothing is enough. So 714 home runs are not enough and neither are 130 stolen bases; Lou Gehrig dissolves into Cal Ripkin, Babe Ruth into Roger Maris into Mark McGwire; Olga Korbut was ancient at twenty-two, and Nadia Comaneci's perfect tens had to be improved on in Moscow. How much sand had to be dug out of Los Angeles in the summer of 1984? Brian Boitano won gold in 1988, but wept in frustration at Lillehammer in 1994. How many times did Carl Lewis have to prove that he was the world's fastest human? Yesterday an African-Anglican was faster than the African-American. Today an African-Canadian is faster than the African-Anglican. Tomorrow a golden shoed African-American is unbelievably faster than mythic silver shoed Mercury.[341] One thinks of John D. Rockefeller. When asked how much money it took to satisfy a man, he replied, "Just a little bit more."

How Super is the Super Bowl? Duane Thomas, the star running back in New Orleans with the Cowboys in ancient 1972, was Black Sisyphus. A reporter wanted to know how he felt playing in the most important football game in the world. Thomas' answer: "They're going to play another one next year aren't they?" And the next. And the next. Hordes of peasants shoving a rock back and forth, straining to push it through sticks that represent the gate of the enemy's castle: not far, I think, from the king of Corinth.

How crucial is any contest? After four years telecasting with ABC's Monday Night Football, Don Meredith looked down from the celestial booth on the San Francisco game with Green Bay in Candlestick Park and said—on national prime time—for all to hear: "There must be something more important than this."

Don's comment reached far beyond mere athletic mediocrity on the field. City after city, banquet after banquet, year after year—the traveling freak show moved on. Weariness as an invocation to authenticity? The pornography of celebrity status could no longer energize Don's piece of the rock. Two months later *Sports Illustrated* published a feature story on "The Defection of Dandy Don."[342] There *must* be something more important—perhaps at NBC, perhaps in film, perhaps in deepening relationships with one's family, perhaps back with ABC again, perhaps simply a dandy glass of tea in the clear air of Santa Fe.[343] The gods say: be careful—rebel or no—you will push some rock. Camus warns us that genius, after all, is the intelligence that knows its frontier.[344]

Even George Leonard's "ultimate athlete" discovered the mountain. Running the soft rock of his own body up and down the wilds of Mt. Tamalpais near Mill Valley, California, he learned, as he put it, to be "at home in this world." Running for a moment beside some unknown woman, he was overwhelmed by a sense of the erotic freed from an eroticism.

"Everything is erotic—the sun, the mountain, the dust on the trail, the motion of my body, the air I breathe. All things all drawn together, all things yearn and are fulfilled. Just to move to love. No need to seek other meanings for life."[345]

The woman vanished, and Leonard moved inexorably down the mountain, only beginning to suspect that we must think of Sisyphus as happy.

> I continue along the Old Railroad Grade, descending toward destinations that in some sense will always dissolve and disappear before I can reach them. There is something here that I may yet understand: What we run for we shall never reach, and that is the heart and the glory of it. In the end, running is its own reward. It can never be justified. We run for the sake of running, nothing more.[346]

Alexander King dedicated one of his books to his wife, and titled it, *I Should Have Kissed Her More.* How ultimately sad that we repress our kisses, waiting for the eschatological moment, when love transcendent will validate all our trivial attractions to the bodies of earth. Or so reads the first primal myth of eternal reoccurrence.

2. Eschaton and Ecstasy

The second primal story is what I would call the myth of Armageddon. John the seer sets the scene, where the spirits of devils go forth against the kings of the earth: "And [God Almighty] gathered them together into a place called in the Hebrew tongue Armageddon."[347]

Here the *eschaton* is at hand. In the heart of Palestine, the decisive battle of history will be fought.[348] Here where the great armies from Egypt, Syria, Persia, Greece, and Rome turned this tiny land into a corridor of power, here the cosmic forces meet: angels vs. dragons, legions of light vs. demons of darkness—the Word of God (who leads the forces of righteousness with a sharp sword issuing from his mouth) vs. the terror of Satan (who leads the forces of destruction with foul spirits issuing from his mouth). It is the classic struggle, the ultimate duel, where two contend for what only one may possess. Absolute Good vs. Total Evil. Armageddon is the archetypal contest.

The message in this story also seems clear. It is issued in a time of testing and doubt, a time of fundamental trial when the very future of the people is at stake. History—it says—matters. Life means and means intensely, and we are moving somewhere in the civilizing process: alpha and omega, beginning and ending, creation and consummation. The *eschaton* is not empty, but filled with radical purpose. History matters—the Apocalypse shouts again— and all that matters will be decided today.

That is what we wanted to hear, this confident voice that conveys order moving across the face of the deep and challenging chaos, from political conservatives, the Christian Coalition, and even David Koresh deciphering the seventh seal at his Rancho Apocalypse. How acutely we suspected that the princes of this world would not go unchecked. Today, righteousness is crucified, but tomorrow, rightness is risen. Today, the flesh suffers, withers, dies. But the seals are broken open and—wondrous to behold—the seven bowls are poured out to reveal the great secret.

> The seventh angel poured his bowl into the air; and there came a great voice out of the temple of heaven, from the throne, saying, "It is done!" And there were voices, and thunders, and lightnings; and there was a great earthquake, such as was not since men were upon the earth, so mighty an earthquake, and so great. [349]

And the great city—say it not in Pasadena—was split into parts! Sisyphus be damned! This life of death is no life: it is the spirit that endures. If you are faithful in resisting the beast, you will win this primordial struggle. "If God be for us, who can be against us?" That, in the myth of Armageddon, is not a question, but an exclamation.

An Answer of Some Significance

We have reached, I think, the core of our love of contest. Beyond money, sheer excellence, and personal identity, there is this triumphant challenge to indifference and sameness: the annihilation of routine. The eschatological battle vindicates our existence. It is the final appeal. Winning gives instant immortality; losing is symbolic death.

General Douglas MacArthur understood. His famous benediction still graces Mitchell Stadium at West Point:

> Upon the fields of friendly strife
> Are sown the seeds
> That, upon other fields, on other days,
> Will bear the fruits of victory.

MacArthur would later, with profound arrogance and keen generalship, incur the wrath of his commander-in-chief, Harry Truman, by insisting that stalemate in Korea was no substitute for the glorious Apocalypse. He must cross the Yalu, must be allowed to bomb the Chinese. And when fired by Truman for insubordination, he explained it all before Congress and the world: "If we do not find some more equitable way to peace, Armageddon will be at our door." MacArthur apparently would have loved to open that door, stride through, and take his place in the pantheon of the gods. It would have been the Superest of Bowls! Is his shade stirring as the North Koreans rattle their reactor rods? As Bob Dole promised to pursue terrorists to the ends of the earth? As Bill Clinton wags the dog?

This lust for the *eschaton* was Richard Nixon's tragic flaw—as the angels poured out his tapes. No leader in our history, not Johnson in the Tonkin Gulf incident, not Kennedy contemplating the Cuban blockade, not Reagan reacting to tragic Russian paranoia, not even Bush drawing a line in the desert sands, appeared more empowered by the myth. Vietnam was on the plains of Megiddo. Here history would be written and it must not record that Nixon presided over America's first defeat in war. Free world vs. Communist Enslavement. South vs. North. West vs. East. The primordial struggle must not be questioned: The Beast is numbered—and we know who he is, and attack on him is not a matter for debate.

Nixon was never convinced that Watergate was important. It was, in his mind, a "third-rate burglary," and not a fit subject for the imperial power to discuss. He wanted to be remembered as a great statesman—on par, say, with Churchill, rallying the world in the greatest of wars. That's why he couldn't bring himself to burn the tapes, whose existence brought him down. They were his record of power. Homer would have loved writing about a Quaker whose *hubris* robbed him of the simple gifts of his heritage. Thou shalt not bear false witness, unless by telling the truth you lose the game.[350] The same Billy Graham who supported the war in Vietnam, delivered the eulogy sermon for Nixon at Yorba Linda, April 27, 1994. Surrounded by Marines, casket draped with an American flag, wreaths from around the world, all of the American presidents since 1972, the leaders of congress, and a national television audience, Graham invoked the democracy of death. We shall see him again in heaven—no doubt along with Kennedy, Johnson, Patton, and MacArthur: listening to the Mormon Tabernacle choir and watching the angels stir up those seven bowls—just aching for the opening of the seventh seal.

It's all so Super Serious that you have to be Semi-Tough to gain any perspective on the phenomenon. All America sensed the bemused expression of Shake Tiller and Billy Clude Puckett [Burt Reynolds and Kris Kristofferson on film; Frank Gifford and Don Meredith for semi-real] as they listened to the Shoat Cooper describe the patriotic flavor of the Dan Jenkins' Super Bowl: "Several hundred trained birds—all painted red, white, and blue would be released from cages somewhere and they would fly over the coliseum in the formation of an American flag." And as those fine, feathered patriots thrilled the supplicants at our civil religion shrine, "Bob Kellum, the Western TV star, would recite the Declaration of Independence." Then the grand Disneyesque invocation:

> Next would be somebody dressed up like Mickey Mouse and somebody else dressed up like Donald Duck joining the actress Camille Virl in singing "God Bless America."[351]

Watching Whitney Houston sing the *Star Spangled Banner* in Tampa for Super Bowl XXVI, invoking the gods of commerce and patriotism, made us realize that Dan Jenkins is not only a humorist, but a historian.

That mythic January, the people came to Pasadena, and the world watched the most public game: pretending that it—like life itself—matters, hoping that this heroic struggle on the field would provide not merely some break in our journey up the mountain with the rock of routine, but some grand moment—a final victory for our sad little lives. Sisyphus vs. Armageddon—exactly in the sacred ancestral space of all the Bowl games everywhere, looking out over the hills of Hollywood, the fantasies of pleasure, the urban revolution tubercular, endless orangeless counties stitched together with concrete and steel, celebrated and capitalized by Disney's Camelot and a coliseum poised to host the *agon* of Olympia.

As the flashes of lightning, peals of thunder, and mighty earthquakes poured from the angels' Bowl, popular sentiment favored significance. But the honest money—I'm told by Zorba the Greek—was on Sisyphus.

GODOT IN THE GAMEROOM: CAPRICE

Was Aristotle wise? Is John Simon?

John Simon is a film critic: sophisticated, acerbic, relentless, sometimes disliked *and* often respected—rather like Howard Cosell used to be. In a book of film criticism, Simon defends his own work as art, and offers us a proper distinction between art and non-art. "We must not confuse pleasures with higher pleasures," he tells us, "fleeting with lasting goods, laughter with laughter that taught us something...." We are "dual creatures," and we can appreciate *both* "Bach and the Beatles," "Kafka and comic strips." We can enjoy a great dancer's arabesque *and* a champion tennis player returning "an impossible smash."

> But it is wrong to call the tennis player an artist, wrong to prefer Super-man to Joseph K., wrong to equate a popular song with a concerto. Not morally wrong (though, in some cases, that too), but esthetically wrong.[352]

This strikes me as a debatable point—an invitation to deepen our analysis of sport as ritual for body religion. I might, on occasion, prefer concertos to Big Bad Voodoo Daddy, and Joseph K. has a certain complexity which makes him by and large more interesting than Superman. But is Simon some kind of simple when he tells us that it is wrong to call a tennis player an artist? Not *morally*, he insists, but *aesthetically* wrong?

What does it mean to say that something is *aesthetically* wrong? What is an aesthetic moment or object? David Miller, musing on *Gods and Games*, informs us that *Aesthesis* derives from the Greek verb *aisthanomai*, the past-tense form of *aisthesthai*, meaning "to know" or "to sense." That is: to know is to know with your senses. Miller cites several ancient Greeks who use *aisthesis* to mean not only "knowing," but "seeing" and "hearing" as well. And he remembers—even deep into December—that marvelous little play, *The Fantasticks*, where a character implores the listener to "see...with your ears," and "hear...with the inside of your hand." Light and shadow on the green breath of the earth. *Before* life is an ember: "Celebrate sensation."[353]

Aisthesis, then, is seeing and knowing with the whole body, with, as Miller puts it, the wholeness of the body. *Aisthesis is* body-seeing: not cerebration as much as celebration.

I assume that Simon would have no problems with calling *ballet* art. For in ballet, critics would tell us, the intention is clear. It is a serious, disciplined evocation of value through the beauty of moving form, a heightening of sensibility—new levels of possibility made aware to us.

So we might even be willing to label ballet a form of *kinesthesis*. The Greek here combines *kinein*, "to move," and *aisthesis*, "to perceive." *Kinesthesis* in physical education becomes kinesthesia, and is defined as the sense whose end organs lie in the muscles, tendons, and the joints, and are stimulated by bodily tension. Kinesthesia is indeed the muscle sense, the body sense. The science of the muscle sense we know as kinesthetics: the development and discipline of the muscle sense, of the perception of the universe through the receptors of the sense organ—training, if you will, in body language.

If ballet qualifies as art, why not gymnastics? At what point, in other words, does kinesthetics pass over into aesthetics? One watches the Olympic gymnast with something approaching wonder. The grace and timing is so exquisite, the movement so mesmerizing. But Simon might tell us that these are complex exercises—precise movements without meaning.

Perhaps free skating qualifies? Here is grace and poise, gliding and whirling to various musical rhythms, pirouetting and shimmering in kinesthetic sweat. Is it *sliding* ballet at least? Why retain the word "art" only for the classical sweat and audible leaps of the stage?

Yet the level of expectation is somehow different for ballet, rather like the difference between a concerto and a popular song. A concerto requires more intellect, more perception, more concentration, as does ballet. Popular songs and skating and gymnastics are so much more simple, so—how shall we say it?—so *easy.* I don't mean easy to do. Who could do what those tiny Russian and Romanian girls did? Who can defy gravity like "little body," Mary Lou Retton, or the gymnastic munchkins at Atlanta? It is easy, however, to *watch.* It demands nothing of us that would alter our perception of the world—or heighten it. At least, this is what aesthetics purists would tell us.

That is, non-art only entertains us, it does not *confront us*—as Lahr suggested. And so Simon says [haven't we all played this!] that tennis is not art—can under no circumstances be art, because there is no possible way that a tennis stroke, however beautiful, however graceful, would confront us: challenge us to be other than we are, raise the quality of our humanness.

So ballet is not a game, but tennis is. Gymnastics is a form of exercise, but ballet transcends exercise. Then Bill Bradley describes basketball as "brutal ballet." Some motion pictures are sheer entertainment. Others become art. Are there any "strange kinds of clarity" emerging from these meditations?

Wrestling With Playing

I am certainly not the only one to meditate on these matters. Dr. Frank Wilson, a professor of neurology, has written a delightful book, *Tone-Deaf and All Thumbs: an Invitation to Music Making,*[354] analyzing the relationship between the brain and the development of musicianship. In the first paragraph, he compares music and athletics, underlining the physical renaissance that George Leonard had called the "rediscovery of the body"—the explosion of interest in participation in sport:

> This excited awareness of the body's physical potential, and the great popularity of novel approaches to the exploration of that potential, make the time ripe for a new slant on one of our most venerable pastimes—music. At first glance, the notion of the musician as an athlete seems contrived, if not downright comical. By what stretch of the imagination can one consider a violinist even remotely akin to a wrestler? Glad you asked.[355]

Wilson goes on to draw an explicit comparison between the musician and the athlete—-despite "the stereotyped and mutually uncomplimentary notions that you might encounter in football locker rooms and recital halls." While the musician concentrates on improving control of the muscles of the upper extremities (the hands), the mouth and the air passages, the athlete develops mainly the trunk, the leg, and the upper arm muscles. Musicians mostly stay stationary (with spectacular exceptions at, say, a drum and bugle corps show), while athletes are usually moving: pursuing opponents, teammates, or some inanimate object quite passionately.

Yet the relationship is clear:

> In certain sports, most notably gymnastics and ice skating, and of course ballet, the striking parallels of these physical disciplines are unobscured....When the necessary moves have been mastered to a certain level of expertness, the athlete or performer moves to a sort of summit experience—live performance—during which the effort is made to perform flawlessly.[356]

My college choral conductor used to chide the administration for putting so much money into sports, and not enough into choirs. "You can't lose a concert," he would say. But, of course, you can "lose" a musical performance, as Wilson points out. Both the athlete and the serious musician want to "win"— although the musician might be more interested in communicating sheer excellence than in winning approval—read applause.

What Wilson wants is for music to join in the rediscovery of the body, "this revolution in people's attitude about fresh air, fitness, fun, and a new waistline."[357] He does not want music to remain "a spectator sport."[358]

Fred E. H. Schroeder has written an entire book relevant for this kind of meditation, entitled *Outlaw Aesthetics: Arts and the Public Mind.*[359] One chapter—"Ballet, Boxing, Bullfighting and other Sports"—is particularly intriguing. He wants to answer the question: "How do I know what is 'good' in the arts?" He also wants to understand "art" as a neutral term, closer to artifice and any kind of designed actions, than to more narrow aesthetic forms.

Within the bounds of this permissive definition, we may consider as arts all forms of athletics, most particularly ballet and professional wrestling, which tend to be the most theatrical variants of their art categories.

Now, we commonly think of professional wrestling as fake—not like that NCAA drab sport indulged in by Garp. Which means, of course, that it is most definitely a form of theater: a scripted play. Schroeder calls it "a dead-end form of theater," by which he means that no "wider horizons are opened to the imagination." This "theater"—snubbed by "serious" critics—does not engage us at our deepest level. The elite mantra is intoned: Tennis players cannot be artists.

But wrestling also has affinities with dance. Both are rehearsed, have dramatic structure, communicate in bodily movement, with broadly based ethnic traditions (Schroeder mentions Japanese Sumo wrestling and the Bharata Natyam dance of South India).

From my experience in Japan, the relationship between wrestling, dance, and religion is particularly instructive in Sumo. The Sumo ring is actually conceived as sacred space, marked off by the *kanagawa*, which also surrounds sacred trees, rocks, etc. all over Japan—and which is worn by the Grand Champion as he comes out before the beginning of the matches to celebrate his position as Yokozuna with ritual dance. The wrestling circle is covered by a canopy exactly matching that of a Shinto shrine, and the referee is a kind of priest, insuring that the ritual match will be conducted "correctly." All Sumo wrestlers engage in pre-match ritual, which includes stylized leg lifting and the throwing of salt. Lifting might be helpful in limbering up, but salting? That is strictly part of the sacred existential space: to purify the ring in accordance with Shinto "doctrine" that life is fertility, reverence for nature, *and* purity.[360]

"Dance" in Sumo is almost frozen in time, but it shares this "fixed" quality with more recognized formal dance, as in *The Nutcracker Suite*. Much popular art does not have this altar-like rigidity. In fact, it almost by definition thrives on "progression," innovation, bad taste excursions into the offensive, street smart aesthetics. Probably not many lovers of Bach think Nine Inch Nail very good art. Break dancing started in the streets and has yet to make it into the New York Ballet, which practices what anyone would call cultivated art. Both are quite athletic. Mikhail Baryshnikov always appeared to be in supple physical condition, and, within invented limits, tested excellence with gross or discrete motor movements with every leap.

The experiments in the streets and the clubs change almost as fast as one can learn them, as if the experimenters are more interested in cult language for the in-group than perfecting technique. Cultivated dance fixes the "best" of these innovations and preserves them in repertory—what Schroeder unfortunately names, embalming. These preservations are more like resurrections, so powerful and moving that they do not dissolve into yesterday's top forty, but take new life every time they are performed.

Is the distinction we are looking for embedded in the word *permanence*? After all, we must imagine Sisyphus as happy. What are we to make of these revisionist definitions of art? Are there any principles here for understanding aesthetics?

Let me make this point as unmistakable and non-mysterious as possible. With all authority created, life centered on the body, all things permissible within those bodily limits, it follows that no hierarchy of values can ever be established as absolute—no matter how high on the best seller lists the books of virtue climb.

Does this mean the end of any distinction between art and non-art? What we have is art as feeling and experience, as energy forming itself into imaginative bodies. So *aesthetics* and *kinesthetics* in some sense coalesce: one can no longer say art for ballet, or non-art for gymnastics, if both *confront us*, involving the totality of bodily expression, extending the limits of our possibilities, delighting our eyes, and inspiring our own performances. Art and absolutes always play the infinite game on a finite field.

Now, any event or activity or object may potentially "confront" us. Looking at a mail box may trigger memories and even metaphysical anxieties, thinking of a letter you once received from him or her—or for that matter the IRS. How does art "confront" us—and can tennis players *playing tennis* do that? Schroeder suggests an arithmetic image that has merit.

Ordinary events—even popular arts—are not self-sustaining. They are thinly layered and tied to the moment, products of their time and place and nothing more. Their artifacts belong in the category of *landeskunde* and might possibly survive in one of those folk museums somewhere. But arts—in Simon's sense—are multilayered, deeply rich in design, and, while produced in time and place, transcend those to enlarge our humanity.

So Schroeder gives us an equation: an eternal denominator and a shifting numerator. Imagine, he says, that we place two art works together [he suggests Myron's *Discobolus* and an action photograph of John L. Sullivan, or perhaps Martha Graham's *Appalachian Spring* and a 1944 world series game]. All four selections are clearly placed in time, but not equally "dated." Sullivan and the baseball game seem somewhat mundane in comparison to *Discobolus* and *Spring*, which have a "inherent universality" that transcends the Attic Peninsula of 450 BCE and the Manhattan Island of 1944.[361]

"Inherent"? From what stance could one possibly say that Martha Graham's work was "inherently" universal but not a picture of a boxer? Suppose, for example, the picture were of Joe Louis fighting Max Schmeling. Now we have the Brown Bomber versus the Brown Shirt: black American and white German. Louis lost and then in the rematch destroyed Schmeling in the first round.

The Fight for Dignity

This is time and place, popular culture, the art of self defense, a creation of the moment—to be forgotten like a thousand other boxing matches, surely belonging among marginal nameless numerators that fill up our sad little lives. But then a little girl in Stamps, Arkansas, listens over the radio to a boxing match. She is in her grandmother's family store ["the Store"], where friends and neighbors had taken every "last inch of space," every chair and stool and box and lap filled with palpable nervous energy. Her Uncle Willie had turned the volume as loud as it would go so that all of the youngsters outside on the porch could hear. The anxious mood was carried by dark hope:

"I ain't worried 'bout this fight. Joe's gonna whip that cracker like it's open season."

"He's gone whip him till that white boy call him Momma."[362]

The girl listens as the white announcer calls the fight for "the ladies and gentlemen" all around the world, missing, she thinks, the irony of addressing all those Negroes, sweating and praying, glued to their "master's voice" as "ladies and gentlemen."

The static intonations rise. Louis is on the ropes, pounded by a left to the body, and a right to the ribs, and he may be going down.

> My race groaned. It was our people falling. It was another lynching, yet another Black man hanging on a tree. One more woman ambushed and raped. A Black boy whipped and maimed. It was hounds on the trail of a man running through slimy swamps. It was a white woman slapping her maid for being forgetful.[363]

Was this just another fight? Or was it something like "your whole being at stake here"? The black youngster knew differently.

> This might be the end of the world. If Joe lost we were back in slavery and beyond help....Only a little higher than the apes. True that we were stupid and ugly and lazy and dirty and, unlucky and worst of all, that God Himself hated us and ordained us to be hewers of wood and drawers of water, forever and ever, world without end.[364]

But the Brown one recovered and blasted the great white hope to the canvas, with the "winnah"—and still heavy weight champion of the world—Joe Louis. "The Store" had become sacred space, just like that ring so far from Arkansas.

Thus does little Marguerite Johnson describe a boxing match she heard in her uncle's store, "a night when Joe Louis had proved that we were the strongest people in the world," an event that transcends time and space and confronts white America with the coming new day—when tall Maya Angelou says to all America at the inauguration of a President from Arkansas: "Good Morning." When deep Maya Angelou takes us "Down in the Delta" at Christmas to meet the ghost of slavery past.

Body and Imagination

The new consciousness "community" has dared to entertain this astonishing hypothesis, formulated theologically at Chalcedon, that body and mind are *distinguishable* but not *separate*. Formulated metaphorically in *Cyclosis*, the astonishment translates as grace: we think with our whole bodies. So convolutions on a horizontal bar may be physically simpler than *Swan Lake* ballet movements, but they are no less "artistic." For the aesthetic (the knowing, perceiving, art sensibility) fundamentally plays with the universe: pokes at it, cuts it up and pastes it together in collages, intersects its time flow, arranges its wave lengths, squeezes its textures, frustrates its natural rhythms, smears it, multiplies it, laughs at it, laughs with it, represents it, makes it present.

Only one thing it does not do. It does not conquer it. Art does not have dominion—authority—over the world. It caresses it and loves it. Domination is madness: a forgotten way. "It is the curse of theology," writes Gerardus van der Leeuw, "always to forget that God is love, that is, movement. The dance reminds us of it....Whoever does not dance runs, races, waddles, limps—that is, he dances badly. We all must learn once to dance so that once again a general consciousness of life can be created...." [365]

Non-seriousness then is that quickness, that readiness to move, that facility, adroitness, poise, mercurial magic that puns with the Word made flesh, accepts no situation as unredeemable, no solution as final, no formulation as divine, no death as despair, no life as paralyzed. Non-seriousness pricks our pretensions about ourselves, pipes a tune and says, come dance with me.

As David Miller pointed out, that is the fundamental meaning of the Greek *aesthesis:* non-seriousness. The "aesthetic" man is dangerous, for he will not take our pretentious nonsense seriously. Artists who would not shape their work to the community standards ["the express image of noble character"] were "unwelcome" [compelled "on pain of expulsion"] in Plato's Republic. Of course. They will disrupt utopia, frustrate any organized effort to freeze spontaneity, turn every portentous and heavy academy into a circus.[366]

And when *aesthesis is* combined with *kinesthesis,* what power is generated to redeem our exhausted, moribund, bureaucratic, serious world. Think of it: the art of motion, honing the raw processes of energy and exploding daily into shocks of delight.

How Long Can We Wait?

Athletes do raise the question of meaning in "what you call your life." Think of Samuel Beckett, a French-Irish writer of the strangest kind of fiction, of which the most famous is called *Waiting for Godot.* It is a play that might start someone meditating on metaphysical education.

Two tramps wait by a leafless, lifeless tree on a bare stage—wait for some mysterious stranger named Godot, who they hope will give their lives significance. They pass the time with small talk, little games, but Godot never comes. *Two* other strangers arrive named Pozzo and Lucky: Pozzo a brutish, bullying, bureaucratic type; Lucky a luckless servant, carrying Pozzo's bags, entertaining him, and occasionally even thinking for him, all on command. In the exact center of the play, Lucky delivers his only speech, a seemingly meaningless paroxysm of words, pouring out and tumbling over one another with no obvious coherence, almost as if his blocked circuits suddenly were turned loose all at once and his verbal switchboard jammed with noise sounding like thought.

But one must *hear* this noise—particularly anyone interested in physical education and sport, who still is wondering why anyone would question Simon's simplicity: no tennis players can be called artists. Find a copy of the play and turn to Lucky's "speech." Take a deep breath. Deeper than that. Say the following invocation aloud: "...personal God quaquaquaqua with white beard quaquaquaquaqua..." Can you feel the Beta waves wavering? Alpha ocean shimmering?

Now recite, with accelerating dispassion, Lucky's entire outburst, allowing the sports for all seasons mantra to glide into your consciousness: tennis [bracketing football, running, cycling, swimming, flying, floating, riding, skating, golf—not to mention dying] tennis. Recite it "for reasons unknown," beyond rivers running through the earth gone cold and unfinished labors abandoned and who can say what time will tell us "in spite of the tennis...."367

Four times the phrase appears: "in spite of the tennis"—like a litany, almost a requiem mass. *Is* it gibberish? Beckett playing with words and *us* ? Is he painting from within, etching feelings, leaving the surface in this ontological burlesque show? Suppose—we're only playing here, of course—that the two tramps are body and mind, know that they are somehow not separate, and are waiting for some outside force to unify them, give them meaning and purpose. But Godot never comes.

I do know that it is a useful fiction that body and mind are separate, but the games we devise to pass the time are ludicrous obscenities if they do not confront us with this wholeness for which we do not have to wait because it is here and always has been. And Pozzo and Lucky suggest—to me, not necessarily Beckett or anyone else [surely this is nonsense]—the tramps everywhere institutionalized in culture: separating off kings and subjects, lords and vassals, masters and servants, professors and students, male and female, mind and body, concertos and popular music, art and non-art, Simon and me.

The center part of the play—our play (what you call your life)—is this explosion of the body, the body that speaks and thinks. And what does the body say? That "God"—that abstract notion of disembodied ideal authority—has been born again as creative imagination, that theology of oppression—of superiority of one class over another—is quaquaquaquaqua, that our advances in civilization have been ritualized in the arts of contest, that all the physical culture we developed to support the commerce of that civilization has been transformed from preparation and relaxation to be only the thing itself.

Tennis...in other words...I resume...is no longer the gentlemen's respite from the game of economic life where Pozzo—the tyrant the industrialist the economist the technician—has produced a world where physical man as earth—man and earth—woman as earth—as in the plains the mountains the sea—by rivers running water running fire—beings—who are finally *Lucky* to be purely and freely and bodily and only *human*....tennis... the stars... so calm… you and I… unfinished…

It may be that, after all, *Waiting for Godot* suggests nothing of this, but only that we are all tramps and must pass the time as best we can—say, in writing books. For my own part in passing, I would suggest that sensuous sport is love in a body under challenge, designed to expand our unique human capacity for sensitive joy. Seriously now, Aristotle should have written about it.

PART THREE

DEATH

CHAPTER SIX

INVINCIBLE SUMMER:
THE BODY AS MORTAL

SIR, WHEN ANY MAN KNOWS HE IS TO BE HANGED..., IT CONCENTRATES HIS MIND
WONDERFULLY.
SAMUEL JOHNSON

AND YOU CAN GET CAUGHT HOLDING ONE END OF A LOVE, WHEN YOUR FATHER
DROPS, AND YOUR MOTHER; WHEN A LAND IS LOST, OR A TIME, AND YOUR FRIEND
BLOTTED OUT, GONE, YOUR BROTHER'S BODY SPOILED, AND COLD, YOUR INFANT
DEAD, AND YOU DYING: YOU REEL OUT LOVE'S LONG LINE ALONE, STRIPPED LIKE
A LIVE WIRE LOOSING ITS SPARKS TO A CLOUD, LIKE A LIVE WIRE LOOSED IN
SPACE TO LONGING AND GRIEF EVERLASTING.
ANNIE DILLARD

SOME DAY, AFTER WE HAVE CONQUERED WIND AND WAVES, PERHAPS WE WILL
LEARN TO HARNESS THE POWER OF LOVE. THEN MANKIND WILL HAVE DISCOV-
ERED FIRE FOR THE SECOND TIME.
TEILHARD DE CHARDIN

"Time is a river which sweeps me along," wrote Jorge Luis Borges. But
he knew that he was the river. What time is it? I write this it is 6:10 New
Year's Eve, 1998, having just watched a television retrospective on the year's
most dramatic events. 12:00 will bring the last night of the first morning of
the last year before the new millennium. And that's not a bad time to read
verses from the Bible on time.

But when the fulness of the time was come, God sent forth his Son....
[Galatians 4:4]
Now after that John was put in prison, Jesus came into Galilee, preaching the gospel of the kingdom of God, and saying, "The time is fulfilled, the
kingdom of God is at hand; repent... and believe the gospel." [Mark 1:14-
15]

There are two Greek words meaning *time: chronos* and *kairos. Chronos*
is clock time, calendar time, newspaper time. We can measure it and predict

it. My watch is registering Pacific Standard Time. I will continue to think about time for forty-one more minutes, then shut down my computer [leaving it to worry about the Y2K bug problem] and then turn on ESPN for sports news, where the probability is extremely high that football scores will be heard in my family room. The word in Galatians 4:4 is *chronos*.

But *kairos* is not clock time. It means the right time. The time that cannot be measured or predicted, but somehow is just right. Comedians, actors, musicians all know about this kind of time. Joe Montana knew. His coaches could tell him to drop back three steps and wait two counts, but only he knew *when* to throw the ball. All great athletes have the gift for the moment—for the *kairos*—for the right time. So do real lovers. I have heard that some married folks make love every Saturday night at 10:00, finishing just in time for the news at 11:00. But the hands of love don't keep time—they make clock time stand still. The word in Mark 1:15 is *kairos*.

In the spring of 1993, a new watch, developed between the Swiss and the Japanese, went on the international market. There were no numbers on the dial. A circulating wheel of colors was covered by another wheel, with a pie shape wedge cut out to reveal the different hues as they made the twelve hour circle—providing the clues to time. The trade name was ingenious: *Chromachron*. And the chromae offered for chronating ranged from orange at one through red at three, blue at six, and yellow at twelve.[368] Actually it was up to the wearer to decide what time it was by what colors were showing. The muse—careless about bestowing her virtue—spoke to me about this remarkable development between the two most temporally obsessed countries in the world, where being on time is more important than believing in God. Capitalism, computers at the ready, depends entirely on numbers. I title it

The Color of Time: or, at last, A Real Clockwork Orange

The Greeks had called it *chronos*:
Dividing noon from night.
They also termed it *kairos*:
The Time that means "just right."

But now the Swiss and Japanese
Have changed the clock face clue:
Not "one" or "two" or "quality,"
But Time is just a hue.

How cute and deconstructionist
To color code a dial—
And give our aging eyes and hearts
The Time to reconcile.

Up at Blue instead of six,
Schedule Green for tea,

> Spinning Yellow—working space,
> Red for ecstasy.
>
> I hope the Swiss and Japanese
> Know what they have done:
> Their GNP will vanish when
> The color wheel is spun.
>
> Their organizing Seikos—gone,
> The Alpine trains—on blocks:
> *No* industry can long survive
> When tint transcends the clocks.

You have already guessed that the Swiss and Japanese found out quickly what they had done. This imaginative—and subversive—timepiece is now only a museum piece.[369]

What time is it? It's the right time for reality—to present the truth.

What is truth? Pilate didn't wait for an answer, and he was correct. Truth stood before him. Not that Jesus is the truth, though I'm certain that is what John's gospel means to say. There is no abstract truth, separated from its context: its embodiment. Near the end of his life Yeats finally found a way to say this:

> It seems to me that I have found what I wanted. When I try to put all into a phrase I say, "Man can embody the truth but he cannot know it." I must embody it in the completion of my life. The abstract is not life and everywhere draws out it contradictions. You can refute Hegel but not the Saint or the Song of Sixpence. [370]

There is no abstract freedom to be paraded about in China by an intentional tourist, no glory in capturing a piece of the Wall as a trophy of the revolution. One can speak of this moment in history as being the "right time" but only if we also insist that any "right time" intersects with "clock time."

Someone once asked Yogi Berra what time it was. "You mean now?" was his legendary reply. One remembers how the Zen masters teach the reality of the "present." The *roshi* balances a stick on his finger in front the student. He points to one side of the stick and calls it the past; to the other side and calls it the future. The balance point itself, he says, is the present. That balance point has no precise location, although it is exactly between the past and the future. One carries that present through space, though only the past and the future have concretion. It is as if *chronos* can be specified and measured on the stick, and *kairos* is the balance point, what meditators and mystics and poets call "the still point." The abstraction of *kairos* is embodied in the concretion of *chronos*. The one is eternity, what Tillich called *The Eternal Now*; the other is time, what Heidegger called "existential space."

This is why the gospel speaks of Jesus' coming as *kairos* and Paul's word is *chronos*. It is both. It is another conjunction of time and eternity of divine and human, of what we are and what we have. There are days when the universe changes, when history is hit with such force that it splits in two, when calendars divide, when ordinary days become holy days, when flesh becomes spirit, when eternity "flows over rocks cut from the basement of time." When love embraces a lover.

Until Death Do Us Part

I have always loved the month of August. So deep in summer, a warm canyon of adventure cutting through the year of stress, a floating, lazy time, serenely edging what I was and what I must be. A moment when lions lay with lambs and danced with wolves. I was born in the heart of it and married on its final day. My youngest boy also chose August to begin the politics of love.

We need to give those politics articulation. Marriage is not just a friend-ship recognized by the police (Robert Louis Stevenson), nor the last refuge of the cowardly. Marriage is the ultimate way that we transcend selfishness and seek the adventure of truth. We are not married because some presiding bureaucrat says we are, or even because we say we are. We are only married if we grow together, finding ourselves in the Way and its Power.

That fecund epigram from the *Tao Te Ching*, referred to in the Introduction, might well be in all the marriage manuals: one becoming two, then three, then the ten thousand things. The direction is multiple, not singular. We will become—if our adventure is real—the exponential two: all of us part of all that is. Male and female created he them—so reads the story of that first Eden: yin and yang, positive and negative, birth and death, earth and sky. Marriage is union not just with each other, because what we are, all become. If two fail to grow more loving, we are all diminished.

Marriage—no matter what H. L. Mencken said—is not the triumph of imagination over intelligence. It is not a quaint custom where two people share problems created by the fact that they got married, not a rite of passage from passion to convenience. Marriage, as John Ciardi suggests, is an arch where two lean together to form beauty, strength, and an invitation to enter new worlds. Marriage *is* the politics of love, the way we organize sensitivity and institutionalize joy. Marriage is the way we intoxicate reason and harmonize chaos, invite centaurs to the feast, join with the Lord of the dance, embrace Dionysus as the Christ and turn water into wine. Marriage is the resurrection of the body, the final miracle emerging from the tomb of self to live with and for the other. To know the truth, said Camus, you must be married—for marriage is truth without illusions.[371]

I must confess, with Jean Bolen and assorted Goddesses, that I really do believe in Camelot—that place "where there is not a more delightful spot."

Camelot is the mythic space where people actually do fall in love. Not abstract, saintly, responsible, emotionally correct, disinterested "Christian" love—but old fashioned erotic, melting ecstasy.

In abstract, mundane space everybody *loves* everybody: they sign off on postcards from the lake with it, they chant it in rituals in the church, they describe trips to Greece with it. "Loving" is a benediction, a seal of good housekeeping, a promise not to harm your neighbor. It's good and deep, and in a world where fear has the bit in its teeth, that kind of love is welcome indeed. We all do so admire life lived in benediction.

But *in-loving* is an invocation. It's an invitation, not a blessing. It's a dance on the shores of Crete with the widows of the world, climbing Sinai at dawn with a gorgeous lady from Denmark, stealing Helen again from Sparta after the Odyssey is over and returning to the primal chamber of power under the earth at Knossos, diving through the waves of the Indian ocean straight into the arms of the Javanese goddess of the tides, drifting together through the hanging valley of the Yosemite, suspending time in an old yellow boat down the rebirth of the Merced.

But can we stay in love, stay in the magic of summer? Lewis Carroll, in *Alice in Wonderland,* reported on the changing seasons of romantic fantasy. The sunny sky pales, echoes fade, and memories die: "Autumn frosts have slain July."

Autumn frosts do slay summer. It is the most painful kind of homicide— for they kill our chances of giving ourselves completely to the other. Age becomes increasingly a matter of survival—a desperate struggle with diminution, a narcissistic agon urged on by physical deprivation and the deepest kind of fear that nothing matters very much. Marriage becomes sheer co-dependency, rather than spontaneous relationship. Feeling gives way to symptom. Experience settles into reminiscence. Ecstasy cools to comfort. Adventure is grounded by order. Eros diminishes to support. Kisses give way to analysis. Those frosts are the ultimate felons, and summers lie terminal under their embrace.

The warmth of August, a minister and his sons, call up that marvelous remembrance: *A River Runs Through It*. Norman Maclean's father, a Presbyterian minister in Montana, is sitting out in the woods near the river where his sons, whom he has taught, are fly fishing. He is reading his Greek New Testament. In their family, Norman tells us, there was "no clear line between religion and fly fishing."[372] God might not have been a mathematician, but the boy knew "He" could count, and "only by picking up God's rhythms were we able to regain power and beauty."[373] Norman asked what he has been reading and his father answers, "A good book."

He has been casting his eyes at the gospel of John, the hymn to the Spirit of creation made flesh in Jesus as the Christ: "In the beginning was the *Logos*" [translated as "the Word"]. He had always thought that water was here first, the primal substance out of which all things came. But he is listening more carefully now, and hears "the words" that are "underneath the water."[374]

The young man decides that his father thinks this, not because it is given in the world, but because he's a preacher first—and then a fisherman. But his father insists, with the thoughtful exegesis of a literate fisherman: "The water runs over the words."

Norman's brother Paul has joined them, casting and catching a powerful fish that he plays skillfully, swirling it out of the water on to a sandbar where the shocked fish "consumed the rest of momentary life dancing the Dance of Death on his tail."[375]

As the story closes, death also takes his brother and his father, and he, old now, still fishes in the cool of the evening at the Big Blackfoot River, in "the half-light of the canyon"—alone with his memories and hope.

> Eventually, all things merge into one, and a river runs through it. The river was cut by the world's great flood and runs over rocks from the basement of time. On some of the rocks are timeless raindrops. Under the rocks are the words....[376]

Maclean never tells us what those words are—but I think I know—and they create and sustain all of creation. Those words are the *cause* of the world. The words are: **I'm in love with you.**

That is what I wish for my own children and their wives, for all couples that enter into the covenant of marriage: that they stand together—playing, embracing, laughing, creating—and always in love.

THE TIME OF OUR LIVES: REALITY

Reality has a shape. It is an incarnation. It is either in time—in the body of the world—or it doesn't exist at all. This is what Steven Hawking meant when he said that the concept of time has no meaning before the creation of the universe.[377] Hawking is responding to Kant's *Critique of Pure Reason* where equally compelling arguments are set forth that the universe both did and did not have such a beginning. Augustine, not Kant, had it right, says Hawking:

> When asked: What did God do before he created the universe? Augustine didn't reply: He was preparing Hell for people who asked such questions. Instead, he said that time was a property of the universe that God created, and that time did not exist before the beginning of the universe.[378]

It seems to me that there is also a sense in which time does not exist until we do. *Chronos* is a way of talking about our reality. I was born on August

14th. I was not, and I will not be, but, right now, I am. *Kairos* is the *am,* and *chronos* is the *I.*

And it is extremely important to speak of my death date as well as my birth date. Time somehow must also end when I cease. This is why, among all the animals, human beings build tombstones. We scatter ashes in Paris, celebrate the day of the dead in Mexico, separate out bones of the monks on Mt. Athos, dance with skulls around our necks in West Africa.

Death is always a primal act. Its reality frames who we are and we cannot allow anyone—or any doctrine—to steal it away. We are only given one—Lazarus and Dracula to the contrary—and it must be laid down intentionally in time and space. Woody Allen wrote with inerrant irony: "It's not that I'm afraid to die, I just don't want to be there when it happens."[379]

I watch the pathetic grasp of those who think that not going "gently into that good night" means pretending that death is a demon to be exorcised from life. Norman Cousins wrote a chapter in his *Anatomy of an Illness* entitled "Pain Is Not the Enemy." We should write now that—Paul to the contrary— "Death is not the enemy." It is not some kind of defeat.

The Time His Father Died

Joe Mathews was the most powerful speaker I ever heard. He was my ethics professor at Perkins School of Theology in the fifties, but left to form the Faith and Life Community at the University of Texas, eventually moving his organization and vision to Chicago, where it became known as the Ecumenical Institute. As far as I know he never published, except for one short piece, but he changed every life he touched with his invasive, comical, prophetic, rhythmic stutter—stripping away pretensions and calling us to decision: to pick up our lives and lay them down across the "barbed wire" of history. He often said that he ran for God, but never was elected. Those he offended—and they were legion—replied that he wasn't even campaigning in the right district. He's dead now, and his Institute has dissolved into something utterly secular: International Cultural Policy. Even the magazine (*motive*)[380] that published his lonely article is gone. It was called "The Time My Father Died."

The *chronos* was November 9, 1963, just thirteen days before another father was taken. But Kennedy was only forty-six when the shock of assassination silenced the country. Joe's Papa was ninety-two, surely no occasion for the usual sociology of death (litanized by Elisabeth Kübler-Ross): surprise, denial, anger, bargaining, depression, and acceptance. At ninety-two, there can be only acceptance—and sometimes gratitude.

Certainly I was grateful for such comments. But I found myself perturbed too. Didn't they realize that to die is to die, whether you are seventeen, forty-nine, or one hundred and ten? Didn't they know that our death is our death? And that each of us has only one death to die? This was my father's death! The only one he would ever have.

The family gathered, clarified their self-understanding, and embodied that understanding in a plan of celebration. Death must be seen as a lively part of a man's life, a crucial point in the human adventure which transposes to every other aspect of life, an event to be received in humility and honored with dignity.

But during the rituals surrounding death there intrudes the great conceal-ment, the efforts of our culture to disguise this climax to the human drama: the decorous caskets, satin head pillows, deflecting perfumes and rude cos-metics, Sunday clothes and immortal vaults. All these were empty of sym-bolic meaning, serving only to deceive by simulating life. They seemed to say: "Nothing has actually happened."

Do we think we can be victorious over death by denuding it? Stripping it of its rightful power? How indignant to steal from death its own icy majesty. Do we worship life so desperately that we cannot grant its cessation? Doesn't the constructed smile of the dead mock our powerlessness in the face of final-ity?

Mathews had entered the reality of existential space during his time as chaplain in World War II, on beachheads in the islands of the Pacific—remembering the soldiers he buried: "There was great dignity in the shelter—half shrouded, in the soiled clothing, in the dirty face, in the shallow grave." Death at last had to be recognized as death.

The funeral parlor existed to erase any such recognition. When the fami-ly insisted on an utterly simple pine coffin, the kind used in pioneer days in the country, all the undertaker could produce—under great duress—was a pauper's casket, complete with pillow and lined with a cheap imitation satin. They asked that their father's body be made ready in his pauper's coffin for the celebration.

Several hours before the funeral, Joe went in to be alone with his Papa, to sense in that private moment something of the presence of his public life. He could scarcely believe his eyes. The undertaker had stolen away his father.

> My father, I say, was ninety-two. In his latter years he had wonderfully chiseled wrinkles. I had helped to put them there. His cheeks were deeply sunken; his lips pale. He was an old man. There is a kind of glory in the face of an old man. Not so with the stranger lying there. They had my Papa look-ing like he was fifty-two. Cotton stuffed in his cheeks had erased the best wrinkles. Make-up powder and rouge plastered his face away up into his hair and around his neck and ears. His lips were painted. He...he looked ready to step before the footlights of the matinee performance.

With a ferocity only available to a man whose family is being attacked, Joe raged at the mortician—who hurried to bring him material for a restoration. Joe rubbed off the powder with alcohol, wiped away the lipstick and rouge, relined the face—and watched the body in the coffin become his Papa again. In that resurrection into death, Joe realized that he had straightened not the body of his father but his father: "It was my father in death."

They entrusted his Papa to the ceremony celebrating his life, but when it was over, the death march, once explosive in symbolic force, had lost its power. For at the grave-site, the morticians—seemingly incapable of allowing the earth to be natural—had recreated that artificial world of green, covering every scar of the grave with simulated grass.

> I wanted to scream. I wanted to cry out to the whole world. "Something is going on here, something great, something significantly human. Look! Everybody, look! Here is my father's death. It is going on here!"

The graveside service ended as Mathews lifted up scripture and poetry that his father loved, and placed him gladly in the hands of the One in whose hands he already was. He reached outside the artificial green, plunged his hands into real dirt three times, and three times tossed that good earth onto his Papa in his Papa's grave—all the while singing the three-fold majesty of life: *In the name of the Father and of the Son and of the Holy Ghost.*

Death is not the enemy. It is not some kind of defeat.

The Time My Mother Lived

My father died when I was nine and I have no memory whatsoever of the funeral. He died in the home of my grandmother at 336 Elm Street in Coshocton, Ohio, where the Merediths—my grandfather, my father and his brother, Lawrence, for whom I am named—had a canvas manufacturing plant. My father was an athlete, a musician, and a lover, miscast as a wandering sales executive. He never went to church and he never read a book. I scarcely knew him. I had no epiphany, except a feeling of the night he died as strangely still. I had no sense of this being my father's death since I did not know his life. I did not want to shout out anything at all.

His death did bring about a happening of consequence: the family scattered, my oldest brother and mother to New York City, my sister to Washington, D. C., and my middle brother and I to Calvert, Texas, with our grandparents. We would never all live together again.

When we arrived in Texas, grandmother took us to the little school, where—for reasons no one told me—I was enrolled in the fourth grade, instead of the third where I belonged. Whatever incompetencies and shortcomings I have, whatever psychological aberrations, whatever intellectual and technical disabilities I have formed, whatever cosmic information I lack, whatever abnormalities I exhibit, I blame it absolutely on not being enrolled in that grade. Fulghum made a fortune telling America that all he needed to know was learned in kindergarten. I'm certain I've lost a fortune by not learning the secret wisdom revealed in the third grade. What *do* they teach in that mysterious grade?[381]

My grandmother died when I was twelve. For some reason—space I think—we were sleeping in the same room, my brother and grandfather in another. I could feel her slowly shift from present warmth to absent cold, as if something tactile had been withdrawn. I could almost touch the moment she left.

My oldest brother was being given a chance to attend Southwestern University, the first chartered university in Texas, and my mother moved from New York to Dallas to be nearer to us. My brother, Mac, joined Spence at the college, and I was sent to Dallas for the rest of my high school years—eventually following my brothers at Southwestern.

I learned to know my mother. Her affection for me was absolute and, though she was probably the most unusual person I have ever known, she instilled by some sort of parental photosynthesis that all would be well with whatever I did. "Do what you want to," she would say, "unless there is some reason why you shouldn't."

Our "wanting" was always marked "insufficient funds"—a day away from joining the street people. She worked at some selling job for a while, and I was hired at the YMCA as a craftshop instructor. For a long time we rented a room—with one bath down the hall for the entire floor, and its only luxury a minuscule hot plate. I wore the same clothes to high school every day until they disintegrated—and seldom had a hair cut. Today that would qualify me as in-group grungy—with a shot at MTV.

Perhaps poverty was appropriate: Mother was a writer. She once wrote a column for the *Chicago Daily News.* She wrote for *Nature Magazine* and newspapers in St. Louis, Dallas, and Mississippi. She had one book manuscript that was destroyed in a fire (*The Unseen Becomes Visible*), and one that made it into print (*Poems That Make Sense*). She despised housework, cooking, and wasn't particularly thrilled with child bearing, not to mention the process by which such an event is usually preceded.

Mother was an Emersonian fundamentalist, who thought God wrote the Bible, but whispered a few extra divine sentences in Concord, Massachusetts. She decided that when Jesus said to pray after the manner of the seven line prayer in the Sermon on the Mount, he meant it *literally*—and she never prayed in any words but those. I found it unimaginative, but it certainly saved time on her knees. She was thrilled to have a daughter who helped run the government [audit it actually, through the Organization of American States], one son a medical doctor, another a minister, and her baby boy a professor of religion. She never knew how little of her kind of religion I professed. She was so proud to be the one to buy my crimson doctoral gown for Harvard commencement—and never ceased lamenting the fact that I insisted it not be silk. She was to the manor born and should have been in a palace somewhere,

where eccentricity could have been construed as a royal touch, and protocol protect her actually being in this world. Mother often wished she had been born an orchid, for then she could have lived on air.

She dreaded her in-laws because they expected her to be normal, which she clearly was not. She slept on the floor beside her bed so she wouldn't have to make it up in the morning, battled the birds in the early light for fresh figs in the yard, refused to cut her hair *ever* and just as steadfastly refused to go to any hair salon. She typed with plugs in her ears so she couldn't hear any distracting demands on her concentration—including a stray request or two from her children. She memorized everything she might have to say in public, including "hello," and had obsessively specific ideas about nomenclature. She never understood why people called me *Larry,* since that was *not* my name, and she resolutely refused to be called "grandmother"—answering only to her own suggested name: "Daddy's Mama." She felt uncomfortable with daughters-in-law and people in general, but especially women—whom she found manipulative and predatory. She read French and Latin, loved Shakespeare, and played Beethoven on the piano.

And she adored word play. One of her verses makes wonderful nonsense:

> I often have wondered—
> And never have guessed,
> Why de-feathered chickens
> Are said to be dressed.

Mother always wanted to live to be one hundred. She died in summer at the age of ninety-three at my oldest brother's home. There was no question of a coffin. From California, Washington, and Mississippi, we journeyed to tiny Calvert, Texas to place her ashes in the family plot. We gathered at a motel a few miles outside the town. Mac and Sis and I were sitting in the room when Spence walked in with a covered package of some sort. It was supper time and, as the door opened, I remember thinking how thoughtful of my brother to bring in some food so that we could all relax and talk in private. It is intrusive, tasteless, but redemptively comic recall. The package was our mother.

Cremation dissolves death. Like some short cut through despair, this tiny jar holds imagination in ash, indistinguishable from the magma clouds that give birth to the world. The molecules disassemble and memory congeals into fiery flakes, the final transubstantiation. You are infinitely opened to mystery when you can hold your mother in your hand.

We decided that because Mother rose so early every day, we should have whatever ceremony we chose just before dawn. It was absolutely dark at the cemetery when we arrived with ashes and shovel. The victorious irony was not lost on me. This woman, who had despised her imprisonment within the Meredith prejudice, had vowed to outlive their disdain. They, too, had all gathered in that piece of earth, buried so close together by my grandmother's design that her son's widow could not be close to him, even in death.

Nevertheless, we had determined that—however apart their lives had been—that neither death nor enmity, would do them part. In the blackness, we dug down, directly over my father's grave, like some sort of medieval thieves providing ritual artifacts for the cults. All of us dug, not knowing how deep to go, cutting through time. I was digging when the shovel struck something very hard. We had reached our father's casket, disturbing its rest of forty years.

Epiphany had finally come. The dark had silvered; we could see. The family that had never been together was joined, standing on my father's grave, the shovel blade touching the coffin, the handle above hard in my hand linking me with a man I never knew; my oldest brother, his wife and children, who had taken responsibility for our mother when she could no longer care for herself; my brother with whom I had lived in Calvert and walked by this place so many times on my way to school; my sister, who knew us all before we were born—all now distinguishable in the growing light, looking at those small slabs with our communal name gouged out of granite.

It was over. In the full light of morning now I looked down to see where my uncle was buried. The slab carving was clear: *Lawrence Meredith*. I was overwhelmed by a sadness difficult to manage. He—all of them—were so unhappy, so unfulfilled, with such potential and unusual talent, generosity and unaccountable malevolence. They hated my mother's idiosyncratic eliteness, and she had outlived all their recriminations and cruelty: their attempts to kidnap me and break up our home, my grandfather's incandescent temper and my grandmother's obvious favoritism towards the little blond boy that took the place of her dead son and carried his name, their callous indifference towards the brother I adored.

What word play could catch this moment—the time my mother died? I remember standing inside that family plot with her after my grandfather was buried. Her word play had no light touch: "I've done it. They're all under the ground and I'm on it." *Stabat Mater*. Now she too was surrounded by the silence, that required embrace beyond love or hate. *Requiem aeternam dona eis, Dominie.*

Death is not the enemy. It is not some kind of defeat.

The Time My Mind Was Concentrated

Maya Angelou taught me something extraordinary about death. We had just picked her up at the Stockton airport coming in on a private flight from Palm Springs, California, where she had given a speech at noon. We had to rush her to a friend's home where she could get her breath, and a bite to eat, before a late afternoon convocation, where our university would honor her. Immediately—*immediately*—following our convocation we had to whisk her at the speed of light to the University of California at Davis, for an 8:00 P.M. address/performance. Every shift was a stress fracture of time. On the Lincoln Continental Shinkansen ride for that sixty five mile trip in forty-five minutes, I was having flashbacks of an old folk song sung by Cool Hand Luke when his mother died:

I don't care if it rains or freezes as long as I got my plastic Jesus....

Bolted firmly to the dashboard of your car. One of those awful pink, iridescent, glow-in-the-dark statues, the St. Christopher of Southern Protestant pick-ups. Keep it with you, is the folk song imperative, when you travel into the unknown dangers of the road....

And more to the speeding point, sung by Luke faster and faster: go get yourself a "sweet Madonna." Not one of those graceful, ethereal, lovely Ladies Dressed in Blue, transparently a Mother of God. But get one decorated in rhinestone, garishly upright on a "pedestal of abalone shell." Then those lightning miles won't be "so scary."

Long as I got the Virgin Mary assuring me that I won't go to hell.

That scene—with Paul Newman strumming the banjo, singing this silly blasphemy, eyes moist with anger and sadness, the rain behind him in the window of the prison barracks as if the heavens felt his pain and rage—that scene was intruding as we flew across the valley. The film *Cool Hand Luke* was actually filmed in Stockton, just a mile from our house, beyond the edge of town in a grove of oaks. The site is now a gentle park, surrounded by subdivisions creeping steadily northward across the richest farm land in the world. The inexorable logic of capitalism, like some mindless virus destroying its host, is exercised by the need to flee the city. And who will exorcise the exercisers? It is a fascinating irony to me that the park which carries the name of Maya Angelou's mother, Vivian Baxter, isolated in one of those wealthy subdivisions, is just north of the cinematic prison which held the freest spirit of them all.

In the midst of this maelstrom, rolling up to Pacific's administration building, Doyle Minden, head of public relations for the university, asked Maya if she didn't need time to be quiet, compose herself, and think about her speech. But she continued to talk to us, looking directly at us all the while, responding to every turn in the conversation. She told us that a long time ago she came to terms with death: realized that each moment might be her last, and that this person—that face—might be her last sight on this earth.

I was mesmerized by this almost accidental confession: Maya Angelou—world artist and platform celebrity without peer—is consciously present to each ordinary moment. She pays attention. It was Zen and the art of Lincoln Continental maintenance.

We took her in to meet the president and selected official types—and ten or twelve administrative assistants, just minutes before the procession. As we stood to join the faculty, she looked every person in that room in the eye, called each one by first and last name, and thanked them all for honoring her by their presence.

Maya Angelou taught me something extraordinary about life. I pay attention.

THE DEMOCRACY OF DEATH: COMMUNITY

A central design of religion is to modify "life" with "eternal." What gives religion its "persistence" is the fact of death. Human beings simply will not believe that they are made to die. As Zorba told the boss, "What's the use of all your damn books if they don't tell you why men die?"

In one of the longer books ever written to tell us why, Sri Aurobindo articulates a winsome denial.[382] It seems that the lust of the embodied self (in every individual creature) seeks to realize itself first by increasing growth and expansion—by feeding on the environment, by absorption of others or what they possess. This is Hunger in all its forms. Hunger produces Division—competition for the sources of satisfaction, and Division finally produces Death—the eater is finally eaten. But this Hunger must give way, according to Aurobindo, to the law of love; Division gives way to the law of Unity; the law of Death gives way to the law of Immortality. [383] Kazantzakis, pay attention. This is *the* ascent. The only epic, the spirit script, is the story of this ascent from nature to higher consciousness.

Forty years ago, Jessica Mitford's irreverent analysis of *The American Way of Death*—written when she was forty-five—revealed what everyone knew: we are so afraid immortality might not be true that we are only too willing to pay funeral managers, who undertake cosmetic denial of death.[384] As Queen Victoria says to Orlando in Virginia Woolf's androgynous fairy tale: "Don't grow old."[385] Not being afraid of, Virginia Woolf took her own advice.

It may be that death is not so frightful as growing old. Zorba said that he was afraid of only one thing:

> "What scares me, boss, is old age. Heaven preserve us from that! Death is nothing—just pff! and the candle is snuffed out. But old age is a disgrace."
> [386]

I suppose Katharine Hepburn got it said for all of us who are beginning to experience that lethal diminution, that attrition of capacity, that twilight of potentiality, that funereal obsession with order, that insolence of pain, that terror of incontinence, that anger at indifference, that paranoia at inattention, that patronizing of the young, that loss of mobility, that fading of eros, that creeping of conceit, that residence in the past: "Old age is like watching a car wreck in slow motion." If Dr. Chopra, or Pat Robertson, or Muhammad, or anybody else can make an offer of immortality sound convincing—or even inviting, the whole world will buy a ticket on the train that runs forever.

The Prince of Darkness in the Big Valley

I HOPE SOMEONE THOUGHT TO BRING A WOODEN STAKE.
[POLITICAL OPPONENT WATCHING
THE FUNERAL OF RICHARD NIXON]

I often wondered why Dracula was such a popular myth. I realize, of course, that it is another tale of forever, and that should be enough—my apologies—to get our teeth into. But the basic story seems so silly, and the number of times it is told has to be overkill on immortality. Who are more numerous, the living or the dead? The realist would answer, the living, because the dead are no more. But the dead seem to have considerable life in the mythologies of the world—most particularly that bizarre nocturnal bloodsucker who will not die.

From *The Vampire Chronicles* to Francis Ford Coppola, from the drooling parodies of *Love at First Bite*, *The Fearless Vampire Killers*, *The Rocky Horror Picture Show*, and Don Rickles ingesting *Innocent Blood*, to the astounding image of José Ferrer—who once won an Oscar for *Cyrano de Bergerac*—playing second fang to a blood lust canine in *Dracula's Dog*, from the Austrian literary history *The Vampires of Styria* to the teutonic horror of *Nosferatu*, from Frank Lugella to Peter Cushing to Martin Landau in *Ed Wood*, the story invades our nights. Scarcely a year goes by without another retelling—I should say re-Counting—of the immortal thirst of the impaler of Transylvania, the lethal insomniac and enemy of light. He has—fundamentalism to the contrary—set a world's record for resurrections, well ahead of remakes of *Beau Geste*, Richard Nixon, *Rocky*, JFK conspiracy theories, or even the myth of the evils of feminism. And this is the '90's. If AIDS can't kill him, nothing can.

Bram Stoker began it all in 1897, and the twentieth century can't seem to be satiated with stories about the prince of darkness, rather like the Count himself as he lives on by the blood of his endless victims. My first glimpse of the great monstrous one was in 1938, when he was impersonated by Bela Lugosi, frightening and somehow funny at the same time, sinister *and* ludicrous—his Hungarian vampirese one of the most recognizable cultic accents in the history of movies. My most introspective glimpse was one Easter season: Saturday, April 10—Black Saturday after Good Friday at that—attending a play at the Stockton Civic Theater, written and directed by Dr. Sy Kahn.

Kahn has known struggles for freedom up very close. He was a supply soldier seeing action in the Pacific during World War II, all the way from New Britain and New Guinea to the Philippines. And he kept a diary of the entire three years he served, writing in it every day, even in battle—*even* watching kamikaze planes explode on sister ships, the diary then tucked away inside a gas mask or a field telephone case, in exceedingly ironic safety. It is published by the University of Illinois Press under the title *Between Tedium and Terror: A Soldier's World War II Diary, 1943-45*, as far as anyone knows the only complete diary written by a member of the armed services in that war.

On May 26, 1944, in Hollandia, New Guinea, Kahn made this entry:

> These past few days I've been haunted by thoughts of death. I am not, I can honestly write, afraid of it.... The few times that I thought it was imminent I have just gritted my teeth and waited for oblivion. [387]

It is a moment of soft memory, this young Jewish soldier, keeping this record as his "mark against oblivion," asking his ship comrade to see that the diaries get home, "just in case." It is a moment of profound reflection when he writes: "Sometimes it seems to me a tragedy that we are animals capable of sentimentality." [388]

Kahn's play is based on Stoker's novel, and in his director's notes, published in the playbill, offers the following rationale as to why Dracula "persistently tantalizes us on some level of consciousness."

> I subscribe to the idea that each human being has a dark side, a shadow self, and until each of us recognizes that, and comes to terms with it, the shadow self will manifest itself in various ways, some harmful to the self. Indeed, groups, even whole nations, have a collective shadow self, expressed in aggression, war, racism, scapegoating and genocide.[389]

In Kahn's *Dracula*, the Count is made to say: "I am the shape you dream," and it is in these shapes that we find the seductive power of our darker impulses. Ultimately, Kahn tells us, Dracula is the symbol of death itself, the "price of our mortality." At the final moment of confrontation between the Count and the "psychiatrists" seeking to destroy him, he gives away his blood sucking game: "Each of us owes God a death."

So instead of Dracula giving immortality—creating an undead—he is actually an agent of God. Not a prince of darkness but an emissary of light, as his other name implies. Lucifer, after all, means "made of light." It is the young maiden that old Dracula seduces, draining her blood that he may live. Ironic isn't it? Death must live in order for life to be. Both Kahn and Stoker name Dracula's primary "victim" *Lucy*, the woman of light.

It is quite rare to see a vampire story where the victim is old, although Anne Rice does manage some aging sustenance. Death, it seems, must begin with the young, fastening his lips to fresh flesh, drawing out virginal power.

Isn't that how salvation is supposed to come in the spring of youth: by the shedding of innocent blood? Dracula is repelled by the cross because there the sacrifice promises eternal life in the spirit—a declaration of war on the fragility of the life of the flesh. Surely, the only way to end the threat of death is to kill death itself, drive a wooden stake through its heart, behead the body, and stuff garlic in its macabre mouth.

Why? What have the heart and head and mouth to do specifically with the death of death? Isn't all this a bit melodramatic, Halloweenish, and really rather funny? Actually, a mouthful of garlic alone ought to do the trick—it certainly would kill everybody around Dracula, if not the old vampire himself.

What gives Dracula peculiar power is the unmistakable union of sex and death, and, like all myths, makes it a story about us. Norman Mailer points to this union in *The Prisoner of Sex* when he makes the "outrageous" statement that, for all men, intercourse is an attempt to kill the women: the penis impales the "partner," and because of this "death" men live on. Is it any wonder that the search for the historical Dracula always points to Vlad, the Impaler?

The Count of course *is* making "love" to each of his victims, a dark oralism sealing off a vortex of light. He kisses Lucy in agonizing eroticism, brings her alive with such force that she faints in organismic death. And all the men in the play kiss Lucy in simulated passion—masquerading as lovers, parents, protectors, doctors. The covert sexuality of the Dracula myth couldn't be more overt. They, too, are messengers of death, as all sexuality is, as all survival is: all of us live by the death of the other. The maniacal Renfield of Kahn's play is forever chewing up little insects, to remind us that we too will soon be chewed as the host of the world—in this Transylvanian communion of inevitability. Our passion for each other can never be satiated: we are nymphomaniacs of the life force. So the wise of the world remind us: *desire* is poison. No human being can ever be satisfied, simply because each owes God a death. Sexuality is a promissory note on that inexorable payment.

When the Irish Stoker visited the austere castle soaring out of rocks in the land beyond the forests ("trans"–"sylvania"), his careful notes tell us that the prince of the castle was Vlad the Impaler—the fifteenth century blood lust genesis of the myth. How must he die forever? The myth is instructively neat. Drive a wooden stake into the heart that pumps our blood, and, by metonymy, monitors our deepest emotions and feels our agony at ceasing to be. The axe cuts the head that remembers who we were, that thinks we were not made to die, that dreams of ecstatic union. The garlic seals the mouth that presses down in soft invasion, that murmurs symbolic sounds, that drinks away our ultimate weakness. Heavy, Slavic, horrowshow.

That Black Saturday was lightened by the fact that Dr. Kahn's son and two grandsons were in attendance. Dr. David Kahn is also a director, an actor, a teacher, and a writer—pursuing a career at San Jose State. Some years ago, he had, in fact, played Dracula in a production at Fallon House Theater in the Sierra foothills, directed by his father.

Surely we have some profound clue here, some serendipitous insight into the nature of things. Life, as Gibran writes, has longed for itself. And for a moment, the man who was between tedium and terror is between eternity and time. He has pressed down in soft invasion, and memories now pulse in bodies good and grand. He watches one child immortal on stage, and another reborn as audience.

The grandchildren sit patiently through the exposition and the philosophy, waiting—as they tell us during intermission—for the "scary parts." They *like* the creepy doors opening by themselves, the howling banshees beckoning mortals away, the flaring black cape enfolding the pale and submissive girl, the anxious plotters of Dracula's demise, the body unharmed by bullets and disappearing before our very eyes, even while being subdued by those European biologists of the mind, and the terrible, candlelit corpse being driven into everlasting life by our own fear of death. Perhaps in the interplay of day and night, they somehow sense that, in the exact meeting of light and dark, the world shifts the cycle of mortality. *It is life that is immortal, not us.*

We should all be little children here, waiting with some anticipation for the "scary parts." I remember Edward Abbey's description of death in his grand literary canyon, *Desert Solitaire*. Sent out to find a lost hiker, Abbey found him bloated like a balloon on a mesa not far from Moab, Utah. The smell of decay was "rich and sickening" as he and his companions stuffed the remains into a body bag and began the journey back to civilization, making jokes about the "old fart" that had wandered so far off the road.

> If he'd meant anything to us, maybe we could mourn. If we had loved him we would sing, dance, drink, build a stupendous bonfire, find women, make love—for under the shadow of death what can be wiser than love, to make love, to make children?—and celebrate his transfiguration from flesh to fantasy in a style proper and fitting, with fun for all at the funeral.[390]

And yet there was another feeling—alive, as Abbey suggests, in each of us "as we lug these rotting guts across the desert..." Abbey's strange and strong sensual word is "satisfaction."

> Each man's death diminishes me? Not necessarily. Given this man's age, the inevitability and suitability of his death, and the essential nature of life on earth, there is in each of us the unspeakable conviction that we are well rid of him. His departure makes room for the living. Away with the old, in with the new. He is gone—we remain, others come. The plow of mortality drives through the stubble, turns over rocks and sod and weeds to cover the old, the worn-out, the husks, shells, empty seedpods and sapless roots, clearing the field for the next crop. A ruthless, brutal process—but clean and beautiful.[391]

Death does not diminish, any more than life exalts. Dracula has not only fastened himself to our necks, but to our imagination: to the flights of fancy that beckon us to film the shadow, to keep diaries of the darkness, to create plays, to make love, to make children—and have them happy to be with father and grandfather—and wait for the scary parts. They will come soon enough.

Aftershock Thanksgiving

On October 17, 1989, at 5:04 P.M., just as the nation tuned in to watch the third game of the World Series being played between the Oakland A's and the San Francisco Giants at Candlestick Park, the Bay Area experienced an earthquake of 7.1 on the Richter scale. The Marina district was devastated by fire, the Cypress expressway in Oakland collapsed, a section of the Bay bridge dropped open, the death toll mounted and hundreds were made homeless. The World Series was postponed for a week and set in perspective for a lifetime. The great quake paused as aftershocks continued to trespass our shaken world. Then gradually the biography, statistics, and geology gave way to the aftershock of recognition: what did it all mean?

The Bay area is not just any area. It was America's golden destiny—rising up on the tides of raw adventure, harboring one of the most beautiful cities in the world. San Francisco is also one of the most controversial cities, mixing gays and straights, drugs and artists, radical politics, religious cultism, minority and ethnic power, and closet Republicanism. For many conservatives across this land, it plays Sodom to Berkeley's Gomorrah.

Was God sending a message to Babylon that his patience with sin was about to run out? A lifetime member of the PTL ["People That Love" or "Praise the Lord]—in the teeth of Jim Bakker's forty-five year jail sentence for preying on the faithful instead of praying for them—suggested on "Larry King Live" that the hurricane which blew off course into Charlotte was a breath of Almighty anger at the shabby treatment of his servant Jimmy. Several callers agreed that Bakker's sentence was too harsh—and one observant soul thought that just being married to Tammy Faye was punishment enough. The investor in Heritage USA then turned her eyes to stone and declared that the earthquake was only the trembling of the lips of Divine Wrath about to pronounce total destruction on the Wicked City of the West. And I rather suspect that even a mellowing Jerry Falwell and Pat Robertson would have trouble suppressing a self-righteous smirk if the whole Bay Area fell into the sea—especially if all the conservatives had access to an Ark sailing up the San Joaquin.

Outrageous reaction? Fairly classical I would say. John Wesley, founder of the Methodist societies in England, was no fundamentalist. He was an Oxford don and sophisticated Anglican who wrote reams of theology and dictionaries in Greek, Hebrew, German, French, and Latin, edited entire libraries, kept written accounts of almost everything he thought, said, or did—and nearly everybody else in eighteenth century England—and published them.

In 1755, a huge earthquake shook Lisbon in Portugal, a jewel city by the sea. Hundreds died and thousands were left homeless. Wesley wrote reflections on the event, which he called, "Serious Thoughts Occasioned by the Late Earthquake at Lisbon," observing that virtue was as scarce among Christians as the "ancient Heathens." Sins of injustice and ambition infected every rank (including clergy), he wrote, and God is most probably not pleased with all of this.[392]

> And what shall we say of the late accounts from Portugal? That some thousand homes, and many thousands of persons, are no more! That a fair city is now in ruinous heaps! Is there indeed a God that judges the world?[393]
>
> Here is a nearer enemy. The earth threatens to swallow you up. Where is your protection now? What defense do you find from thousands of gold and silver? You cannot fly; for you cannot quit the earth, unless you will leave your dear body behind you. And while you are on the earth, you know not where to flee to, neither where to flee from. You may buy intelligence, where the shock was yesterday, but not where it will be tomorrow.... It comes! The roof trembles! The beams crack! The ground rocks to and fro! Hoarse thunder resounds from the bowels of the earth! And all these are but the beginning of sorrows. Now what help?[394]

There is no question about Wesley's interpretation of natural tragedy. God is our friend—if we so choose. That is benevolence enough. But He is righteous enough to be fierce in punishing evil. He who is Light can cover the earth with Darkness.[395]

Is this a possible message a meaning we can take seriously? That God deliberately destroys in order that his will shall be done? It seems to make God into a subject for a horror show, a divine version of the deterrent argument for capital punishment: a judicious execution will publicize the cost of immorality. Pompeii was rich, indolent, and licentious. It is better that Mt. Vesuvius bury a few in ash than that all should perish in debauchery. Is this the lesson: everyone sooner or later sits down at a bitter banquet of consequences?

Yes, say Calvin, Luther, Augustine, Paul, Noah, Moses, Gautama, Zoroaster. Our lady of the PTL has lots of good company. But two voices are not on this list: Job and Jesus.

Job had enough personal suffering visited upon him to qualify as a truly nasty man. Sitting there on his manure pile with running sores, homeless, and reviled by his former friends as deserving this treatment. He was in an earthquake all right—and everything had shaken loose in his ordered life. But when all the arguments were over, there was Job, declaring that he had given occasion for none of these problems. To be sure, he still trusted God, but not because of tragedies—in spite of them.

And Jesus. There are depictions in the gospels that make Jesus appear vindictive and the incarnation of a God of wrath and judgment (the gospel of John, the cursing of the fig tree, etc.). But the Jesus of the synoptics emerges quite clearly as one who rejects punishment as deterrent and wrath as the character of God. Luke's Jesus, immediately following the baptism and temptations returns to Nazareth to announce his public ministry, reading from the prophet Isaiah:

> The Spirit of the Lord God is upon me;
> because the Lord has anointed me to preach good tidings to the meek;
> he has sent me to bind up the brokenhearted,
> to proclaim liberty to the captives,
> and the opening of the prison to them that are bound;
> to proclaim the acceptable year of the Lord....

The quotation is from Isaiah 61:1-2. But in Isaiah there is an added line: "...and the day of vengeance of our God." Jesus seems quite deliberate in dropping that phrase. Luke tells us that after reading the phrase, "the acceptable year of the Lord," Jesus *closed* the book. Indeed I would like to think that he closed the book on vengeance, and that we—from Singapore to Washington—would be well advised to do the same.

The famous passage from the Sermon on the Mount reinforces my wishful thinking. We have been told, he says, to love our neighbors and hate our enemies. "But I say to love your enemies and pray for those who persecute you." Why would you do this perfectly unnatural act of loving bastards who want to see you crawl? "So that you may be sons of your Father in heaven." And how does God react to wicked life on earth? By sending hurricanes, blowing up volcanoes, wrenching Bagdad by the Bay with a piece of his angry old mind?

Jesus apparently didn't think so: "...for he makes his sun rise on the evil and the good, and sends rain on the just and the unjust."[396] We must stand in that indifferent illumination and build conduits of mercy for the torrents to come. Nature may be even-handed, but our hands must reach out to lift up the fallen and share in compassionate community.

San Francisco is the home of just such a community: Glide Memorial United Methodist Church, in the heart of the Tenderloin District—in the shadow of the gigantic Hilton Hotel. The minister is the Reverend Cecil Williams, an African-American from Texas, and the director of its programs is Janice Mirikitani, a Japanese American from the San Joaquin Valley. Both take the Mark Twain quip seriously: religion as *dangerous* if we get it wrong. At Glide, the quip is turned upside down: religion is dangerous if we get it *right*!

Using religion as escape from the world of human need is getting it very wrong—an opiate indeed, so Cecil and Jan and the entire Glide community spend twenty-four hours a day every day getting it right. The record of that commitment is found in Cecil's two books: *I'm Alive* and *No Hiding Place* [397] And his social gospel comes not out of Marx, but straight from a radical view of Jesus:

> Long ago I decided I wanted abundant life here, right here in this life. I looked in the Bible—I really did—and I found that the Jesus I know, the one who liberates oppressed people, is written about in those pages. The Jesus in Luke 4:18 says he came to preach the good news to the poor. The good news the poor want to hear is that they are free now. They are free from hunger, free from sub-standard housing, free from the need to use or sell drugs to survive. The Jesus I read about in Luke isn't going about saving folks for another life, by and by. Jesus liberates, here, now.[398]

Glide is an American laboratory for Liberation Theology. Cecil calls it "a theology of recovery," a four step program, designed to help anyone trapped by dependence discover the real meaning in his/her life. Glide outreach moves through *recognition* ("no secret is too terrible, no memory is too horrible, no rejection is too harsh),[399] *self-definition* ("The names we call ourselves matter. People with drug problems must decide, ' Am I an addict or a recovering person?'"), *rebirth* ("Rebirth happens when we go beyond wearing our real names like name tags and start living from the inside out."),[400] and *community* ("When you are in a community that won't lie to you—a community that allows you to express your anger and rage—then black folks, all kind of folks, can get healing").[401]

Shortly after the earthquake, Pat and I, along with one of my religious studies classes went to Glide to celebrate with Cecil Williams and the Glide community that had done so much to minister to the suffering caused by the quake. More people were made homeless in the Tenderloin than in the Marina District, and in response the church provided food for seven thousand a day. Such muscular compassion prompted Dan Rather at CBS, Peter Jennings at ABC, and Geraldo (belying his sensationalist reputation) to cover the ministry—and *Life Magazine* featured Glide as "A Church for the 21st Century."[402]

In the midst of his message that Sunday, Cecil was seized by these thoughts:

> We divide ourselves up all the time—rich and poor, black and white, Christian and Jew. Then the earth shakes and evens us all up for a while. For a moment everybody's poor and we can see what it means that God has made of one blood all nations.

This is what I call the *democracy of disaster.* Disaster is not necessarily tragedy. The tragedy is our wretched human need to invent caste systems that insulate us from community, so that it seems to take floods and fires to even us up. As Robert McAfee Brown put it in his *Christian Century* response, published the following week: "Earthquakes wipe out distinctions. The lowliest can have as chilling or thrilling a story as the most privileged." [403]

It seems to take the plagues for Pharaoh to set the prisoners free; and a world war to teach us that women are as capable as men in the work place—and that blacks can fly airplanes. It takes a madman with a AK-47 gunning down little Southeast Asian children on the Cleveland School playground to make us realize, just for a moment, that all colors and races bleed red and that all children are vulnerable. Yes, we have boat people in our schools. But the message from the assault rifle of Mr. Purdy is that *there are no people in this world but boat people.* We are all in the same boat: fragile creatures of bone and tissue with a chance of survival only if we realize we are one people.

Even John Wesley knew there was another message in destructive forces. In a tiny piece he called "Advice to a Soldier," he spoke with moving simplicity to the final tremor in our lives:

> Death levels all; it mingles in one dust the gentlemen, soldier, clown, and beggar; it makes all distinctions void. When life ends, so do they. Holy or unholy, is the one question then.[404]

Wesley understood the democracy of disaster, surely one of the most final and appropriate—if not particularly sweet—uses of adversity: that moment when castes crumble, when we overcome only because we are undone, when black and white are forced to be together, when there really is neither Jew nor Greek, Armenian nor Turk, Iraqi nor Israeli, Cambodian nor Stocktonian, English nor Portuguese—when Mexico City and San Francisco become the one village it takes.

Good Grief, Charles Schulz

So this is one clear message and we must be thankful for it. But there is that other—that shadow companion message—a penetrating, but quite different aftershock: the destruction of naiveté, the end of the world of childhood.

"Old men are fond of little certainties," wrote Tennessee Williams. To which I might add: young men want identity and middle aged men need power. (Women are speaking for themselves.) Large certainties incubate the desire for control, for domination. From the Garden of Eden comes the word: be fruitful, multiply, and have dominion. Children, of course suspect that they are not in control—inhabiting bodies that drive them, obeying rules they did not make, living in institutions they did not create, relying on parents who seem gigantic and invulnerable. Then, theological extrapolations conveniently replace the gradual demythologizing of the Super Parent.[405] If the earthly father falters, the heavenly father will not. If the mother is given to corruption, there are everlasting arms. Freud rightly saw that these extrapolations were wish fulfillments—illusions with no future in the reality principle. And religion—he reminded us—is the custodian of illusion. Whole institutions have been designed with just one major task: to prevent us from growing up, to keep us submissive members of the family of "God."

The summer of 1989 was also the fortieth anniversary of the *Peanuts* comic strip, that whimsical, amusing, and penetrating gang of "Li'l Folk" (the original title of the strip). As we all know now, this is no kid stuff. Robert Short's *The Gospel According to Peanuts*, published in 1965, made sure of that. The book sold over ten million copies (through 1999), and Charles Schulz credits Short's slim volume as one of the four most important events in the life of the strip, forcing us to see the biblical and theological ambiance surrounding Charlie Brown as Everyman and Snoopy as redemptive presence.[406]

But as nice as he is about allowing Short to use the cartoons for a neo-Calvinistic homily on original sin, the gospel according to Schulz is quite different than the gospel according to Short. A former Sunday School teacher and still a member of the Church of God (headquartered in Indiana), Charles Schulz now describes himself as a "secular humanist"—that horrid phrase so detested by conservatives in America. And what he means by that he drew into a cartoon rather obviously omitted by Short.

Peppermint Patty asks Charlie Brown what security is. The question prompts him to think about those wonderful days when, as a tiny child, he could be riding with his Dad after a family outing, and coming home at night, curl up in the back seat of the car, knowing that all was well.

> "Security is sleeping in the back seat of the car—when you're a little kid and you've been somewhere with your Mom and Dad and it's night, and you're riding home in the car, you can sleep in the back seat."
>
> "You don't have to worry about anything. Your Mom and Dad are in the front seat and they do all the worrying…They take care of everything…"

Peppermint Patty exclaims: "That's real neat!"

Then Charlie Brown goes on: "But it doesn't last! Suddenly, you're grown up, and it can never be that way again! Suddenly it's over, and you'll never get to sleep in the back seat again. Never!"

Peppermint Patty's eyes get big with fright as her little pigtails jump up and she reaches quickly for Charlie Brown. *"Hold my hand, Chuck !!"*

Warm and comfortable in our father's car, all the driving left to someone who cares and can get us home safely, it is terrifying to have this taken from us. Schulz tells us that the context for this nostalgic strip was a journey back to St. Paul after his own children had grown and gone and his father had died. Twenty years after he left Minnesota for California, he visited his father's barbershop—a business trip that became a pilgrimage to his childhood. The same chairs were there, and the place where his father would rest his lighted cigar, the same mirror and linoleum squares on the floor. It was so overwhelming that he stayed in the shop only one or two minutes—and has never gone back again. Schulz recalls this visit and the cartoon strip in a film essay on his life entitled *To Remember,* by Karen and David Crommie. As the film ends, he is driving a car in France, revisiting the site of a French chateau turned barracks where he was stationed in World War II.

What does life mean? It means, says Schulz, that at some point you can no longer ride in the back seat, with the blessed assurance that all will be well.

> You grow up. You have to sit in the front. You have to do the driving and all the responsibility is yours. Maybe this is what maturity really is. Maybe maturity is being reconciled to the fact that you cannot go back. You can't sleep in the back seat any longer. You have to sit in the front. You have to drive your own life.

It is gentle and wistful—this comic book litany of yesterday. You have to grow up. You have to move to the front. *You have the drive the car yourself.*

Well and good, we say. Time to grow up, to take responsibility for ourselves. So we become literate, inculcated with the values of our clan, adroit in business, marry the partner of choice, plan and produce children of choice, calculate financial stability, order our lives. Then one crystal autumn day, with the euphoria of our national pastime rising in a cathedral of contest, we drive the car ourselves out over the bridge that crosses into the future, confident of our ability to help bring that future into being. The time is 5:03. Time to give thanks.

But for what? For invulnerability? For the protection of God?

The *Titanic* was unsinkable, the Maginot line unbreachable, the Great War ended all wars, Spirit Lake—nestled at the foot of Mount St. Helens— was perfect peace. And here we are moving over a mighty span of steel and stone.

What does life mean? It means that the world is a gift, with all its possibilities, but that we have this treasure in earthen vessels. We are called to receive the world, love it, use it, and leave it finer and richer for those who come after us if we can. That is the message at 5:03.

But then it is 5:04. What does life mean in the aftershock of recognition? Can we still give thanks? Our innocence and our arrogance have ended. Now we know that the ultimate metaphysic of an earthquake is its unpredictability. We can track a hurricane, set out tornado watches, draw a precise timetable for the advance of killer bees, give flood and tidal wave warnings, even project a reasonable percentage of disease probabilities. But those great plates under the surface of our civilizing culture seem beyond our instruments. The fault, dear Brutus, is not in the stars, but just under our feet. *Per aspera ad astra.*

We have enough possibilities to make us interesting, we have enough certainty to make us responsible, and we have enough caprice to make us humble. Our precious earth comes with only one guarantee: it must be passed on to someone else. The rain may fall on the just and unjust, the ground may shake so that every mountain shall be brought low and every valley lifted up, but when we embrace each other in compassion, respect, and delight, the glory of the Lord shall be revealed, and the sun will rise on a world at peace.

It is 5:04. It is also *kairos*.

FIRE AND ICE: CREATIVITY

What is life about? How do you know when you're alive? Did Charles Schulz *live* before *his* death in 2000? What is the answer to Zorba's question?

Robert Pirsig, a college philosophy teacher who never finished his doctorate, once set out to answer the question: What's best? He and his disturbed son Chris climbed on a motorcycle in Minneapolis and rode all the way to San Francisco, filling a journal with observations and probes, technology and philosophy—which grew into a manuscript of four hundred pages.[407] Pirsig wanted to share those reflections and sent the manuscript to several publishers—all of whom turned it down. Who would read the diary of a failed teacher, running from life with his maladjusted child? No sex, no plot, no exposé: just a therapeutic odyssey. Keep it to yourself. One hundred and twenty one consecutive publishing firms agreed. The one hundred and twenty-second editor refused to say no, citing the fact that although the book wouldn't sell a thousand copies, it still had enough "quality" to appear in print. Millions of people bought a copy of *Zen and the Art of Motorcycle Maintenance*.[408]

No one thinks these metaphysical wanderings a masterpiece, not even Pirsig.[409] He explained its success as a "culture-bearer"—a book which, almost accidentally, challenges cultural value assumptions, as *Uncle Tom's Cabin* galvanized an entire culture's shift of assumptions about slavery. In 1974, *Zen* challenged our ideas of mental illness, of education and of material success.[410] But I think it was more than this. The book hit the "Me Decade" dead center: the national paranoia of Watergate, the leaderless government, the end of the Vietnam export of blame for the ills of America, that forced calm which gave us the uncomfortable chance to talk to ourselves about what's best. And it was set in that most American of modes: the picaresque story of the open road. It was the mythic adventure of the West on two wheels, the landscape of the soul, big sky and big questions, father and son: *Easy Rider* in reverse, drug free, and with a happy ending. They are together and free inside the Golden Gate.

> Trials never end, of course. Unhappiness and misfortune are bound to occur as long as people live, but there is a feeling now, that was not here before, and is not just on the surface of things, but penetrates all the way through: We've won it. It's going to get better now. You can sort of tell about these things.[411]

Remember the ending of another culture bearing novel, written just on the cusp of the civil rights revolution—an incredible first book that swept the nation? Ralph Ellison's *Invisible Man* had journeyed from South to North, from patronizing, fawning Booker T. Washington in Alabama, to Ras the Destroyer and the Harlem riots, living out his blackness under the streets of New York, stealing light from white power—knowing full well that his dark presence is visible inside the white man's fear. "And who knows but what on other frequencies I speak for you."

Did *Zen and the Art of Motorcycle Maintenance* speak for us? *Could* we tell about these things? Pirsig wrote it, but could *he* tell?

Young Chris decided to join the Zen Center in San Francisco, a way of continuing the journey I suppose, this time into inner space. Pirsig returned to the East to live and write, remarried and moved to England. On Saturday, November 17, 1979, Chris was murdered—stabbed to death by two men in a robbery attempt, just outside the Center at the corner of Haight and Octavia Street. The men apparently were enraged that he had no money on him. At the funeral Pirsig learned that Chris had bought a plane ticket that very morning for England. What is life all about? Where did his son go?

Where indeed. *Where* do any of us go? One moment, like Chris, we are "occupying time and space on this planet"—deal with money, arrange our rooms, address our responsibilities. Then that second moment that suddenly seems to cancel the first. Pirsig wonders: "Did he go up the stack at the crematorium?" Perhaps somewhere in the "little box of bones" given back to him? Even above the clouds somewhere? "None of these answers made any sense." [412]

Before we can answer the question *Where,* we must ask the question *What.* Pirsig refuses to believe that the oxides of Chris's flesh and blood were Chris. *What* was Chris? The answer that does make sense is this: what Pirsig missed so badly was not an object but a pattern, including the flesh and blood—but that was not all there was. The pattern was larger than that, larger than both father and son. The pattern was their complete experience of maintenance and insight into the nature of the journey.

> Now Chris's body, which was part of that larger pattern, was gone. But the larger pattern remained. A huge hole had been torn out of the center of it, and that was what caused all the heartache.

Rather like the sensations in an amputated limb, the "pattern" that was Chris was searching for location that was no longer there. Pirsig begins to

understand why grief work clings to material "representation" of the torn relationship: "The pattern is trying to hang onto its own existence by finding
some new material to center itself upon."[413]

The new material in Pirsig's life is a baby daughter named Nell, a time in
Sweden to write his sequel, published—after *one* editor read it—in 1992 as
Lila (another odyssey, this time boat maintenance on the Hudson). He still
thinks we have won.

I agree that *he* has won. But why? Divorce, murder, insanity, rejection,
utter paranoia at speaking in public? [Pirsig compares lecturing to parachute
jumping and will not do either one.] The hidden substance underlying all the
accidents of his life, the very possibility of pattern, is creativity. He wrote
Chris and himself into health, wrote Chris out of the crematorium and into his
daughter. He even allows her to play with the computer keyboard creating the
last line of his article for the *New York Times*:

ooo1099ikl;i,pykmulmmmmmmmmmmm 1 1 1

The editors, creating a pattern of their own, left it in. It is Nell's "first published work."

What's it all about? It is love making flesh. It is flesh making words. It is
weaving fresh patterns across the spaces of our isolation. It is holding up
those patterns to the light of our imagination and looking for quality. "Making variations on a theme," said Douglas Hofstadter, "is really the crux of creativity."

The conjunction of light with death is not usually marked by conscious
art celebrating life on earth. We are seduced by all those spools of radiance—
luring us into the great beyond and going gladly. I always wondered why they
played "Nearer, My God, to Thee" at funerals.[414] Why should we think that
somehow we are closer to God in death than we are in life? If we are serious
that body and soul are one, then it should follow that life and death are one.
Not identical—one. So just as I don't actually want to live forever—doesn't
seem much of an option, really—I don't want to die forever either. Perhaps
those creative folks who imagined re-incarnation were early stress-reduction
specialists. While there is not much I can do about it either way, there are
those who aren't intimidated by such impotence.

Making Light of Death

The book shelves are full of light these days: Shirley MacLaine's *Dancing in the Light* (she's crinkly-eyed certain that past lives lead to a future
union with the lightness of being—and that there is no darkness at all),
Melvin Morse, *Closer to the Light: Learning from the Near-Death Experiences of Children*,[415] and the sequel by Dr. Morse, written with Paul Perry,
Transformed by the Light: The Powerful Effect of Near-Death Experiences on

People's Lives..[416] Morse provides us with call letters for this real-close-but-not-quite-yet phenomenon: NDE. And we get the NDE (near-death experience) schematized so you can know if you've had one. There are nine essentials for the "full-blown" experience, but in NDE, all will have some and some will have all.[417] The essentials range from "a sense that you are really dead" [sounds reasonable enough] to "a reluctance to come back to the body [even more reasonable, given the condition of some bodies].

The most successful charge of the latest Light brigade is Betty J. Eadie's *Embraced by the Light*, the winsome story—shouldn't we call it *autothanatography?*—of yet another woman who found death's door to be revolving. Translated into twenty-one languages, two million hard cover copies sold, on the best seller list in the *New York Times* for over a year. Bidding for paperback rights started at $1,500,000 and was snapped up in twenty seconds—in the universe of publishing, considerably faster than the speed of light. Betty J. Eadie, whatever other experiences she may have had, is rich.

How is the journey made? Souls come up from earth as pinpoints or beacons of light. And this seems natural enough, especially if one had ever seen the cover of *Life* for December, 1990. The question posed by the special issue was striking: "Who Is God?"—the question in big, bold white against a deep blue galactic backdrop filled with stars and planets, all pictured as pinpoints of light. George Bush, I'm sure, must have had a copy close by to remind him of his benevolent vision for the country.

Eadie had been in a hospital for a partial hysterectomy [See Freud and Johnnie Cochran]. She "died" there in that hospital from a hemorrhage: grew weaker and weaker—and then some enormous energy took her out through her chest above her body. She looked back, hovering above the bed, near the ceiling and then up—heard a rushing sound—and was sucked up by some tremendous force. Moving forward through it, she felt great tranquility, then approached a pinpoint of light—light recognized as love. She went forward and the Being of light—which now she clearly identified as Jesus—embraced her. Jesus told her—in a rather jovial style—that her mission wasn't complete and he sent her back: "You died but it is not your time."

To set her journey to heaven and back in context, Eadie is a Roman Catholic and her mother was full blooded Sioux—a fairly fertile soil in which visions can grow. She confessed that she always had a tremendous fear of death and not a good relationship with God—both problems taken well care of by her NDE. She waited nineteen years to tell this tale, until the doctor, who she says signed the death certificate, was himself in the other end of the tunnel—probably for good. No medical records are available, since only Eadie can release them, something she doesn't feel constrained to do as yet. Perhaps another nineteen years.

What *is* all this? Hallucination of a dying brain—a dream—a scam—creative fiction—real? *What?* Some kind of transcending encounter? Is this life after death?

"No such thing as death," she says in a lecture question session, televised from one of her "missionary" appearances—with a gentle, candid, unpretentious style. If she's conning the public, she deserves an acting award to place over her bank account. Heaven? Full of loving guardian angels, majestic mountains, "each little droplet of water that cascaded over the fall had a tone, each pleased God by its very existence." A garden of intense color where each flower was illuminated from within: "Each rose was beautiful and had a melody." [418]

Psychologist Susan Blackmore (*Dying to Live: Near Death Experiences*) has reviewed hundreds of these NDE cases and sheds some candid, gentle, precise neurological light on these strange matters. When oxygen stops in the brain, the inhibitory system fails very fast and the brain goes wild and produces energies that are relevant to our lives—the "my whole life passed before my eyes syndrome." These images are like dreams, but we are cut off from our normal outside world and these images feel completely real.

Tunnel and bright light—reported by nearly everybody in the NDE lexicons? The visual cortex has lots of cells devoted to the middle of the visual field and very few towards the outside. Now traumatized, they all start firing randomly—and what will that look like? Exactly like a bright light in the middle of the visual field—and as the oxygen level drops one would get the sensation of rushing forward into that light. It's a brain function—a phenomenon of the body—just like everything else.[419]

This may be the greatest wonder of all: each day death strikes and we live as if we were immortal. We should be looking for quality of life, not another denial of death that promises life after death and distracts from the urgency of life before death. I don't want to be embraced by the light. I want to embrace my wife and play with my children. I don't want to hover above my gray likeness and then soul travel to God. I want to live with my talent and love the earth. I don't want to swirl into eternity. I want to stay in summer.

What's best? Knowing that we did our best. That we gave our potentiality form. We painted it, wrote it down, traced its trajectory in the arena, pressured harmony on threads, edited images into giants, challenged the politics of literary reputation, sculpted the sides of caves, released seed into swirling receptivity, designed rhythms in air, caressed wood, and wired our world by the calculus of excellence. We danced.

In *The Color of Money*, Fast Eddy—an aging hustler now, and once again played by Paul Newman, takes a young hot shot pool player as his protégé on the make. But it isn't enough to teach. Fast Eddy wants to play again. Re-entering the world of fast money and competition, he meets his pupil in the championship match—and beats him, only to find out that Vince, his condescending protégé (played by Tom Cruise), has *let* him win. In a hallway, Fast Eddy confronts Vince in an exorbitantly poignant moment—remembering perhaps the time so long ago he himself had run the table just to show how beautifully pool could be played—and says *very* softly: "I wanted your best game."

What's best? Your best. Surrounded and audited by everyone else's best. When the goats were cast out into everlasting darkness, bleating about the sheep that got to lie down in green pastures, the Almighty Judge was heard to whisper: "I wanted your best game."

"Best" is a Chalcedonian word: it is both divine and human, unconfused but inseparable. It is community and person, like an ellipse with two foci: I and us. The I exists as a pattern woven into all that is and cannot be understood outside that pattern. Inasmuch as you have done it unto the least of these, my brothers and sisters and forests and rivers, you have done it unto me. *Excellence* is an empty word without a *world* in which to be excellent. It is to be judged by inclusive potentiality. Today's Fast Eddy will slow tomorrow, but he will never know that without being at the table where everyone brings his best game. Jim Valvano was famous for his ebullience, his courage in the face of cancer, and this coaching philosophy: "Always give yourself a chance to win." North Carolina State couldn't win all the time, few people beat cancer, and everybody dies. But that's not the point. Did you write it out? Did you go to Crete and build a ramp to the sea? Did you learn all there is to know about Jack London? Did you make a film every day and make love every night? Did you draw a round headed kid who owned an imaginative dog? Did you raise your voice where the caged bird sings? Did you review the nation from the firing line of total intellectual war? Did you spend every ounce of energy you possess in the Tenderloin helping people define themselves? Did you leave the insulation of Newport Beach and risk sacrifice in the revolutions of South Africa? Did you burn out exercising your genius for hearing harmony?

The Dead Teachers Society

I have always been clinically paranoid about wasting anybody's time—and equally obsessed with openness. I never saw openness as contrary to wisdom, but rather as the very heart of wisdom. The Buddhist teachers in Japan have a way of showing this to their students. A master will offer tea to the student, giving him a full cup. Then the master will pour tea into that full cup, causing it to overflow. The lesson is obvious and subtle at the same time. Obvious truth: one cannot learn if one brings a full cup already to class. Subtle corollary: there is always new truth pouring in on the old, refreshing, replacing—and overflowing any efforts to contain it.

I have never liked canned jokes—even though I'm open to a good one. Did you hear the one about...? No, but I'm about to... and I resent it. It's rather like going to the morgue. The *one about* is already dead—it's fun frozen in a locker. A fine comedian playing prophet can resurrect the corpse and we all applaud, but living humor is something different, something immediate—a series of synaptic leaps that requires instance for life. That's why comedy is the most difficult form of art, why Robin Williams is rightly seen as a genius of sorts—in his own words "a cesspool of consciousness." Real humor is Zen: it is an excruciatingly accurate reception of the environment. That's also why laughter is the hallmark of humanity.

A joke is a full cup of tea. It's a way of denying humor by embalming it. Jokes are for fundamentalists. Telling a joke requires nothing from the audience but submission, acquiescence to pre-scripted titillation. It's the old dualism all over again: it's a group out there to be conquered by me in here. "I killed them," the victorious evangelist of authoritative wit reports. Staged humor becomes nothing more than another weapon in the war of control: disarm the enemy, catch them with their guard down, and waylay them with the Word. It's really not very far from "Have you heard the one about…" to "I have the truth." The "funniest" people in the south—Howard Butt, Jr. (his father owned the very serious HEB Food Store chain), Jess Moody (he officiated at the not-so-funny marriage of Burt Reynolds and Loni Anderson), Charlie Fox (he metamorphosed from marquee Baylor cheerleader to sesquipedalian Harvard Ph.D.)—were revival preachers and Youth for Christ evangelists, all of whom must have had a copy of *101 Snappy Stories That Preachers Tell*, and spent a lot of time squirreling away nutty pieces from the *Reader's Digest*. A rather accurate description of Southern Baptist sermons was a part of this repertoire: three jokes and a death bed story. And that's no joke.

I feel the same way about canned classes. Write out the syllabus, require the specific reading, schedule every lecture, arrange the visuals, pre-set the exams. Might as well film it: *The Dead Teachers Society*. Students are presented with a full cup, which you—as infinite resource—pour into their infinitely empty cups. Isn't that the way it's supposed to be?

Education is not a tea party; it's a dance. It is miraculous reservoirs of energy and imagination that you have invited into your life and if you are not closed in your openness, they may invite you into theirs. Wisdom is not the property of either teacher or student. It resides only in the partnership—or (at the risk of a court case) the embrace.

It seems to me that a college partnership should do three things: inform, entertain, and inspire. In some weird way, I always wanted to convert the classroom into sacred space, a temple of my unfamiliar, and play priest by encouraging the supplicants to defrock me. If you thrive on deference, it is a fairly dangerous way to teach, rather like the ancient Aztec game of "basketball" where teams fought each other to force a huge stone ball through a hole in a wall—and the captain of the *winning* team was beheaded as symbol of victory.[420]

In the Course of Human Events…

In my years of teaching, the class which came the closest to providing the ambiance of openness and, to paraphrase Valvano, gave us a chance to gain wisdom, was the one I hosted for sixteen years—that gives this book its theme: *Religion of the Body.*

The general point of view was developed in a formal lecture by the instructor, one of the few in the entire semester. It's not that I am opposed to lectures—an old evangelist thrives on seducing audiences. But lectures are too often narcissistic and evasive. They are pastimes that pre-define the journey. Even the tools they provide distort the investigation of the world. As the saying goes: to those with a hammer, all problems look like nails.

The consequent "lectures" then became a kind of introduction for the guest—or guests. The guests were carefully chosen to open up the world beyond the classroom—and their presence required some explanation. I *never* talked about a subject in class if I could find somebody who knew more about the subject than I did—and since I know very little about a lot, that meant guests every week. In all classes, not just Religion of the Body. Professors can easily become isolated inside their own consciousness—and some design barricades of arrogance or territoriality that exclude inconvenient questions. One of the reasons I liked the Cluster concept of college was that it *forced* the professors to interact every day and in every class with the presence of men and women from other disciplines and other perspectives. One can easily maintain sovereignty over a group when by definition the king cannot be criticized—rather in the same way that Suharto remained president of Indonesia for thirty years. And this way of being in education is quite as hard on the students as it is on the teachers. Many students *want* Messiahs for masters. Why should they pay a fortune to realize that they must educate themselves?

But how long will we go on wallowing in someone else's expertise—what I call the *substitutionary theory of atonement in education.* Jesus does for us what we could never do for ourselves—we are sinners, but he is perfect. When he speaks, we listen, memorize, and repeat. When he is silent, we pause and pray for receptivity to his next utterance. Substitute *teacher* for *Jesus* and authority is back in the classroom. Just answer "here!"

I prefer the Abelardian theory of atonement: Jesus inspires us by his example into participating in redemptive activity. He doesn't do it for us; he calls us to follow. And what is it that he does? He studies his own tradition, engages the masters in conversation about the finer points of that tradition, and then makes his own judgment as to which part he will accept, which he will reject, and which he will change. He is not a robot—he is a redeemer: one who has developed authority in himself, beyond that of his teachers. His version of the ten commandments is *not* the one Moses left. "You shall not kill" memorizes the robot, and that is that. Not a bad idea to refrain from killing, says the Redeemer, but that's too superficial. You should not even be *angry* with your brother or sister. And, next thing you know, the one who says never to be angry is creating havoc in the temple, furiously ripping up furniture and flaying the skin of the merchants of sacrifice. Jesus is not even trapped by his own rhetoric.

So I have had guests. Lots of them. Not because I agreed with them, but because we must deliberately seek out people who have something we need to know. Who *are* somebody we need to know. Judges, orthopedic surgeons, evangelists, mimes, psychologists, philosophers, transsexuals, bisexuals, gays, gynecologists, fine artists, martial artists, therapists, historians, rolfers, meditators, Olympic athletes, all-pro football players, film stars, Pentecostal choirs, feminists, traditionalists, Buddhist monks, Scientologists, sociologists, and—don't breathe a word of it—Christian ministers. Guests. Lots of them.

The Library of DNA

Each year, I would ask students to choose the most "powerful" female guest. The clear winner was always Vivian Baxter. Lady B, as she was called by her friends in the community—and on her license plate in fact, was our neighbor—literally. I always loved her wit, élan, and earthy approach to heavenly matters. She was in her middle seventies then, irascible, radiant, and dressed to the nines. She brought with her to class an amazing expanse of feminine space: multiple marriages, poverty, high society in St. Louis, nurse on the high seas, gun carrying-poker dealer, church pillar, cigar-smoking sensualist, unshakable faith in God—and the fact that she was Maya Angelou's mother. She died in summer of 1991.

Tom Robbins once suggested that the most interesting library in the world is DNA. Maya's mother, who lived in Stockton from 1967 until her death, had that warm, regal bearing and throaty, mischievous, confident voice spinning out stories like some mythical pistol-packin' mama, who knew God personally, but could take care of business on her own. Vivian Baxter was always "preparing for the worst and hoping for the best," and her infectious energy reminded us that we can pray and party at the same time. She taught us that it is possible to turn the many "winters of discontent" into "invincible summer."

In that convocation in 1993 when we honored Dr. Angelou, when the ovation for her inaugural poem was still ringing over our country, and "the horizon leaned forward" from the Capitol steps all the way to Stockton, when she melded imagination and form in celebration of the human possibility and moved us beyond cynicism and despair—teaching us all that, no matter what time it is or trouble we have, to say *"Good Morning!"*[421]—on that May afternoon the miraculous library was opened to us.

In honoring Dr. Angelou, we literally celebrated the American Dream of Education. Out of poverty, racism, urban jungles and rural isolation, out of the shock of sexual abuse the jinn of reading were unleashed, and the little girl from Stamps memorized entire Shakespearean plays, devoured classics of world literature, became fluent in a dozen languages, and riding the magic carpet of learning has become America's First Lady of Performing Letters. And just as this Caged Bird sings, so can we all.

Liberal education is a tautology. Safe sex may be possible and certainly wise, but there is no such thing as safe education. Perhaps Mortimer Adler was correct when he attributed the phenomenal success of Allan Bloom's book to its title—the mind (American or otherwise) was made for opening not closing. Ask not what your college can conserve; ask what it can liberate.

There is a soft, winsome moment in *The Wizard of Oz* at the end of the yellow brick road, when the scarecrow, after the long adventure, stands before the fearsome Wizard himself in the Emerald City and asks for a brain. "I can't give you a brain," he replies, "but I can give you a diploma."

A lifetime ago I left Dallas and went to Georgetown, Texas, on an asphalt road and entered the university, as naïve a young scarecrow as ever walked into Oz, following my high-achieving, brainy brothers into the fabled land of mighty wizards. I suppose I performed well enough to warrant a diploma—I was, as they say, in the upper third of the slow group. But the wizards were wise, and instead of giving me a brain, Southwestern University gave me an education—and encouraged my heart to pursue the adventure of ideas.

Today I realize just how long I have been a part of the college world. Fifty years since the president handed me that diploma. But I never left the educational community, marrying a beautiful young teacher from Kansas—of course—and traveling the road from Texas to New England to California, from Austria to the Far East and the islands of spice, professing my faith in the freedom of inquiry and redemptive awareness of context. I consider myself a marginal man in the world of education. I do not speak from the Olympian heights of the Ivy League, or the broad vistas of the Carnegie Foundation. They didn't even know my name at *Cheers*. But I have not been wholly inattentive, and I hope not insensitive.

What I have learned in my own presumptuous attempt at wizardry is that we are guests in the lives of our students. We can teach only by invitation, and then not for long. When the student is ready to receive, we may begin the fragile process, which consists primarily of arranging ambiance and secondarily of provoking and honing skills. The effectiveness of the teacher resides in the sense of rhythm between motivation and content. The wisdom of the teacher resides in the ability to humanize the seven deadly virtues: seriousness, responsibility, tolerance, competitiveness, talent, confidence, and obedience.

And the artistry of that teaching process is to help students **see** when they look, **imagine** when they see, **think** when they imagine, **feel** what they think, **symbol** what they feel, and **trust** what they symbol.

The teacher is not just an intellectual with credentials to inculcate the uninitiated. I have learned that we must be *sorcerers*. We specialize in revealing sources: the way political decisions are made, the structure of matter, the genesis of social interaction, how languages insinuate patterns of thought, the chemistry of consciousness, the alchemy of economics, the metaphysics of movement, the rituals of belief, how poems mean, how music plays, why people laugh.

I have learned that education is not a virtue. It is not some kind of substance which we can add to a person who earns it through disciplined investigation of the world. It is rather more like a grace, like a sacrament, where the celebrant is the student. We may, in fact, provide the elements of curriculum, ivy-covered ecclesiae, and a tradition of probability. But we have no final authority and no real power. Only the student has these.

The educational process may be virtuous, but education itself is a gift, given in the occasion of discipline, but not because of it. The wise teacher—rather like the wise parent—is quite content to make his presence more and more unnecessary, and thank the student for that precious, fleeting hospitality.

The Musical Christ

What's it all about, this life before death? It's about placing your talent at a center of the world's need, and refusing the seduction of mediocrity.

I wanted to see *Amadeus* in Austria. Forman released the film in 1984, when we were in Graz, and I would see those ominous posters with the black and white mask announcing something hidden and classically European. That it would be in German was appropriate—though a student translator at the screening would be helpful. We went by streetcar to the theater, but it was sold out, and we had to settle for *gemütlichkeit* at a local *Stuberl*—the Austrian idea of seminar education. So it was that I waited to see the film with students in America, after the Academy had given it highest accolades, when the only translation I needed was aesthetic.

The film purported to be about Mozart's genius, a kind of musical Christ sacrificed for his art by the jealous Viennese court composer Salieri. Mozart is played out as a giggling, farting buffoon with the miraculous talent of being able to write music as if he were taking dictation from God. As Salieri puts it, reading the original and unchanged scripts was like looking through a "cage of strokes at an absolute beauty." He vows to hinder and harm God's creation for giving him the "ability to recognize the incarnation" without granting the talent to match his creativity. This hindering takes the final form of hastening Mozart's death by encouraging him to finish a Requiem Mass that Salieri has secretly commissioned and financed, a struggle so intense that it burns out any life left in the exhausted genius, leaving him dead at thirty-five. Since no one knew of the composition, and Salieri was writing out the music dictated by the dying man, he would then be able to claim the requiem as his own, and finally share in the glory reserved for this musical Word made flesh—while its real creator lay decomposing [*sic*] in a pauper's grave.

Salieri—this being a highly romanticized film—gets what he deserves:

madness and commitment to an asylum, where he himself tells the tale as an extremely unctuous confession, calling himself Saint Mediocrity and faking identities to the last, absolving all the mediocrities of the world.

The film isn't history, but neither is history. Salieri was a respected composer, the most popular in Europe, including much affection from Beethoven and Schubert. Mozart himself sent his children to learn music from Salieri. While he surely envied Mozart—may have hated him, there was no truth to the vicious rumor that he poisoned him. Salieri did make it more difficult for Mozart to get a good appointment in Vienna, and the rumor—later molded into an opera by Rimsky-Korsakov entitled *Mozart and Salieri*—caused the old man to make an "official" death-bed statement: "I did not poison Mozart."[422] Forman's film (and Peter Shaffer's play) draw little inspiration from actual events.

The title concentrates the film. "Amadeus" is brutally ironic, since it means "lover of God." In the case of the film, *Amadeus*—familiar as one of the names of the genius [Johann Chrysostom Wolfgang Theophilus (Greek for Amadeus), and the name to whom the gospel of Luke is addressed]—refers not to Mozart at all, but to Salieri: the true believer who cannot accept the obvious fact that the world is not fair. It is Salieri, not Mozart, who was poisoned—by the lethal drug of comparison.

On the surface, *Amadeus* is a most violent film, more so than the cartoons created by Stallone and prime-time TV. Here Mediocrity *murders* Genius. But behind the mask of glorious sound and desperate envy, the film asks an even more brutal question: what music have *I* written? Harlan Jacobson writes: "If Forman has elevated Mozart as an incandescent presence to equal and surpass for a time the force of Salieri and all he represents, then the film really sharpens the core question of self-confrontation, 'Am I Mozart, or am I Salieri?'"[423] I believe this question is misleading, because the question implies an absolute difference between the rule and the exception—and the truth is that we are both. Attempting to borrow strength by wearing Achilles' armor will only get you killed without ever going into battle for yourself.

Forman is not only presenting Mozart; he is presenting himself. *His* music is the superb editing and pace of the piece, the brush of the camera catching the ingratiating contrast between giggle and glance. Like Kazantzakis' neurotic Savior, he has given birth to his own Christ, and we behold what glory there is in all the details on the screen.[424]

David Thompson disliked those details, complaining that they were all surfaces, as if depths do not really exist: "And what a surface! Breasts, keyboards, masks, nipples of Venus, wigs, pens, papers, a billiard ball, even the last shower of lime turned into paste by the rain. Good enough to eat."[425] There was "something wrong, he said, "and it's not disguised by polish and reticence." That something, he contended, was Forman's failure to let us see *why* the music seems "beautiful." And the crime against "history" was not Salieri as a "lizard of murderous envy" or Mozart as a "brat."[426] It's presenting Mozart as not knowing what's going on.

Fair enough, except that Thompson is not writing just about Forman, but also about Thompson. He thinks Mozart knew what he was doing. So what? Whatever Mozart did, we are not likely to penetrate his consciousness. We are moved to listen to his music, watch Forman's film, and read Thompson's commentary. And in each instance—enthralled, entranced, or enraged—the question intrudes: what music have *you* written? Am I Thompson or am I Forman? William Palmer got it right when he called *Amadeus* "a biography of the imagination"[427]—at least it sounds right to someone who's writing a theology of the imagination and smuggling it in as a religion of the body.

Karl Barth's love of Mozart is legendary. Writing a generation before Forman or Shaffer, Barth addressed a "Letter of Thanks to Mozart":

> If [one] really digests your musical dialectics he can become young and become old, he can work and relax, he can be gay or depressed; in short, he can live. You know now, far better than I, that much more is necessary for that purpose than the very best music. But there is much which helps men to this end…and other music which cannot help toward it. Your music helps….
> [428]

Barth claimed that the dialectics in Mozart mirrored life in its two-sidedness, but that he always "turned right rather than left"—hence his "triumphant charm." Accepting the limits of his art form, he says "how everything is." [429] What this tells us about Mozart is problematic, but what it says about Barth is that this music moves him. So much so that he writes this rhapsody to the musical Christ: "whether the angels play only Bach in praising God I am not quite sure; but I am sure…that *en famille* they play Mozart and that then also God the Lord is especially delighted to listen to them." [430] His essay on Mozart is his creative way to fix a pleasure that passes in the moment it is felt, an appropriation of evanescence, a witness to the Word. It has a relationship to the actual sounds that he hears, of course, and he writes in a kind of counterpoint to Mozart's melodies, as if, somehow, his writing allows him to be in Mozart's presence.

As Laurence Perrine suggested in *Sound and Sense*, the relationship of interpretation and criticism to the art form itself is rather like looking at a cone of illumination emanating from a flashlight. Close to the source the cone is almost identical in size to the lens, but immediately begins to spread in all directions, ever larger—until it dissolves somewhere in infinity. Therefore, when we hear a word like "horse," it can have multiple meanings and variations: "sawhorse," "black horse," "filly," "stallion," "pale horse of death," etc. But in no case can the word mean "cow." Just so, when we hear Mozart's *Magic Flute*, our mood is somehow bound to the actual notes but quickly spreads out—opened up by the orchestra playing it, the chorus singing it, our hearing apparatus, our own cultural background, the day of the month, the position of Mars, the speed of the galaxy, and God's willingness to turn off Bach for a few hours. [431] But, in no case, is the mood likely to be similar to listening to *The Phantom of the Opera*.

Music—all art—is a communal resurrection. The source can be delineated but not sealed. Art escapes the death of definition and we are invited to join in its freedom. This is why fundamentalists and fascists everywhere destroy art and crucify imagination. They would rather turn off the light or block the lens than explore the reaches of its rays. There's dark enough without arrogant ignorance. Turn on the searchlights and let those silver pencils write against the night.

The Ascending Christ

A great many stories have circulated about the life of Jesus, twenty or more gospels—fragments of up to fifty. There is a miracle tale for every taste—including several scintillating virgin births and the boy wonder, who could make clay pigeons fly. There are sermons on mounts and plains, a stack of ripostes guaranteed to irritate the most irenic of Pharisees, a riveting story of debauchery by a boy who had everything, puzzling interpretations of Roman occupation, legends about donkey rides to Egypt, a collection of brutal execution notes, a death no one could forget—and a few imaginative stories of bodies coming out of tombs.

One artist, not long before the end of the first century, took it upon himself to present his own understanding of the man from Nazareth:

> Forasmuch as many have taken in hand to set forth in order a declaration of those things which are most surely believed among us, even as they delivered them unto us, which from the beginning were eyewitnesses, and ministers of the word; it seemed good to me also, having had a perfect understanding of all things from the very first, to write to thee, most excellent Theophilus, that you might know the certainty of those things wherein you have been instructed.

So begins the gospel of Luke. The author gathers the tales and scripts, sorts them—culling out the ones not suitable to his vision, and edits them into a kind of play—a drama built on the metaphor of ascent. His Jesus enters the stage of history as the Bread of Heaven and must therefore be born in the house of bread, called *beth lehem* in Hebrew. The prologue therefore is filled with heavenly choirs exalting the low estate of those who give birth to the body of the highest in a place of food. [1-2] The prologue continues with inauguration of his mission by placing him in the line of the prophets of Israel and tempting him to appeal to miracle rather than message, by turning stones into earthly bread. His refusal to invert his calling closes the prologue. [3-4:12]

The first act opens in low-lying Galilee, far to the north—as the mountains of Judea break down into the hills of Nazareth, where Jesus identifies himself with the liberation of the oppressed. [4:18] The prophet delivers his most memorable message on a level place on the plain, [6:17-49] and gathers disciples from around the shores of a gentle lake to join him in preaching and healing. [9:1-2] In the midst of this ministry on the plain, Jesus takes three disciples up into a mountain, where he is revealed to them, not only as a prophet, but as the Son of God [9:28-38] Returning to the work in Galilee, his performance finds new intensity, sending out multiples of disciples to spread the message with a new urgency [10:1-2]—to reopen the prophet's call for a consuming fire instead of peace. [12:49-53] Act One closes with the rising opposition of the religious establishment, stunned by the parable of the profligate boy who was found, and the elder son who was lost. [15]. As the curtain drops, we sense the inevitability of the final conflict in Jerusalem.

Act Two takes the new Israel from Galilee to Jerusalem, rising through the central highlands of Samaria [17:11], straight up to the sacred heights chosen by David, the beloved Messiah, to rule the Kingdom of God. The drama moves into fervent pitch as Jesus deliberately symbolizes his own Davidic succession [19:37-38], the very week of the Jewish celebration of deliverance, provoking the Temple authorities to accept his challenge. They seize him and in collusion with the civil authorities he is tried, condemned, and crucified. [23:13-24] Jesus is taken to the hill above Jerusalem and his body lifted up above the place of the skull. His tortuous death, exposed above the city of kings, ends Act Two.

The climax of the drama unfolds in Act Three, where some, who had followed Jesus from lowly Galilee into the heights of Jerusalem, now find his tomb empty. The stage is made luminous with the presence of men in dazzling apparel, who remind them that this inexorable drama began long ago in Galilee: that he has risen. [24:7]. Jesus appears center stage now, surrounded by adoring, exultant believers. He gathers them together in Jerusalem, telling them to witness to the new kingdom by going down from the mountain in Judea, through Samaria, and on to every corner of the world. [Acts 1:8] He moves to the back of the stage, and as everyone gazes in wonder at the great Mount Olivet which looms over the city, he *ascends* into the heaven from which he came.

The geographical artistry is apparent: earth is human, the heights are cosmic. The ministry moves gradually *up:* Galilee, Samaria, Jerusalem, Mt. Calvary, Mt. of Olives, Heaven. And because Jesus connects Earth with Heaven, we too, shall one day ascend.

No one, I suppose, will miss the connection. Both Luke and Acts are addressed to the same Theophilus, which translates in Latin as *Amadeus*. And this author moves freely among all those materials. He alone places the "Sermon on the Mount" on the "plain." His gospel is unique among the Synoptics in recording a journey through Samaria *up* through the highlands—and the story of the "good" Samaritan. The other two are quite content to have Jesus avoid hated Samaria completely. He alone has an ascension and heavenly host singing at the birth in Bethlehem's manger. "Lovers of God" have to recognize why they have been given that name. We must not hurt or hinder this incarnation.

What connects earth with heaven? The ability to transcend the limits of history and produce something new. That is what we mean by the word *mundane*—we mean earth bound. This is the final miracle of human life, the astonishing grace of passing over the waters of chaos and creating something we can call good. Of burning out in the passion of sorcery. Some think the world will end by fire, some by ice, mused Robert Frost. And the Spirit prompts transcendent rhyme: From what we know of great desire we "hold with those who favor fire."[432]

Jesus wasn't resurrected by God; he was resurrected by Luke. As long as we refuse to exercise our gift, the grave in the garden will be filled. Death will have the victory. *The unexamined life may not be worth living, but the unlived life is certainly not worth examining.*

Am I Luke or am I Kazantzakis? Perhaps I am both resurrection and dance.

The Dance of Death

I remember being moved and mystified by Bergman's *Seventh Seal*, the 1956 film that made him internationally famous. The image of the grim-lipped knight playing chess with Death has become a staple of our popular culture [see *Bill and Ted's Excellent Adventure*] and shadows all the symbol laden film texts. Antonius Block played well enough to delay that final move until he reached his home—where Bergman creates immortality in the face of Death. There in his castle at last, reunited with his wife, he and his fellow travelers listen to a description of the end of time from the book of Revelation.

The scene is worth resetting. The wife emerges from the shadows: "I heard from people of the Crusade that you were on your way home. I've been waiting for you here. All the others have fled from the Plague." She looks at her knight as he stands in silence: "Don't you know me anymore? You too have changed." She stepped forward close to his silence: "Now I can see that it's you. Somewhere in your eyes...somewhere in your face...but hidden and frightened is that boy who went away so long ago." Block's dispassionate reply: "It's over now and I'm a little tired." " Are you sorry you went?" "No, but I'm a little tired." She moves her hand gently to his face: "I can see that."

At last his own hand moves to hers. "Over there are my friends." "Ask them in. I shall prepare a meal." Block's face dissolves into a woman's—his squire's sensuous companion, a full screen close-up as the wife's voiceover is heard reading from the eighth chapter of the book of Revelation:

And when the Lamb had opened the seventh seal, there was silence in heaven for about the space of half an hour. And I saw the seven angels which stood before God; and to them were given seven trumpets.... The first angel sounded and there followed hail and fire mingled with blood, and they were cast upon the earth: and the third part of the trees was burnt up, and all the green grass was burnt up. And the second angel sounded, and as it were a great mountain burning with fire was cast into the sea, and a third part of the sea became blood....

All the while she is reading, the castle pilgrims look anxiously—ominously—around, waiting for something invisible, some unwanted guest.

And the third angel sounded, and there fell a great star from heaven, burning as it were a torch.... And the name of the star is called Wormwood...

Then Death appears. All the pilgrims approach the figure as the Knight as earthly host greets him: "Good morning Noble Lord." The wife adds her greeting: "I am Karin the Knight's wife, and I bid you welcome in my house." The others speak: "I'm a smith by trade and not a bad one if I say so myself. My wife Lisa—curtsy for the great lord Lisa. She's a bit difficult to handle and we quarrel....but no worse than others." The Knight—his head in his hands—behind the others intones: "From our darkness we call out to Thee...O Lord! Have mercy on us! We are small and frightened and ignorant." The Squire takes up the litany:

In darkness where You are supposed to be...where we all probably are—In darkness You will find no one to listen to Your cries or be touched by Your sufferings. Wash Your tears and mirror Yourself—Your indifference.

The Knight lifts his hands together in supplication: "God You are somewhere." O God the absent being who *must* be somewhere, "Have mercy on us!" Jons the Squire stays in character toward his fretful master: "I could have given you an herb to purge your worries about eternity." But even though now it seems to be too late, "You feel the great triumph while you can still roll your eyes and move your toes." Karin bids the Squire "Quiet! Quiet!" "I shall," he murmurs, "but under protest." The woman kneels. A shadow climbs across her face: "It is the end."
She closes her eyes and dissolves into Mia—outside the castle, whose face is startlingly bright. The camera pulls back to reveal the child (Mikael) and Jof. The Holy Family prepares to resume the journey of life. Jof looks to the horizon and sees what the seventh seal has revealed: "I see them. Over against the dark, stormy sky." They are all there. The Smith and Lisa. The Knight. Raval. Jons and Skat.

And Death the severe Master invites them to dance. He tells them to hold each other's hand, and then they must tread the dance in a long line. And first goes the Master with scythe and hour-glass, but Skat dangles at the end with his lyre. They dance away from the dawn and it's a solemn dance away toward the dark lands—while the rain washes their faces from the salt of their bitter tears.

As Jof pronounces the phrase "bitter tears," the young, smiling image of Mia and child appear. Mia lovingly chides her husband—who she knows will never leave her for war against the infidel: "You with your visions and dreams." They move off into the future as a choir suggests "Gloria."

And so the scene is played out. The voice of the *eschaton* is heard amid ominous thunder and jagged sheets of light, each pilgrim's face starkly framed in black and white. Death appears and leads them out across the horizon, silhouetted in the dance of death.

1956 was the year I was married, starting out on a pilgrimage of my own, moving to New England for graduate school, with the possibility of family and a vastly new life in education. And now after all these years, a teaching career, three boys—grown and doing passingly well, I see what Bergman was telling me—what Koresh in Waco and biblical scholars and symbol mongers everywhere wanted to know—the message of the seventh seal, so startling that it silenced all of heaven.

The Knight had chosen death the moment he embarked on the Crusades. Raval, the seminarian from the theological college at Roskilde, had convinced him to spend ten years in God's army. But the blasphemous, loyal Squire understands the waste of it all. He calls the clergyman Doctor Mirabilis. Caelestis et Diabolicus.

Why—quite literally in God's name—did the Knight leave his wife, running off to slaughter the infidel and drive Islam out of the Christians' sacred space in the Holy Land? His sacred space was with her, giving birth to life, not taking it away. No wonder he was so moved by Mia and Jof and their tiny child, creaking along in their little cart, stopping to entertain, singing and seeing visions of the Mother of God. It is those creators—not the crusaders—who bring us hope, not because they will not die, but because they embrace each other, make love and not war, juggle, laugh—and see death as a dance.

As this century dies, in a satirical resurrection, film critic Edward Guthmann imagines re-making *The Seventh Seal*, this time as a comedy. The year 2000 could then bring us "Waterboy" Adam Sandler as Death, playing chess against the mournful Knight—the same Max von Sydow, who danced across the horizon in 1956.

It is a sign, this "second coming"—a juggling of the chess pieces, mixing black with white and holding Death in check by making fun of it. It's as if the master of the meaning story (who could not stay in the summer of love) could only face winter by laughing at his own masterpiece. George Bernard Shaw—whose own wit danced with death—once said that life does not cease

to be funny when we die, anymore than it ceases to be serious when we laugh.
If I ever die, I would like this to be my epitaph:

Lawrence Meredith
He loved his wife and his boys.
He liked Jesus, the Boston Celtics, and Dr. Pepper—
And sometimes he was funny.

CONCLUSION:

THROUGH A GLASS GLADLY:
WHAT IS TRUTH?

I FEEL A SPECIAL GRATITUDE TOWARD BRAINS, EVOLUTION AND THE GRAND
CANYON. WRITERS SOMETIMES FEEL AS IF THEY HAVE BEEN TAKEN OVER BY A
BOOK: IT DEVELOPS A LIFE OF ITS OWN, PROCLAIMS ITS OWN IMPERATIVES,
ALMOST WRITES ITSELF ONCE THE FRAMEWORK HAS BEEN ESTABLISHED; ONE
HAS SOMEHOW TO LIVE UP TO ITS EXPECTATIONS.
WILLIAM CALVIN

THE AUTHOR IS CONCERNED WITH THE PROBLEMS OF HIS ART AT THE TIME,
ABOVE ALL, OF HIS CREATION. BUT THE MEANING WHICH HE PRESENTS TO THE
SENSES WITH HIS WRITTEN WORDS HAS ALREADY CONCERNED HIM, BEFORE HE
SITS DOWN AT HIS DESK. HOW WILL HE RELEASE THE MEANING IN THE MYTH...?
PANDELIS PREVELAKIS

ENJOY YOUR BODY. USE IT EVERY WAY YOU CAN. DON'T BE AFRAID OF IT OR OF
WHAT OTHER PEOPLE THINK OF IT. IT'S THE GREATEST INSTRUMENT YOU'LL EVER
OWN.
KURT VONNEGUT, COMMENCEMENT AT MIT, 1998

It is time to sweep up the glass fragments and put my house in order.
"Now we see through a glass darkly," sang the apostle, and who would want
to claim more? There have been men and women among us whose lives were
eyes, who searched out the glass, and examined every fresh fracture. "Thinking," they said, "is more interesting than knowing, and less interesting than
looking."[433]

Now in this moment let us be honest. Those who see, who darkly see, do
not by simple virtue of their perception, achieve immortality. If bullets kill
them, if diseases ravage them, if accidents annihilate them, they live only as
long as their transcendent values live on in us who are inspired by their vision.
We are this day called into life by the death of those who have given us birth,
whose own history must not only be remembered but imagined. The woman
who gave birth to me also created this metaphor:

A seed
Is concentrated

Memory—
The life it knew
Springs into
The life it remembers

Birth, Imagination, Death. This book has developed a life of its own, and demands that I conclude by revealing to you the secret code that unlocks these writings. That code—the *pesher* to understand this religion of the body—is a special sacred number. You may have noticed that the offerings of this manuscript have been brought in threes: three parts, with diminishing chapters, each reincarnating the cycle of potentiality, creativity, mortality: the body as final wisdom. This wisdom is hidden in a most traditional story of three: those silhouetted monarchs riding across the horizons, guided by heavenly light toward the fullness of time.

Matthew started it all—even without giving "men" a number. The first gospel alone tells the story of their marvelous visit to the Christ child: the kings humbling themselves before the infant King of Kings and presenting the little one with three regal treasures. Tasteful and expensive, those first Christmas presents—gold, frankincense, and myrrh—and destined to begin a custom deeply symbolic of our respect for deity and our love for each other. But those royal treasures compromised human love: they were expected.

The famous starlight carol tortuously explains this predictability for any who might have missed it—as each Magus, in turn, exposits his gift. Melchior offers the gold "to crown him again," while Gaspar is wafting incense for divine worship. Then it's melancholy Balthazar's turn—and is he ever morose!

Myrrh is mine: its bitter perfume
Breathes a life of gathering gloom:
Sorrowing, sighing, bleeding, dying,
Sealed in a stone cold tomb.

A depressingly appropriate offering for one who is destined to die for the sins of the whole world.

These star men—these astralogicians—ought to shed more light on the gospel of Jesus Christ than this. After all, their holy day is called *Epiphany*: the day when Jesus is manifest, unmistakable recognition of who he is, surrounded by light, revealed as glorious. The date of this Epiphany (the visit of the wise men to Bethlehem) is traditionally January 6—twelve days after December 25, the Augustan winter solstice. [434] Those magi started something with all their gift bearing, and I wish they had understood more about the gospel before they dragged those ponderous offerings to Mary's baby.

There is another carol uniquely expressive of Christian joy over Jesus—more than many of the so-called religious songs. And ironically enough it takes its title from this number chronicle of the wise men's visit: the raucous mathematics of "The Twelve Days of Christmas." Everyone knows at least the first line of this cumulative and delightfully capricious carol: "On the first day of Christmas my true love gave to me…..a partridge in a pear tree."

A partridge in a pear tree. What an odd choice for a Yuletide present—for anyone, much less your true love. It sounds more appropriate for a toga party at Animal House. And the gifts get odder and more ludicrous as the carol accumulates: two turtle doves, three French hens, seven swans a-swimming, ten lords a-leaping, and finally thundering with twelve drummers drumming. Halford Luccock, a professor of preaching at Yale, once wrote a wry commentary on this silly song:

> Nonsense? Not by a jugful of wassail. It is a profound philosophy of giving. It celebrates the high wisdom of completely inappropriate and large-ly useless gifts. And a good thing to remember just before Christmas. A par-tridge in a pear tree—what on earth could one do with that? That's the beau-ty of it! That makes it something to sing about! And folks have been singing about it for several hundred years. Would they have sung about a floor mop (highly appropriate for housecleaning) or a tea kettle or a foot warmer? Not much! [435]

Real wise men and women, I contend, constantly delight each other with a lovely sense of impractical warmth and useless fun. The true mark of human love is not mere faithfulness—dogs, horses, and intolerable bores can manage this. Human love is also intuitive surprise, the amazing freedom to surrender our clichés and live life, at least occasionally, beyond our routine and propriety: that serious non-seriousness that annihilates routine.

A partridge in a pear tree is unnecessary, unwieldy, outrageous, and expensive. But the point is neither outrage *nor* expense. The point is that men and women cannot live by logic alone. For redemption, for ecstasy, for joy, we need the magic of surprise. Our lives are really desperately predictable—as *Passages* and any social psychologist can tell us: birth trauma, bonding, growth, individuation, love, work, parenting, the Super Bowl and the Final Four, mid-life crisis, symptoms replacing emotions, Wheel of Fortune and Jeopardy, grandparenting, exeunt, the Final One.

Call it the Myth of Sisyphus or the daily grind, we all know what is meant by the circularity of experience. The evangelists who write beer commercials throw them into our living rooms: you only go around once and you have to grab for all the less-filling, great-tasting gusto you can. Luxurious environment, power, elite leisure, gourmet food and sex, altered states of conscious-ness, extraordinary feats, even service to humankind—a kind of getting high on doing good and being right.

The good news that came to Bethlehem is so different from this despera-tion. Jesus disrupted expectations from the very beginning—so much so that scholars now seeking to determine what he actually said use, as one of the *cri-*

teria, the culturally *eccentric* character of the saying. Israel's hopes were for a political Messiah, modeled on David's kingship, who would fulfill the Law, overthrow the hated Romans, unite the people of Yahweh's promise, and lead them back into international power. Jesus broke the Law, overthrew no one except the commercializers in the Temple, went around eating and drinking with riff-raff, spurning power, talking ambiguously and attractively about a kingdom of love. He was as unpolitical and unpredictable on Jerusalem's cross as he was in Bethlehem's manger.

> They were all looking for a King
> To slay their foes and lift them high.
> Thou cam'st a little baby thing
> To make a woman cry.[436]

Releasing Magic—not anticipated Magi—is what we want: new fantasies, redemptive surprises, even acrid ecstasies will do. And, experiencing the freshness, you will instantly be able to feel the difference.

I have discovered a partridge in a pear tree test for the wise ones. Whenever presents are being opened, look very carefully at your true love. Watch her eyes as the swans swim and pipers pipe. Watch his face as the maids milk. Carefully now. Is she going out of focus? Is he fuzzy? And while you are looking, think of this ancient Eastern story I am going to tell you.

Once upon a time there was an old Chinese named Lu Chen who started disappearing. He would disappear, but only a part at a time. Perhaps an arm or a foot fading away and then reappearing without warning. Lu Chen did not seem alarmed, but rather amused—although he was careful to avoid being seen during these spells. He could always tell when a spell was beginning for he would become fuzzy and couldn't be seen sharply. This continued for a long time. Then, instead of just a part of him disappearing, his entire body would fade to translucence and back—over and over again. Finally, Lu Chen stopped fading and retained his complete form for many years. All during this time he struggled to explain these bizarre happenings—but to no avail.

One night, as he sat gazing toward the heavens, his attention was drawn across the sky to a single star. He stared at that star until, to his utter astonishment, it disappeared. At that moment, Lu Chen understood everything that had happened to him. He stood up, bowed in the direction of the missing star, and vanished completely—never to be seen by anyone again.

Perhaps Lu Chen was the wisest man of all. He brought to life the gift of his own mortality. It is the ultimate non-sense to suppose that we shall not all disappear. While the birth star shines, we do well to worship its wonder.

But in the midst of our inexorable diminution of energy and élan, it is not wise to worship stability and unimaginative responsibility. There is no such thing as a solid, fixed, world. It is all risk, vulnerability, and vanishing. Christians are supposed to be free—not immutable. It would be the unforgivable sin to allow boredom to steal our moment: to mistake getting dull for grow-ing up, to repress Saturday night live into Sunday morning dead, to freeze becoming into being. The treasures we hold as immortal have a rhythm of evanescence: they do not remain, but like Lu Chen's star astonish us by their going. Beauty fades, music dies in the moment that it is born, turn around and your children are grown and gone, laughter stills itself, and love—the great-est gift of all, so seemingly solid and eternal—love too, as we all know, van-ishes the moment we try to possess it.

So be it. Away with all this talk. Deck the hall with partridge feathers. Bring an uncaged bird Jeanette, Isabella. The holy and the non-sense are both full grown. Wassail, you crusty old kings, melt your gold into capricious bands of fun. Forget your lugubrious frankincense and myrrh and start leap-ing with the lords and ladies. Drum cadences to the starlight and play the merry organ.

It is very late, and I feel a certain fuzziness coming on.

Epilogue:

The Parable of the Climbers

Long having wander'd since, round the earth having wander'd
Now I face home again, very pleas'd and joyous,
(But where is what I started for so long ago?
And why is it yet unfound?)
                                        Walt Whitman

Perhaps there isn't anything to be found—and going in itself is finding.

In the Spring of 1998, I did wander back to the place where this odyssey began—returning to Japan, and slouching even more slowly towards Kyoto. We had docked in Osaka, the last foreign port on a voyage of discovery that took us—quite literally—around the world. I had accepted an offer by Dean Seymour Drescher, of the University of Pittsburgh, to join the faculty for the Semester-at-Sea (February through May), to teach religious studies and film on board the *S.S. Universe Explorer*.

This latest wandering included incredible seascapes, schools of dolphins arcing in oceanic ballet, hitting the muddy bottom of the Saigon river, hiking in cloud forests, dancing at Carnaval in Brazil, leaping with Masai warriors at the foot of Mt. Kilimanjaro, stroking lethal snakes in a Taoist temple, observing Hindu holy men process in one of the seven sacred cities of India, listening to Archbishop Desmond Tutu celebrate the rainbow people of God shining through the revolution, hearing the American ambassador to Vietnam (himself a prisoner of the North Vietnamese for seven years) call for healing and understanding (a country—not a war), floating through the miraculous Chinese scroll mountain scenery of the Li River near Guilin, realizing the depth of poverty in the third world (*ranchitos* in Venezuela, *favelas* in Brazil, informal housing in South African townships, *dalit* villages in India), climbing to the top of the Himeji Castle—where *Shogun* was filmed, viewing a herd of three hundred elephants lumber nimbly across the Amboseli plain, striding with the junkanoos in Nassau, staring soberly at the cells that held Mandela for twenty-seven years while three million whites tried to hold thirty-seven million blacks in the prison of apartheid, watching land and light recede—days turning into weeks emptied out of time, anonymity dissolving into persons, handshake into embrace, anxiety into ennui, anticipation into nostalgia.

So we floated through sights and insights around the world. In Japan we went back to Kyoto on a temple and shrine practicum, and found, near the Heian Shrine in Okazaki, the house where our whole family had lived in 1975, as part of Pacific's cluster college non-western program. There was, in that temporal return, indeed a "spirit of place." I knew that here my life had opened out on a new world, that I had been "born again"—had gone from Bethlehem to the wisdom of the East. Round the earth having wandered, it has been a "long, strange trip," and, as part of the grateful living, I give thanks for the gifts of the wise ones, wherever they came to us.

Our boys are men now. The oldest—who carries the burden of my name—is a neurologist in Colorado; the youngest, Mark, a lawyer on the East Coast. Our middle son teaches science in Stockton, and has never failed to find us wherever the journey has gone. My children have all brought gifts, too. Among them, this simple secret: "You don't stop climbing mountains because you get old; you get old because you stop climbing mountains."

While we were in Indonesia, Steve came to visit us in late June, and he and I climbed Mt. Merapi—all the way to the boiling crater. (When we returned to our house the next afternoon, we found out that the volcano had been officially closed to hikers due to the danger of increased seismic activity and threat of eruption. The bemused guides never seemed to mind, but I think they were in touch with some other world. I should have learned to read Indonesian.)

Merapi— "mountain of fire"—is one of the most destructive volcanoes in the world, monitored from six vulcanologist posts, with Indonesia's best scientists alerted to its compressed power. Only twenty miles away from Yogya, it looms 10,000 feet, clouds of smoke ascending every day, like Vesuvius over Pompeii—erupting on an average of every five and one half years. In 1006, it buried Borobudur, thirty miles away, with ash so deep that the Buddhist monument was not visible for nearly eight hundred years, and it has killed fifteen thousand people in twenty-five eruptions since 1930. In the summer of 1996 it vented lethal gasses and began new lava flows—once again terrifying central Java and sending eight people to their death.

I loved living under that volcano. I understood why it was a sacred mountain—its symmetry was alive, a conduit to the gods. The university students held ritual initiations by firelight on its slopes, and, one spring weekend, invited Pat and me to join them. Walking at night through jungle and rock, we arrived at open spaces, where one could see the streaks of red descending from the summit—like arteries venting plasma of fire. There was no sign of fear, as the students sang Javanese folk songs, laughed easily, and prayed their Muslim prayers. The coolness of the evening air was such a welcome shift from the humid streets of the city below. The sense of connection with young people everywhere was calming, and their acceptance of us as their elder guests—and friends—was overwhelming. I knew that I would come back and climb to the top of Merapi before we left Indonesia. It was the one thing I *had* to do. I had walked on the slopes of the Matterhorn, climbed Mt. Sinai at dawn, put my foot on the congealing lava flow on Hawaii's benevolent mountain, looked up from the roof of India at the Himalayas, and stumbled up seven thousand steps to the top of Taishan, the holiest of mountains in China. There is a saying that the day begins on top of Mt. Taishan.

The day begins on top of every mountain. When I was a boy in flat river bottom central Texas, I would listen enraptured to the tales of Richard Halliburton on the "royal road to romance," wondering what it would be like see the world from the heights. As the preachers spoke of the children of Israel at the foot of the holy mountain, I had visions of God's great power writing with a finger of fire the way things ought to be on earth. It had to be, I thought even then, a volcano: pillar of smoke by day and for the dark of the wilderness journey, molten light.

In the fall of 1983, following Kazantzakis' own odyssey in *Report to Greco*, we were guests of the Greek Orthodox monks at St. Katerina, built like some sacred fortress at the foot of Sinai to guard the very presence of God. On the Arab bus through the Sinai desert, we had met a young couple from Denmark, who were determined to make the ascent of the mountain, and encouraged us to go with them. They were both so blond and tall, and she was quite beautiful. I remember her sleeping across the aisle from us, her soft print dress blown aside by the wind, the curve of her breast visible and inviting, erotic in the afternoon sun. A priest on Mt. Athos, a father Isaiah, had explained to me only a month before that there was no need for women on their Holy Mountain. The Virgin Mary—just before settling in Ephesus—was supposed to have been shipwrecked there with John, the disciple entrusted with her care. The incredible isolation and beauty of that peninsula have sheltered the devotion of monks ever since. The mountain, he explained, rose seven thousand feet directly out of the sea, with a perfectly conical shape. "Look at it," he said, "it is like the body of Mary." So it was on the breast of the Virgin where the monks now lived. I was glad that climbing mountains seemed religious.

Since our Danish friends possessed no clerical credentials, they had to sleep outside the monastery walls, a happy advantage for climbers—because the gates inside were locked until long after one must begin in order to arrive at the summit for sunrise. They promised to meet me just outside the gate and show me the right path to follow, if I could find a way out in the middle of the night. When the priests filed down in the chapel for prayers at 3:00 A.M., I went with them and waited for an eerie, black robed figure to glide by, a huge key dangling from his waist—like a medieval monk out of time. Hooded and silent, he led me down stone steps, through a tunnel, to the wooden iron latched door, and with the keys of the kingdom itself, opened it.

She was waiting, clearly outlined in the moonlight, and took me to join her husband at the start of the path. We climbed. Past camels and Arabs resting, their fires not yet extinguished. Past shadow and rock, up great slabs of steps cut into the mountain by pilgrims, monks, religious entrepreneurs. We had almost reached the top when the light began to break all around. We were facing east as we came to the place where tradition says that Moses' visage was transformed by Yahweh's presence, a halo around his head. The faithful had constructed an arch out of stone, through which one must pass on the way to the summit. The husband went first and, still some steps below, I looked up to see her pass through. The sun, which had found her in the bus, now found her in the arch—turning her blond hair translucent and her skin radiant. I knew, in that moment, what epiphany was: Sinai's divine energy streaming from a body. And I also knew why Moses had stayed up on that mountain for such a long time. God really was a woman.

I am not a trained archaeologist, but on top of Sinai that morning I made an incredible find, which I've never reported in print before this moment. It is at least on par with the discovery of the Dead Sea Scrolls, the Celestine Prophecy, and the Gospel of Thomas—but with even greater potential to frighten the orthodox. So I have carefully guarded the secret I found there.

Walking by myself to the very edge of the mountain top, standing on what surely must have been the very spot where Moses received the revelation from Yahweh, I looked down at my feet and saw two ancient tablets, with strange markings etched in the stone. I scooped them up and hid them in my camera bag and began the long descent. As I passed through the arch, gripping the bag with paranoid excitement and moving down by the late morning climbers, I met my wife, slowly moving up the path we had taken. She had come up with just a little fruit to refresh us for the journey down. We sat together away from the climbing path, where we could see St. Katerina through a deep cleft in the volcanic chain, and the Sinaitic wilderness beyond to the northeast.

I lifted out the slabs of stone to show her my profound discovery, and a miracle happened. Even without special glasses provided by an angel, I could read the strange, ancient script. As I translated, Pat wrote it down, word for word, complete and inerrant, as if from the very mouth of the Lord himself. The words, incredibly, were some kind of holiness code—a primal decalogue. Could it be that Moses picked up the wrong ones, and that I had stumbled on the original commandments—still ashen from the capricious finger of God?

I. Thou shalt climb mountains—and imagine worlds.

II. Thou shalt love the earth and embrace all of her gifts.

III. Thou shalt not take life in vain, nor be afraid to experience love.

IV. Thou shalt have fun with thy family,

and especially shalt thou play with thy children.

V. Thou shalt remember every day and keep all of them holy.

VI. Thou shalt not exploit thy neighbor or anyone else.

VII. Thou shalt be passionate and thoughtful in the pursuit of justice.

VIII. Thou shalt be free and willing to dance with a stranger.

IX. Thou shalt not commit arrogance or self pity.

X. Thou shalt be willing to forget principle and do the right thing.

But Sinai has been dormant for centuries. Now, at last, Steve and I stood on the slope of Mt. Merapi—looking up at an actual pillar of fire.

Beginning to climb at midnight in a penetrating mist with swirling winds, we were almost turned back at the saddle, huddled around a fire built by the guides—Javanese shaman straight out of Carlos Castaneda. But in a miraculous instant the morning light broke through, and one wizened guide—smoking God knows what substance—took us to the summit. Standing on those warm, sulfurous rocks, we could see the Indian Ocean to the south, the Java Sea to the north, and great green volcano slopes of sister mountains stretching out east and west—like the dawn of creation itself. It was—as they say—transcendent.

Standing there, I remembered another parable, told and retold around the campfires of the world. We are all like climbers on a mountain, heading for the highest—the goal, so we think, of life. There are very many paths that lead upward—and the view from any one point on the journey will look different than from any other point. And in fact some climbers appear not to be moving at all for a while, but resting, perhaps unable to go on—or simply enjoying the view where they are.

But we must never insist that any other person use our path, or insinuate that our road is the best—or even that everyone must get to the summit. Salvation is being thankful for the gift of the mountain and the joy we experience in sharing that gift with all our fellow climbers.

APPENDIX

Answers to Questions

For those who are curious as to the "correct" answers to the Lake's question in the *Mahabharata,* here they are, just as Yudhishthira articulated them in that exile in the forest, resurrecting his brothers, and allowing them to fight the great internecine war—thus founding Indian civilization. [See Endnote 419, Chapter Six.] The reference point in this journey follows.

What is quicker than the wind? Thought ....[Ch. Four]
What can cover the earth? Darkness ....[Ch. Six]
Who are more numerous: the living or the dead?
    The Living...[Ch. Six]
    Why? The Dead are no more.
Give me an example of space: My two hands ....[Ch. Four]
Give me an example of grief: Ignorance..........................[Ch. Three]
Give me an example of poison: Desire ....[Ch. Six]
Give me an example of defeat: Victory ....[Ch. Five]
Which came first: day or night? Day
    How much first? But it was only a day ahead............[Ch. Two]
What is the cause of the world? Love. ....[Ch. Six]
What is your opposite? Myself ....[Ch. Two]
What is madness? A forgotten way ....[Ch. Five]
What in each of us is inevitable? Happiness....................[Ch. One]
What is the greatest wonder?
    Each day death strikes and we live as if we were immortal.
    This is the greatest wonder ....[Ch. Six]
And the last question is Yudhishthira's to the Lake.
Who are you that is asking these questions?
    I am Dharma. Your Father.
    I am Constancy, Rightness, the form of Love.
    I am all forms.
Source: *Mahabharata*

Epigraph Credits

Preface

1. Virginia Woolf, quoted in William H. Calvin, *The River That Flows Uphill* (San Francisco: Sierra Club Books, 1986), p. 488.
2. Friedrich Nietzsche, *The Gay Science*, trans. Walter Kaufmann (New York: Vintage Books, 1974), p. 343.
3. Question posed to the author by a nuclear engineer, now retired, from the staff of the Hanford plant in Richland, Washington.

Chapter One

1. William Blake, "Jerusalem," Geoffrey Keynes, ed., *Poetry and Prose of William Blake* (Bloomsbury: The Nonesuch Press, 1927), p. 749.
2. Sören Kierkegaard, *Repetition*, trans. Walter Lowry (New York: Harper Torchbooks, 1964), p. 104. First published in Copenhagen, 1843. [Quoted in Richard M. Zaner, *The Problem of Embodiment: Some Contributions to a Phenomenology of the Body* (The Hague: Martinus Nijhoff, 1964), p. 85].
3. E. L. Doctorow, *Welcome to Hard Times* (New York: Bantam, 1960), p. 149.

Chapter Two

1. William Shakespeare, *Hamlet*, Act 1, Scene 1, Marcellus to Horatio.
2. Simeon the New Theologian [quoted in *Parabola*, Volume XV, Number 2, May, 1990.]
3. Bertrand Russell, quoted in Vale and Juno, eds., *Modern Primitives* (San Francisco: RE/SEARCH Publications, 1989), p. 201.

Chapter Three

1. John A. Wheeler, quoted in Calvin, *The River That Flows Uphill*, p. 399.
2. J. Krishnamurti, "Listening to the Silence," *Parabola*, May, 1990, Volume XV, No. 2, p. 80. Reprinted from *Think on These Things* (New York: Harper and Row, 1964).
3. James P. Carse, *Finite and Infinite Games* (New York: Ballantine Books, 1986), p. 78.

Chapter Four

1. William Irvin Thompson, *At the Edge of History* (New York: Harper Torchbooks, 1979), p. 162.
2. Gloria Steinem, Introduction to Jean Shinoda Bolen, *Goddesses in Every-woman: A New Psychology of Women* (San Francisco: Harper and Row, Publishers, 1984), p. xii.
3. *Life,* December, 1990, Introduction to "The Face of God," p. 47.

Chapter Five

1. Thomas Merton, *The Way of Chuang Tzu* (New York: New Directions Publishing Company, 1969), p. 107. Copyright 1963 by The Abbey of Gethsemani, Inc., 1977 by the Trustees of the Merton Legacy Trust. Reprinted by permission of New Directions Publishing Corp.
2. Nikos Kazantzakis, *Report to Greco*, trans. P. A. Bien (New York: Bantam Books, 1966), p. 158.
3. Skip Bayless, *God's Coach: The Hymns, Hype, and Hypocrisy of Tom Landry's Cowboys* (New York: Simon and Schuster, 1990), p. 90.

Chapter Six

1. Samuel Johnson. James Boswell, *The Life of Samuel Johnson* (New York: The Heritage Press, 1963), Vol. II, p. 393. See *Encyclopaedia Britannica,* Volume 13, 1957 edition, p. 115-116, and *Twilight,* with Paul Newman and Gene Hackman.
2. Annie Dillard, *Holy the Firm* (New York: Harper and Row, 1977), p. 44.
3. Pierre Teilhard de Chardin, *Toward the Future*, trans. René Hague (New York and London: Harcourt Brace Jovanovich, 1975), pp. 86-87. [This translation emphasizes the poetic quality of Teilhard's mysticism.]

Conclusion

1. William Calvin, *The River That Flows Uphill*, pp. 488-89.
2. Andonis Decavalles, *Pandelis Prevelakis and the Value of a Heritage* (Minneapolis: The North Central Publishing Company, 1981), p. 39.
3. Kurt Vonnegut, Commencement Address at MIT, 1998. I owe this reference to Don Meredith.

Epilogue

Walt Whitman, *The Selected Poems of Walt Whitman* (New York: Walter J. Black, Inc., 1942), p. 117. See Walter Grünzweig, *Constructing the German Walt Whitman* (Iowa City: University of Iowa Press, 1995). A hugely instructive book on Whitman's literary voyage into Germany, by one of Europe's brightest cross-cultural scholars.

The final "commandment"—so recently "discovered" on Sinai—was also revealed to Joseph Fletcher by oral tradition from a friend, who heard it from a cab driver in St. Louis, where the Western Exodus begins. [See *Situation Ethics* (Philadelphia: The Westminster Press, 1965), p. 13.]

NOTES

Foreword

1. Nikos Kazantzakis, *Zorba the Greek*, trans. Carl Widman (New York: Simon and Schuster, Inc., 1952), p. 185.

Introduction

2. Emma Goldman repeated this often: "If you do not feel a thing, you will never guess its meaning."

3. I often wondered if Yukio Mishima hadn't found the perfect solution to the puzzle of production. He began writing at midnight, worked until eight in the morning, slept then until around 2:00 P.M., had breakfast, went for workouts in the gym or dojo (lifting weights, practicing martial arts and such), then went to parties and assorted social events—always excusing himself at the stroke of twelve for another round of literary work. After his master work was finished, he excused himself from life at the stroke of a ritual sword.

4. Cf. Reggie Miller's "clarity" against the New York Knicks (Indiana Pacers), NBA playoffs, June, 1994.

5. See Adam Smith, *Powers of Mind* (New York: Random House, 1975), "Quarterbacking in an Altered State," pp. 185-190.

6. William Calvin, *The River That Flows Uphill* (San Francisco: Sierra Club Books, 1986), p. 383.

7. Ibid., p. 369.

8. See Edward O. Wilson, *On Human Nature* (Cambridge: Harvard University Press, 1978).

9. See Huston Smith, *The Religions of Man* (New York: Harper and Row, Publishers, 1986), p. 189, "Entering the Zen outlook is like stepping through Alice's looking glass." Smith compares it to finding oneself in a topsy turvy world—a wonderland in which everything is quite mad—stunning paradoxes, conundrums, flagrant contradictions and wild non sequiturs. Smith, I think, has gone too far. He should have stopped with the glass itself.

10. (Los Angeles: Jeremy P. Tarcher, 1992). Michael Murphy is the co-founder and acting CEO of the Esalen Foundation at Big Sur, California. So massive indeed (786 pages—distilled from the original 1700) that his bibliography runs 85 pages, and the notes another 85.

11. Murphy, p. 586.

12. Ibid., pp. 568-575. See also Chapter Five, pp. 64-159.

13. Ibid., p. 566. In *The Future of the Body*, Murphy has compiled massive evidence that extraordinary energy is available for the transformation of human life, including our ability to alter the environment, heightened vitality, further reaches of cognition, somatic healing, and ecstatic bodily states. He also insists [hence my italics] that the practices which integrate this energy must be nourished by "a philosophy that embraces our many parts."

14. Yi-Fu Tuan, *Space and Place: the Perspective of Experience* (Minneapolis: University of Minnesota Press, 1977), p. 34. Tuan's work is very stimulating, and I acknowledge my debt to him for many of the etymologies of space.

15. Immanuel Kant, *Critique of Pure Reason*, trans. Norman Kemp Smith (New York: The Modern Library, 1958), p. 18.

16. *Kant's Inaugural Dissertation and Early Writing on Space*, trans. John Handyside (Chicago: Open Court, 1929), pp 22-23. Quoted in Tuan, op. cit., p. 36.

17. Trans. John Macquarrie and Edward Robinson (New York: Harper and Row, 1962).

18. Ibid., p. 42. Cf. Merleau-Ponty, *Phenomenology of Perception*, trans. Colin Smith (New York: Humanities, 1962).

19. See Leonard Barkan, *Nature's Work of Art: The Human Body as Image of the World* (New Haven and London: Yale University Press, 1975).

20. Compare Merleau-Ponty's *Phenomenology of Perception* with Kant's *Critique of Pure Reason.*

21. (New York: Vintage Books, 1982), "Natural Shocks," pp. 33-53.

22. (Boston: Little, Brown, and Company, 1973), pp. 19-(31!)-56. See Tuan, op. cit., p. 35.

23. Shunryu Suzuki, *Zen Mind, Beginner's Mind* (New York: Weatherhill, 1977), pp. 25-28.

24. See the interpretation of Luke in Chapter Six.

25. See Needham, ed., *Right and Left*—reference in Tuan, op. cit., p. 211.

26. Cf. Robert Hertz, *Death and the Right-Hand* (Glencoe, Illinois: Free Press, 1960), pp. 100-101.

27. Cf. the discussion of Dr. Diane Borden (Chair, Film Department, University of the Pacific) at the 1994 MLA conference on the work of Norman O. Brown. Dr. Borden was his student in the human consciousness program at UC Santa Cruz.

28. Cf. Thomas Mann, *To Taste and See: Exploring Incarnation and the Ambiguities of Faith* (Cleveland: The Pilgrim Press, 1992). See McFague, *The Body of God: An Ecological Theology* (Minneapolis: Fortress Press, 1993), and Matthew Fox, *The Coming of the Cosmic Christ: The Healing of Mother Earth and the Birth of a Global Renaissance* (Harper SanFrancisco, A Division of HarperCollins Publishers, 1988).

29. Arnold Gesell, et al., *The First Five Years of Life: A Guide to the Study of the Preschool Child* (New York: Harper and Brothers Publishers, 1940), pp. 21-22. See Tuan, op. cit., p. 37.

30. Emily Martin, *The Woman in the Body* (Boston: The Beacon Press, 1989), p.

12.

31. Nikos Kazantzakis, *Report to Greco*, trans. P. A. Bien (New York: Bantam, 1965), p. 168.

32. See Paul Weiss, *Sport: a Philosophic Inquiry* (Carbondale: Southern Illinois Press, 1971).

33. Leni Riefenstahl, *Olympia* 1936 (film of the Berlin Games: concluding diving sequence).

34. George Leonard, *The Ultimate Athlete* (New York: The Viking Press, 1975), "Aikido and the Mind of the West.," pp. 47-59. This transformation is the essence of Aikido—a kind of dancing with the enemy.

35. Bryan Turner, *The Body and Society: Explorations in Social Theory* (Oxford: Basil Blackwell. 1984). Cartesian sociology granted that we have bodies but not that we are bodies. The government of society is conducted by the regulation of bodies: "The reproduction of populations in time, the regulation of bodies in space, the restraint of the 'interior' body through disciplines, and the representation of the 'exterior' body in social space." [p. 2] Quoted in Leslie A. Adelson, *Making Bodies Making History: Feminism and German Identity* (Lincoln and London: University of Nebraska Press, 1993), p. 14.

36. Heidegger's "existential space" and theologians' Chalcedonian Christology.

37. See Genia Pauli Haddon, *Body Metaphors: Releasing the God-Feminine in Us All* (New York: Crossroad, 1988), p. 134. In June, 1999, I visited Wittenberg to see the Katharina von Bora *Ausstellung* (500th year celebration of the birth of Luther's wife), mounted in the monastery built for Augustinian Hermits between 1504 and 1508 and home of the Luthers during the Wittenberg years—almost four decades. Luther called her—affectionately I assume— "Lieber Herr Kätie" ("My Lord Katie"). In some consubstantial way, Katharina *was* his "Lord" —almost literally God's body, both metaphor and matrix of salvation. Cf. *Luther's Works*, Jaroslav Pelikan, editor (Saint Louis: Concordia Publishing House), Volume 1, 1958, pp. 13-15; Volume 22, 1957, pp. 110-111, 133, and particularly p. 10: "God, too, in His majesty and nature is pregnant with a Word...."

38. See John Naisbitt and Patricia Aburdene, *Megatrends 2000* (New York: Avon Books, 1990), "The 1990's: The Decade of Women in Leadership," pp. 228-256. One would hope that the third millennium will be the century of women—*and* men, freed from their anxieties about each other by odysseys in the inclusive world of imagination. Wes Brown is a fellow traveler in this world: "The teacher differs from the therapist in that her point of contact with the student is not the student's anxiety but the student's imagination." [J. Wesley Brown, *Innovation for Excellence* (Lanham: University Press of America, 1989), p. 45.]

Chapter 1

39. *The Collected Poems of W. B. Yeats* (New York: The Macmillan Company, 1956), pp. 184-85.

40. I read everything Wesley ever wrote, or edited—not to mention saddlebags

full of material written *about* him, and produced a manuscript of three hundred pages with more than three thousand references. If not memorable, it was perhaps at least noteworthy.

41. Not that I hadn't read before going to Japan. Of the making of books about the nature of the really *old* time religion there is no end. See A. Graham Baldwin, *The Drama of Our Religion* (New York: Oxford University Press, 1939), pp. 5-16 [my source for the beginning of the *This is religion* sequence]; Annemarie de Waal Malefijt, *Religion and Culture* (New York: The Macmillan Company, 1968), pp. 81-103; Max Weber, *The Sociology of Religion*, trans. Ephraim Fischoff (Boston: Beacon Press, 1964), pp. 1-19 [the laudatory introduction by Talcott Parsons is especially instructive]; John Herman Randall, Jr., *The Meaning of Religion for Man* (New York: Harper and Row, 1968), pp. 13-35; Alban G. Widgery, *What Is Religion?* (New York: Harper and Brother Publishers, 1953), pp. 268-301; Emile Durkheim, *The Elementary Forms of the Religious Life* (New York: Collier Books, 1961), pp. 37-63; Lewis Browne, *This Believing World* (New York: The Macmillan Company, 1926), pp. 42-56; James Bisset Pratt, *The Religious Consciousness* (New York: The Macmillan Company, 1926), pp. 1-21. Pratt's classic definition is on page two: "Religion is the serious and social attitude of individuals or communities toward the power or powers which they conceive as having ultimate control over their interests and destinies."

42. Sigmund Freud, *The Future of an Illusion,* trans. W. D. Robson-Scott (New York: Anchor, 1961), pp. 40-41.

43. *Varieties of Religious Experience* (New York: Random House). The Gifford Lectures (1901-2).

44. John Updike, *Roger's Version* (New York: Alfred A. Knopf, 1986), p. 14.

45 I would, if you could assure me that eternal punishment doesn't include talk-radio or the Jerry Springer show.

46. Malefigt, op. cit., pp. 35-36. See David Hume, *Essays and Treatises on Several Subjects* (London: T. Cadell, 1777).

47. Fyodor Dostoyevsky, *The Brothers Karamazov*, trans. Constance Garnett (New York: The Modern Library College Edition, 1950), p. 308.

48. Ibid.

49. See John Romer's explanation in his film series on the Bible: *Testament.*

50. Carol Ochs, *Behind the Sex of God: Toward a New Consciousness—Transcending Matriarchy and Patriarchy* (Boston: Beacon Press, 1977), p.1.

51. Brooksville, Alabama has arrived exactly here. This small community is hoping to incorporate as a town guided strictly by the hand of God. The King James Bible will be the town charter and the Ten Commandments its ordinances. Says the Rev. James Henderson (who is leading the cosmic incorporation): "When I was a child in the 1940's and 1950's, we had a sense of community…. I've watched the separation of church and state get out of control." [*San Francisco Chronicle*, A5, January 2, 1999.]

52. John Stratton Hawley, ed., *Fundamentalism and Gender* (New York, Oxford: Oxford University Press, 1994), p. 197 ["Fundamentalism and the Control of Women."]

53. Ibid., p. 197.

54. I doubt that these groupings will put me in Thomas Aquinas' class for delineating five ways, but then I'm not attempting to prove anything, except that I've read too many definitions of religion. I'm not holding this kind of activity up as particularly laudable, or even moral, but, as the saying goes, "God is in the details."

55. J. Wallace Hamilton, *Who Goes There? What and Where Is God?* (New Jersey, London, Glasgow: Fleming H. Revell Company, 1958), p. 13. See John Hick, *God Has Many Names* (Philadelphia: Westminster Press, 1982). Hick tells us that the great world religions are many responses to the one divine reality. For the theosophically inclined, see Raghavan Iyer, ed., *Civilization, Death, and Regeneration* (London, Santa Barbara, New York: Concord Grove Press, 1985), "Our Gods and Other Gods," pp. 80-85. This is the gentlest lowdown on the Highest.

56. Edward Tylor, *The Origins of Culture* (New York: Harper and Row, 1958), Vol II, pp. 9-10.

57. *New Standard Dictionary,* p. 2081. See J. Paul Williams, "The Nature of Religion," *Journal of the Society of the Scientific Study of Religion,* October, 1962, pp. 6-7; C. J. Ducasse, *A Philosophical Scrutiny of Religion* (New York: Ronald Press, 1953), p. 130; Peter Bertocci, *Introduction to the Philosophy of Religion* (New York: Prentice-Hall, Inc., 1951), p. 9.

58. *On Christianity: Early Theological Writings,* trans. T. M. Knox (New York: Harper and Brothers, 1961), p. 313.

59. *Introduction to Science and Religion,* p. 17. Cited in Edmund Davidson Soper, *The Religions of Mankind* (New York and Cincinnati: The Abingdon Press, 1938), p. 27.

60. James Montgomery, written in 1818. See Robert Guy McCutchan, *Our Hymnody* (New York, Nashville: Abingdon Press, 1937), p. 329.

61. Hackman, Kegley, and Nikander, *Religion in Modern Life* (New York: The Macmillan Company, 1957), pp 7-8. See Kant, *Religion Within the Limits of Reason Alone,* trans. Theodore Greene and Hoyt H. Hudson (New York: Harper and Brothers, 1960), pp. 41-42.

62. *The History of Religion,* p. 13. Cited in Soper, op. cit., p. 29.

63. *The Idea of the Holy,* trans. John W. Harvey (New York: Oxford Press, 1958), pp. 12-13.

64. *The Sacred and the Profane,* trans. Willard A. Trask (New York: Harper and Brothers, 1961), pp. 20-65.

65. Ibid., p. 43.

66. *On Religion,* trans. John Oman (New York: Harper and Brothers, 1958), p. 106.

67. *The Philosophy of Religion* (London: Macmillan, 1906), p. 215. Cited in Hackman, op. cit., p. 7.

68. Ibid., pp. 38-39.

69. *A Student's Philosophy of Religion* (New York: The Macmillan Co., 1949), p. 47.

70. John Telford, ed., *The Letters of John Wesley, A.M.,* VI (London: The Epworth Press, 1931), p. 216 [May 2, 1784].

71. *The Psychological Origin and the Nature of Religion* (London: Constable &

Co., 1921), pp. 7-8.

72. Wright, op. cit., [See Note 67].

73. *Religion, Society, and the Individual* (New York: Macmillan, 1957), p. 8.

74. Monk, et al., op. cit., p. 3.

75. *A Common Faith* (New Haven: Yale University Press, 1937), p. 27.

76. *At the Edge of History* (New York, Evanston, San Francisco, London: Harper and Row, Publishers, 1971), p. 112.

77. Ibid.

78. (New York: India Library Society, 1965), p. 648.

79. Ibid.

80. Paul Tillich, *Theology of Culture*, ed. Robert C. Kimball (New York: Oxford University Press, 1964), p. 42. Tillich's essay, "Religion as a Dimension in Man's Spiritual Life," pp. 3-9, remains one of the best introductions to religion—and the genesis of my parable of "homeless religion."

81. See H. Byron Earhart, *Religion in the Japanese Experience* (Encino, California and Belmont, California: Dickenson Publishing Company, Inc, 1974), "Secularism: From Ritual to Pornography in a Modern Novel," pp. 231-236. The fundamentalist outcry against "secular humanism" has a point—articulated well by Harvey Cox, *Religion in the Secular City*, (New York: Simon and Schuster, 1984), Chapter 5, "Fundamentalism and Postmodern Society, pp. 72-82.

82. Cited in Donald Swearer, "Contemporary Japanese Religion, An Interpretive Dilemma," *Japanese Religions*, December 1972, Vol. 7, No. 4, p. 44. A *Tanka* has thirty-one syllables. Verification by Dr. Leonard Humphreys, UOP historian.

83. John B. Cobb, Jr., "The Meaning of Pluralism for Christian Self-Understanding," in Leroy Rouner, ed., *Religious Pluralism* (Notre Dame, Indiana: University of Notre Dame Press, 1984) p. 176. See Masao Abe, "'There is No Common Denominator for World Religions': The Positive Meaning of This Negative Statement," *Journal of Ecumenical Studies,* 26: 1, Winter 1989, pp. 72-81. Abe gives us an exceptionally clear analysis of the debate over pluralism.

84. See Shusaku Endo, *Silence,* trans. William Johnston (Rutland, Vermont & Tokyo: The Charles E. Tuttle Co., 1977).

85. See Swearer, op. cit.

86. *Myths To Live By* (New York: The Viking Press, 1990), pp. 82-104.

87. Ken Wilber, *Up From Eden* (Boston: Shambhala, 1986), p. 3.

88. See Arnold Toynbee, ed., *The Crucible of Christianity: Judaism, Hellenism and the Historical Background to the Christian Faith* (New York and Cleveland: World Publishing Company, 1969), particularly Chapter XIV, "Rival Theologies," by Robert Grant, pp. 317-330. Grant writes: "By the middle of the 2nd century AD the surviving Christian literature is almost entirely controversial." (p. 323).

89. See William Johnston, *The Still Point* (New York: Harper and Row, Publishers, 1970), pp. 151-170.

90. Olga Frobe Kapteyn, ed., *Eranos-Jahrbuch 1953* (Zurich: Rhein-Verflag, 1954), p. 294, cited in Campbell, op cit., p. 94, and in Campbell with Bill Moyers, ed. Betty Sue Flowers, *The Power of Myth* (New York: Doubleday, 1988). The quote here is p. 319.

91. Ibid., p. 298-99; p. 303.

92. There were those who saw Campbell's ill-disguised disgust with both Judaism and Christianity as evidence of his anti-Semitism.

93. In Julius Bellone, ed., *Renaissance of Film* (London: Collier-Macmillan LTD., 1970), "The Tao in *Woman in the Dunes*," pp. 340-348.

94. See Campbell's description of this, *Myths To Live By*, "The Inspiration of Oriental Art," pp. 108-114, repeated in Campbell and Moyers, *The Power of Myth*— a lucid summary of this pilgrimage of the spirit.

95. (Tokyo: Japan Publications Incorporated, 1975).

96. *Silent Music* (New York: Harper and Row, 1974), "Brainwave and Biofeedback," pp. 32-44.

97. Ibid., pp. 40-41.

98. McFague, op. cit., p. 192.

99. *Joseph Campbell and The Power of Myth*, introduction to the program on "The Masks of Eternity."

100. McFague, ibid.

101. For a lucid report on Chalcedonian Christology in the history of Christian thought, see Paul Tillich, *A History of Christian Thought* (New York: Simon and Schuster, 1968), pp. 79-88.

102. (New York: Simon and Schuster, Inc., 1972).

103. Needleman, ibid., p. 17.

104. See H. N. McFarland, *The Rush Hour of the Gods* (New York: The Macmillan Co., 1967).

105. In three extended trips to Japan—in Kyoto, Tokyo, Tenri, Tondabayashi, Taiseki, Osaka, Ayabe, and Atami—I visited the centers of a score of these communities, talking with the directors and experiencing the rituals, including a 3:30 A.M. celebration at Konko-kyo in western Honshu and trips to all three "paradises" of Sekei Kyusei Kyo.

106. Ikeda's accomplishments are legion, including his edifice complex (the Sho-Hondo and environs at Taisekiji near Fuji-san surpasses the size of St. Peter's Cathedral), and his political genius (in 1964 a political arm of Soka Gakkai was formed called the *Komeito* [meaning "fair play" party], which ranks as Japan's fourth leading party measured by seats in the upper house of Parliament and by national constituency votes). The *Komeito* party is now officially separate from SG (while retaining its values), and SGI international has separated from the head temple. *Sic transit gloria mundi.*

107. Cited in the *Mainichi Daily News*, Friday, June 6, 1975, p. 4.

108. *World Tribune*, No. 3225, January 15, 1999, p. 3.

109. *PL: A Modern Religion for Modern Men* , p. 7.

110. Cited in Marcus Bach, *The Power of Perfect Liberty* (Englewood Cliff, New Jersey: Prentice-Hall, Inc., 1971), p. 71.

111. Ibid., p. 83.

112. For a competent analysis of the influence of the New Religions on American life in the seventies, see Robert S. Ellwood, Jr., *The Eagle and the Rising Sun* (Philadelphia: The Westminster Press, 1974).

113.   Patrick Smith, *Japan: A Reinterpretation* (New York: Vintage Books, 1998), p. 18. For Smith, "courtesy" might well be part of the mask that Japanese wear to hide their ambivalence toward residual Tokugawa consciousness. He mentions almost nothing about religious life—except reference to the creation myths as a sign of female power in ancient Japan [pp. 140-141]. Smith is a fresh corrective to Edwin Reischauer's *The Japanese Today* (Cambridge Mass., and London: Belnap Press, Harvard University, 1988), and Ezra Vogel's *Japan as Number One* (Cambridge, Mass. And London: Harvard University, 1979).

114.   See the British film documentary, *Where Is The Real Japan?*

Chapter 2

115.   See *Life,* December, 1998, the God in America edition. "God" must still be the Sky Father.

116.   *Fundamentalisms and Society: Reclaiming the Sciences, the Family, and Education* (1993), *Fundamentalisms and the State: Remaking Politics, Economies, and Militance* (1993), and *Accounting for the Fundamentalisms: The Dynamic Character of the Movements* (1994). One of the clearest accounts of the global reactivation of fundamentalism (shocked into reality by the 1978-79 revolution in Iran), is Bruce Lawrence's *Defenders of God* (San Francisco: Harper and Row, 1989). Lawrence worked with Marty and Appleby in the Chicago Project, and is especially cogent on the three "desert" religions (Jewish Collectivity, American Protestants, and the Pursuit of an Islamic State). See pp. 120-226. For a less scholarly, but delightful, analysis of one of the most influential of the American fundamentalists at the edge of the millennium, see the article on Pat Robertson and his media empire in *Playboy* magazine, February, 1999.

117.   John Shelby Spong, *Rescuing the Bible from Fundamentalism* (HarperSan Francisco, 1991), p. 93. The good Bishop writes with clarity, passion, and healthy provocation. Referring to the biblical literalists' own attempt to lock up meaning, he calls it "the Babylonian captivity of the fundamentalists." But he can't let it rest there, chiding the historically illiterate: "I use this expression aware that those who do not know anything about biblical history will also not understand it." [p. 246]

118.   Robert W. Funk, Roy W. Hoover, et al., *The Five Gospels.* (New York: Macmillan Publishing Company, 1993). All of these principals were involved in the Jesus Summit, held in the Bay area in California in February of 1994. The Seminar has now published *The Acts of Jesus* (HarperSanFrancisco, 1998)—what he actually *did*, and started traveling workshops around the country to explain to local communities Jesus' message for "the twenty-first century." The two days cost $50 per inquirer—just enough to keep the scholars out of the red. If you can't attend a workshop, and don't own the CD-ROM with all the extant literary Greek texts (down to 800 C.E.) for your own assessment, don't fret. Read Robert W. Funk, *Honest to Jesus: Jesus for a New Millennium* (HarperSanFrancisco, 1997). You will learn how this "new quest" approaches the journey, and addresses the question: Was Jesus a "Christian"?

119. See Luke Timothy Johnson's widely publicized rejoinders to the Seminar's methods in *The Real Jesus: The Misguided Quest for the Historical Jesus and the Truth of the Traditional Gospels* (HarperSan Francisco, 1997). Also his Internet conversations with Crossan, et al.

120. In 1988, the year of the Dragon—the Chinese really do understand history—came the most bizarre revelation of all. Jimmy Swaggart, television's most watched evangelist, the Beast of Baton Rouge, for more than a decade belching out fire, brimstone, and sulfuric tirades against "pornography and degenerative filth which denigrates all the values we hold sacred," was fingered by Marvin Gorman—a TV preacher in New Orleans that Swaggart destroyed by accusing him of adultery—as himself engaging in illicit sex.

121. Please make allowance for Methodist memory. If the Jesus Seminar publishes a Criswell Gospel, these words will be in gray/blue.

122. In 1995, the membership stood—paused—at 650,000. See Harvey Cox, *Fire From Heaven: The Rise of Pentecostal Spirituality and the Reshaping of Religion in the Twenty-first Century* (Reading, Massachusetts, et al.: Addison-Wesley Publishing Company, 1995), pp. 218-228. My figures come from an interview with Lydia M. Swain, Director International Counseling and Prayer, Yoido Full Gospel Church, Yoido P. O. Box 7, Seoul 150, Korea. The church is located at 11, Yoido-Dong, Yeongdungpo-ku, Seoul, Korea.

123. See Daniel Stevick, *Beyond Fundamentalism* (Philadelphia: John Knox, 1964).

124. This is the title, incidentally, of the novel by Sheldon that is still an all time fiction best seller in this country. The novel's subtitle ["What Would Jesus Do?"] is the source of the nineties' Christ-acrostic marketed on pins, bracelets, and tee-shirts: "WWJD?" My guess is that Jesus would not have done this kind of trivializing of compassion. WWJTWS? [What Would Jesus Think Was Silly?]

125. Cf. Cox, op. cit., pp. 123-128.

126. In the spring of 1990, Kirk Douglas and Jason Robards, Jr. re-inherited the Wind for NBC.

127. John Shelby Spong, *Born of a Woman, A Bishop Rethinks the Birth of Jesus* (HarperSan Francisco, 1992).

128. Ibid., p. 4 and p. 11.

129. Ibid., p. xvi. Spong does exactly what his subtitle implies: he is re-thinking the faith.

130. Ibid., p. 17.

131. Ibid., p. 21.

132. Ibid., p. 29.

133. Vanessa Ochs, *Words on Fire* (New York: Harcourt Brace Jovanovich, 1990), p. 189.

134. Quoted in *Life*, December, 1990, pp. 56-57.

135. Thomas Jefferson, *The Life and Morals of Jesus of Nazareth, Extracted textually from the Gospels in Greek, Latin, French, and English* (Washington: Government Printing Office, 1904), pp. 6-9 [Matthew 5]. *The Five Gospels* is also dedicated to Galileo and David Strauss (who began the modern quest).

136. *San Francisco Examiner*, Sunday, April 10, 1994 A-19.

137. Karen McCarthy Brown, "Fundamentalism and the Control of Women," in John Stratton Hawley, ed., *Fundamentalism and Gender* (New York: Oxford University Press, 1994), p. 175.

138. Ibid. Peter Gomes, minister at Harvard's Memorial Church for twenty-five years, completely avoids discussion of abortion—while addressing women's rights, women in scripture and the church, and homosexuality, in his wide-ranging book *The Good Book: Reading the Bible with Mind and Heart* (New York: William Morrow and Company, Inc., 1996). Biblically, it would seem, fetal "right to life" would amount to "textual molestation." *The Good Book* is, actually, a good book.

139. *Frontline* made it plain that Swaggart was the most talented of the evangelists when it came to show business—and before the fall, eight million watched every Sunday. His "show," with diminished crowds, goes on to this day, drained of energy, and so pathetic that one almost wishes him a testosterone transfusion. Dragons without teeth ought to have the grace to lie down and give it a rest.

140. Jay Leno's comment on the 1999 State of the Union address is illustrative: "President Clinton's speech was 77 minutes. That's the longest he's gone without sex." But fifteen minutes into the speech, we could tell that the Congress was a Greek Chorus for the eros of politics.

141. Bakker may be getting closer as the millennium draws to a close. After being released from prison in 1994 for bilking followers out of $158 million, he was "shell-shocked," and took an unpaid position at a center in Los Angeles that serves the poor and homeless. He has a new book (*Prosperity and the Coming Apocalypse*) and a new wife (Lori Beth Graham). His ex-wife, Tammy Faye, is waiting for her current husband (Roe Messner) to finish a twenty-seven-month prison sentence for bankruptcy fraud.

142. In late June, 1994, the fundamentalist coalition organized an around the world around the clock march for Jesus, beginning in New Zealand, and following the sun for twenty-four hours, marchers moved through every nation so that the entire planet became a witness for Christ every second for one day. Followers of the Son follow the sun.

143. For an early version of the importance of Mary Magdalene to the story of Jesus, see the anonymous fourteenth century novel *The Life of Saint Mary Magdalene* excerpt in Edward Wagenknecht, *The Story of Jesus in the World's Literature* (New York: Creative Age Press, Inc., 1946), "The Conversion of Mary Magdalene," pp. 204-208.

144. Wagenknecht, ibid., p. 204.

145. This idea—our desperate need for Christ rather than Jesus—had its genesis in his intellectual encounter with Nietzsche. See *Report to Greco*, "Paris, Nietzsche, the Great Martyr," pp. 304-325. One year before Kazantzakis was born, Nietzsche published *Die Fröhliche Wissenschaft* (*The Gay Science*)—we should translate *fröhliche* as "happy" in America's gay 90's. In Book Five, he considers believers and their need to believe: "How much one needs a *faith* in order to flourish, how much that is 'firm' and that one does not wish to be shaken because one *clings* to it, that is a measure of the degree of one's strength (or, to put the point more clearly, of one's

weakness). Christianity, it seems to me, is still needed by most people in old Europe even today; therefore it still finds believers. For this is how man is: An article of faith could be refuted before him a thousand times—if he needed it, he would consider it 'true' again and again, in accordance with that famous 'proof of strength' of which the Bible speaks." Friedrich Nietzsche, *The Gay Science,* trans. Walter Kaufmann (New York: Vintage Books, 1974). See p. 287. His reference here is to 1 Corinthians 2: 4—to the demonstration of spirit and power. See Luther's translation: *Beweisung des Geistes und der Kraft.*

146. Kazantzakis, *The Last Temptation of Christ*, trans. P.A. Bien (New York: Simon and Schuster Touchstone edition, 1960), p. 374.

147. Ibid., p. 46l.

148. Ibid., p. 372.

149. Ibid., p. 218.

150. Ibid., p. 237.

151. Ibid., p. 262.

152. Ibid., p. 369.

153. Ibid., p. 42.

154. Gospel of Philip, 63:30-64:10, quoted in Thiering, p. 118; see William E. Phipps,*The Sexuality of Jesus* (New York: Harper and Row, 1973). Also see Virginia Hyde, *The Risen Adam* (University Park, Pennsylvania: The Pennsylvania University Press, 1992), "Resurrection in *The Man Who Died,*" pp. 207-231.

155. Thiering, ibid., p. 117.

156. Ibid., p. 117.

157. "Blasphemy or Artistry?" *New York Times*, August 14,1988, p.22., "Zorba the Christ."

158. See Kazantzakis, *Saviors of God: Spiritual Exercises*, trans. Kimon Friar (New York: Simon and Schuster, 1960), p. 80.

159. Ibid., p. 38.

160. Don Lattin, *San Francisco Chronicle* Religion Writer, April 15, 1994 A-1. Matthew Fox does not denigrate the spirit by all this celebration of body culture. He quotes Harvard philosopher William Hocking to the point: "The prophet is the mystic in action." Action means "tasting and seeing." If you rave with the whole self, you'll "taste and see" that God is good. "Mysticism is about tasting—there is no such thing as vicarious mysticism—The Pope can't do it for you, your parish record cannot do it for you, you can't rent a mystic, not even in California!" [Cf. Michael Tobias and Georgianne Cowan, eds., *The Soul of Nature* (New York: A Plume Book, 1994), pp. 208-209.]

161. See John Osborne's play *Luther*, and his mentor on Luther's psyche, Erik Erickson [*Young Man Luther*]. Stacey Keach's performance in the film version is brilliant.

162. Lattin, op. cit., A-17.

163. "Minister 'raves' about power of renewing rituals," by Kristen Davenport, *The New Mexican* [Santa Fe]. Report on Matthew Fox's Techno-Cosmic Mass at the Transformation and Healing Conference at Southwestern College, Santa Fe. [Fall, 1998]. These "renewing rituals" have now transcended sexual orientation in the min-

istry of Bishop Spong, the United Methodist ministers who risk their careers in blessing gay unions, and in the remarkable work of the Cathedral of Hope in Dallas, Texas. That reconciling church—reported to be growing faster than fundamentalist churches in the "Bible Belt"—has broken ground for a new $20 million "gay cathedral." Architect Philip Johnson says it is "a new kind of architecture freed from the constraints of the straight line." Now that's form *really* following function. [See Carolyn Lochhead, "Gay Canterbury in Bible Belt," *San Francisco Chronicle*, A1-4, April 28, 1999.]

164. (London: Corgi Books, 1993).

165. See N. T. Wright, *Who Was Jesus?* (Grand Rapids: William B. Eerdmans Publishing Company, 1992), "Barbara Thiering: Jesus in Code," pp. 19-36. I am indebted to Dr. Wright for opening up the "riddle" of Barbara Thiering to me.

166. See Thiering, op. cit., "The Pesher Technique," pp. 28-35.

167. Ibid., p. 29.

Chapter 3

168. See Thomas L. Hartshorne, *The Distorted Image* (Cleveland: Case Western Reserve Press, 1968), pp. 15-34.

169. William Irwin Thompson, *At the Edge of History* (New York: Harper Colophon Books, 1972), p. 88.

170. I am exploring this existential space, where the fundamental datum is my body. I am certainly not alone in this exploration. Since I began this journey in Japan in 1975, the market has been flooded with "body" books: body fitness, body therapy, body identity, body politics, body language, body awareness—and not just in America. Leslie Adelson documents this flood with an extraordinary bibliography [*Making Bodies*, pp. 135-136]. Gert Mattenklott's essay in 1988 analyzed the explosion of interest in West Germany [*Körperpolitik oder Das Swinden der Sinne*] tracing the phenomenon to the sixties when Norman O. Brown and Herbert Marcuse's dialectics of eros were discussed by both intellectuals and the revolutionary youth culture. Adelson points us to Kroker and Cook, who actually dispute the materiality of the human body with something called the "panic theory" of postmodern culture: "Once the veil of materiality/subjectivity has been transgressed (and abandoned), then the body as something real vanishes into the spectre of hyperrealism." [p. 135.] See Arthur Kroker, and David Cook, *The Postmodern Scene: Excremental Culture and Hyper-Aesthetics* (London: Macmillan, 1988). As late capitalism moves from "the commodity relation based on wage/labor exploitation" to the "simulated economy of excess," nothing is real except the appropriation of excess. In a chilling phrase—which must be a description of the Reagan years, they tell us that the self of the eighties is "a blip with a lifestyle." [p. 279.] This theme of the "missing matter" of postmodernism is further analyzed in Arthur Kroker and Marie Louise Kroker, eds., *Body Invaders: Sexuality and the Postmodern Condition* (London: Macmillan, 1988). See Peter Brooks, *Body Work: Objects of Desire in Modern Narrative* (Cambridge, Massachusetts: Harvard University Press, 1993) [imagination bringing the body into lan-

guage]; Kenneth Dutton, *The Perfectible Body: the Western Ideal of Male Physical Development* (New York: Continuum, 1995) [explores the ideal of muscularity in Western cultures].

171. Lawrence Durrell, *Spirit of Place* (New York: E.P. Dutton, 1971), p. 36.

172. Henry Miller, *Black Spring* (New York: Grove Press, 1963), p. 43-44.

173. Ibid., p. 44.

174. Edmond Jabès, *Les mots tracent,* edition Les Pas Perdus, p. 37, quoted in Gaston Bachelard, *The Poetics of Reverie: Childhood, Language, and the Cosmos,* trans. Daniel Russell (Boston: Beacon Press, 1969), p. 50.

175. Jabès, *Je bâ tis ma demeure,* Preface by Gabriel Bounoure, Gallimard, p. 20, quoted in Bachelard, p. 50.

176. Ibid., p. 51.

177. William Blake, ''Jerusalem,'' in *The Poetry and Prose of William Blake* (Bloomsbury: The Nonesuch Press, 1927), p. 749.

178. Edward T. Hall, op. cit., p. 12.

179. Robert Sommer, *Personal Space: The Behavioral Basis of Design* (Englewood Cliffs, N. J.: Prentice-Hall, 1967), p. 9.

180. Ibid., p 26.

181. Paul A. Insel and Henry Clay Lindgren, *Too Close for Comfort: The Psychology of Crowding Behavior* (Englewood Cliffs, N.J.: Prentice-Hall, 1978), pp. 100-106.

182. Ibid., p. 103.

183. Ibid. Middlemist should have been retained by Kenneth Starr for Oval Office observations.

184. See Norman O. Brown, *Life against Death* (New York: Vintage Books, 1959), pp. 203-233.

185. Tom Wolfe, "The Third Great Awakening," *New West* 6, no. 10 (August 30, 1976): 27-48.

186. Werner Erhard, *The Graduate Review: EST* (November, 1976), p. 2.

187. See Benjamin Lee Whorf, *Language, Thought, and Reality* (New York: John Wiley and Sons, 1956). Cf. Ralph Berger's use of Whorf in *Cyclosis.*

188. Richard M. Zaner, *The Problem of Embodiment: Some Contributions to a Phenomenology of the Body* (The Hague: Martinus Nijhoff, 1964), p. 81.

189. *PPR*, Vol xiii, No. 2 (December, 1952), p. 169. Cited in Zaner.

190. Zaner, op. cit., p. 81.

191. *Being and Nothingness: An Essay on Phenomenological Ontology*, trans. Hazel E. Barnes (New York: Philosophical Library, 1956), p. 316. See Chapter Three: "Concrete Relations With Others," pp. 361-430.

192. *Metaphysical Journal* (Chicago: Henry Regnery Co., 1952), p. 13. Cf. Zaner, p. 39.

193. Ibid., p. 18. See Gabriel Marcel, *Mystery of Being* (Chicago: Henry Regnery Co.), p. 129ff.

194. Ralph Berger, *Psyclosis: The Circularity of Experience* (San Francisco: W. H. Freeman, 1977), pp. 141-150. Note the citations of Whorf's research into Hopi culture.

195. Ibid., pp. 144-145.

196. Ibid., p. 148. I am indebted to Berger for his analysis of the mind/body problem.

197. Calvin, op. cit., p. i. See p. 129, 260, 366, 397. In fact, just open at random.

198. *What Mad Pursuit* (New York: Basic Books, 1988), p. 156. See the helpful "further reading" section on the "Mind-Body Problem" in *The Astonishing Hypothesis: the Scientific Search for the Soul* (New York: Charles Scribner's Sons), pp. 282-284. Crick's annotations are models of bibliographic wit and wisdom. [e.g. his remarks on Penrose's *The Emperor's New Mind*: "At bottom his argument is that quantum gravity is mysterious and consciousness is mysterious and wouldn't it be wonderful if one explained the other." p. 283].

199. Ibid., pp. 156-7.

200. Not to mention Mathematical Physics and Molecular Biophysics and Biochemistry. See Frank J. Tipler, *The Physics of Immortality* (New York: Doubleday, 1994) and Clifford A. Pickover, *Computers and the Imagination: Visual Adventures Beyond the Edge* (Phoenix Mill: Alan Sutton Publishing, 1991). Writes Tipler: "The brain *is* a computer, and the soul *is* a program. After many centuries of mistakes on what thinking is, and where it occurs, we've got it right at last: The brain *is* a computer in the same sense that the heart *is* a pump." [p. 348]. Pickover's work is a graphic playground of "lateral thinking"—not only action motivated by unexpected results, but deliberately thinking in new directions just for the joy of discovery itself. The term "lateral thinking" is from Pirsig's *Zen and the Art of Motorcycle Maintenance.* Kazantzakis' *Last Temptation* is just such "thinking" about Jesus.

201. Ibid., p. 160.

202. See John de Cuevas, "Mind, Brain, and Behaviour," *Harvard Magazine,* November-December, 1994, pp. 36-43.

203. Lewis Thomas, *The Medusa and the Snail* (New York: The Viking Press, 1979), p. 156.

204. *The Brain* (New York: Bantam, 1984), pp. 36-37, section on Dr. Paul D. MacLean and the Triune Brain. See Leslie A Hart, *Human Brain and Human Learning* (Kent, Washington: Books for Educators, Inc., 1998), Chapter Five, "Where and How Learning Happens," pp. 63-92. Hart reproduces Dr. Paul MacLean's forty year old chart of the Triune Brain, telling us, that while still useful, it has been replaced by the biologically more comprehensive "bodybrain partnership." [p. 69]. Fortunately, the theological Triune model was *always* a partnership.

205. See *Datebook,* article by Jerry Carroll, "Black Magic," April 17, 1994, pp. 25-28.

206. Ibid., p. 28.

207. Michael Heim, *The Metaphysics of Virtual Reality* (New York/Oxford: Oxford University Press, 1993), p. vi.

208. Krueger, in Heim, p. viii.

209. Ibid., p. x. Heim's analysis takes us from "Infomania" (the startling ingestion of the cultural heritage of English-speaking countries by computers), through "The Electronic Cafe Lecture" (cyberlearning as the Messianic nightmare: *Lawnmower Man* as neural omniscience in a celestial electronic body).

210. Ibid., p. 80. Cf. Richard Lenski, on the cyber-equivalent of DNA, *Nature*, August, 1999.

211. William Gibson, *Neuromancer* (New York: Ace Books, 1984), p. 51; *Count Zero* (New York: Ace Books, 1986), p. 38) quoted in Heim, p. 80.

212. Ibid., p. 81.

213. See Fritz Capra, *The Tao of Physics* (Berkeley: Shambala, 1975), etc.

214. Germaine Greer, *The Female Eunuch* (New York: Bantam Books, 1972), p. 22.

215. Cf. Naomi Weisstein, "Kinder, Küche, Kirche As Scientific Law: Psychology Reconstructs the Female," *motive* (March-April, 1969): 78-85.

216. Greer, op. cit., p. 97. Cf. her sequel, *The Whole Woman* (New York: Alfred A. Knopf, 1999).

217. Erik Erikson, "Women and the Inner Space," *Identity, Youth, and Crisis* (New York: W.W. Norton, 1968), pp.261-294. See *Daedalus*, no. 93 (1964): 582-606.

218. Ibid., p. 267.

229. Ibid., p. 281.

220. Francine du Plessix Gray, *San Francisco Chronicle*, 14 March 1978, p. 19.

221. See J. Levy and C. Trevarthen, "Metacontrol of Hemispheric Function in Human Split-Brain Patients," *Journal of Experimental Psychology: Human Perception and Performance, 3,* pp. 299-311. Also see TLC documentary, *The Sexual Brain* ; William F. Allman, *Apprentices of Wonder* (New York: Bantam, 1989), pp. 57-79. Crick calls Allman's writing "breezy" but helpful to the unlearned.

222. Ken Wilbur, *Up From Eden* (Boston: Shambala, 1986), "The Natural Patriarchy," p. 228 ff.

223. Jean Shinoda Bolen, *Crossing to Avalon: A Woman's Midlife Pilgrimage* (San Francisco: HarperCollins, 1994). See Carolyn Foster's review, "An Arduous Journey to Inner Destinations," *Review, San Francisco Chronicle*, May 1, 1994, pp. 6, 9.

224. Ibid., p. 125.

225. Ibid., p. 36.

226. Ibid., p. 37.

227. Ibid., p. 39.

228. Ibid., p. 15.

229. *Ceres* is the Roman name for the Greek Goddess *Demeter*—the Earth Mother of Persephone, whom she rescued from *Hades*—and restored the fertility of the seasons to the world. Hence our nourishing breakfast name, *cereal*.

230. Foster, op. cit., p. 6. See Bolen, pp. 21-32, 83-99.

231. (Reading, Massachusetts, et al.: Addison-Wesley Publishing Company, 1990).

232. Mircea Eliade, op. cit., p. 57. Sacred time, as hinted at by Martin Buber, is an extension of this existentiality, that enables us to be present by means of ritual at the beginning of creation itself. Like non-geometric space, sacred time is not chronological but eternal.

233. F. Matthias Alexander. *The Resurrection of the Body* (New Hyde Park, New York: Dell Publishing 1974), p. 12.

234. Ibid., p. 116. See Frank Price Jones, *A Study of the Alexander Technique: Body Awareness in Action* (New York: Schocken, 1979).

235. Murphy's quirky novel, *Golf in the Kingdom* (New York: The Viking Press, 1972), introduced the world to Shivas Irons and cosmic golf revelations from the Burningbush of *true gravity*—a spiritual backswing still in print. Clint Eastwood will direct a film based on the book starring Sean Connery. If it is ever completed, it may not make money, but it will make a lot of days.

236. Erwin Strauss, "The Upright Posture," in Stuart F. Spicker, ed., *The Philosophy of the Body* (Chicago: Quadrangle Books, 1970), pp. 334-361.

237. Ibid., p. 339.

238. See F. Matthias Alexander, op. cit., pp. xxxix-xl.

239. Wilhelm Reich, *The Murder of Christ* (New York: Noonday Press, 1971), pp. 3-4.

240. Ibid., p. 160.

241. F. Matthias Alexander, op. cit., p. xxxii.

242. Francine du Plessix Gray, *Lovers and Tyrants* (New York: Simon and Schuster, 1976), pp. 310-311.

Chapter 4

243. Thomas Moore, *The Care of the Soul: A Guide for Cultivating Depth and Sacredness in Everyday Life* (New York: HarperPerennial, 1994), p. 155. "In the body, we see the soul articulated in gesture, dress, movement, shape, physiognomy, temperature, skin eruption [*sic*], tics, disease—in countless expressive forms."

244. Even in the nineties, serious psychologists understand. See Daniel C. Dennett, *Consciousness Explained* (Boston, Toronto, London: Little, Brown and Company, 1991), "A Party Game Called Psychoanalysis," pp. 10-16.

245. See Calvin's assumptions about how the brain thinks (*The River That Flows Uphill*), p. 456. His Artificial Intelligence friends asked: Could we design a computer that could get bored? Apparently boredom is extremely important from an evolutionary perspective. Boredom with food promotes diversity in diet; lack of boredom in thought is a graveyard for creativity (p. 414). In partial response to that question, he is saying that it would be interesting to see a computer act "like a frontal lobe patient, who settles on one strategy" and stays with it no matter how infinitely unsuccessful—like a computer without its interrupts working, trapped in a loop. He assumes that real brains take the elements of the problem and free-associate, looking for related schemata, arranging the schemata into multiple "scenarios," discarding the stupid arrangements and looking closely at the possible ones, grading these for quality (your call), and implementing the best one—or dumping the whole problem. Only "thinking" is not that "orderly." Cf. Frank McConnell, *Storytelling and Mythmaking*, (New York: Oxford University Press, 1979), p. 60. McConnell is drawing a connection between stone axes and computers, calling both weapons (as in Kubrick's *2001: a Space Odyssey*): "[T]he axe extends our reign over potential enemies and potential games (not always distinguished from each other in the earlier stages of civilization),

and the computer extends our reign over the world of numbers and chance." In the film it seems to me that it's the boredom of the human computers that is snapped by the willfulness of the mechanical computer so that they commit lobotomy—Simsectomy. A sharp mind with an edge seems to be an appropriate metaphor. Apparently boredom has only increased the sophistication of the axe.

246. Mark Johnson, *The Body in the Mind: The Bodily Basis of Meaning, Imagination, and Reason* (Chicago and London: The University of Chicago Press,1987), "Toward a Theory of Imagination," pp. 139-172. I am greatly indebted to Johnson's fascinating work.

247. Ibid., p. 140.

248. Ibid., p. 151.

249. Ibid., p. 159.

250. Ibid. Johnson refers us to Immanuel Kant, *First Introduction to the Critique of Judgment*, trans. James Haden (Indianapolis: Bobbs-Merrill, 1965), sec. 5, p. 16.

251. See the discussion on the Tugendhat House designed by Mies van der Rohe—Franz Schulze, *Mies van der Rohe: A Critical Biography* (Chicago and London: the University of Chicago Press, 1985), pp. 162-173: "A sense of the actual, the imperative, and inevitable mingle in both statements with the search for the essence, the generalizing truth." [p. 172] His concept of the spiritual seems to have come from a re-reading of Thomas Aquinas in the *Summa Theologica:* "Now we do not judge of a thing by what is in it accidentally, but by what is in it essentially.... For a house is said to be true that expresses the likeness of the form in the architect's mind, and words are said to be true in so far as they are signs of truth in the intellect." Mies's translation into German: "die Übereinstimmnung des Geistlichen und des Sachlichen." Mies van der Rohe worked forever on a project, trying to bring conformity between his mind and the object. He often quoted Max Scheler as saying that truth is the significance of facts ("der Sinngehalt eines Sachverhaltes"). That he believed in some kind of objective standards was shown by his famous remark, "I don't want to be interesting; I want to be good." [p. 173]

252. Johnson, op. cit., p. 162.

253. Actually Nietzsche was writing in the context of how philosophers should think of themselves. There is more than whimsy in his suggestion that they are different from scholars—have a different "digestion." [*The Gay Science,* p. 345]

254. Ibid., pp. 345-346.

255. Kazantzakis, *Zorba the Greek*, p. 124.

256. (New York: E. P. Dutton, 1986).

257. Leonard, pp. 1-2.

258. Ibid., p. 2. See Eugen Herrigel, *Zen and the Art of Archery* (New York: Pantheon,1953),p. 80.

259. Highwater, *The Primal Mind* (New York: Meridian, 1982), p. 137.

260. Diane Apostolos-Cappadona, Liberal Studies Program, Georgetown University.

261. If the snakes are not satisfied, according to the guru, people will fall ill, go blind, and some will suffer from skin problems. At last I know what's wrong with me.

262. Audiences everywhere are drawn to worship by music and spectacle (as the

Roman Catholics have always known). The Indian dance gurus seem to proceed on the premise that "What is pleasing to the people is pleasing to the gods." And are they ever pleased with dances such as Geetanadatan Kalamalandam—done in the documentary by an Ottan Tullal Performer! It is a tale from the *Mahabharata*, where the Monkey God teaches a headstrong hero a lesson in humility. The dance features typical Indian neck movements and muscle separation, and all Kata Kala performers are male. Lest anyone should miss the connection between religion and dance, the Benati Shastra—a 2000 year-old dance manual—gives access to the sacred texts.

263. The ascent is designed to take one through the three divisions of the Buddhist universe: *kamadhatu* (ordinary human life), *rupadhatu* (the life of "form'), and *arupadhatu* (the sphere of "detachment" from the world). Why that magnificent view from the top of the monument would induce "detachment" is very mysterious. But, of course, *any* effort to diminish our celebration of the world puzzles me.

264. See Soedarsono, *Wayang Wong: The State Ritual Dance Drama in the Court of Yogyakarta* (Yogyakarta: Gadjah Mada University Press, 1990), pp. 223-225.

265. See Faubion Bowers, *Theater in the East: A Survey of Asian Dance and Drama* (New York: Grove Press, Inc. 1960), "Indonesia," pp. 191-248.

266. Ibid., p. 192.

267. Ibid., p. 242.

268. Shaykh Umar ibn Muhammad al-Nefzawi, *The Perfumed Garden,* trans. Sir Richard Burton (London: Hunt Barnard & Co., Ltd.—Panther Books, 1963). This is the third volume in a triology of erotic works translated by Burton and Forster Fitzgerald Arbuthnot—the first being the famous *Kama Sutra* of Vatsyayana, and the second the lesser known *Ananga Ranga* of Kalyana Malla. Both of these are Indian texts—and the Malla work is a sourcebook for understanding the libidinal background of the Barong dance in Indonesia.

269. Kay Larson, "Robert Mapplethorpe," in Janet Kardon, *Robert Mapplethorpe: the Perfect Moment* (Philadelphia: Meriden-Stinehour Press, 1989), p. 15. [See John Atkins, *Sex In Literature* (New York: Grove Press, Inc., 1970), Chapter 9, "Kissing," pp. 284-302.

270. See *Everything You Ever Wanted to Know About Sex But Were Afraid to Ask*—not the book, but the film sequence where Woody Allen plays a sperm and Burt Reynolds a genital engineer.

271. See Atkins, p. 284. I am indebted to Atkins for this suggestive history and bibliography.

272. Trans. Ezra Pound (New York: Collier Books, 1961). Chapter 11, "The Mechanism of Love."

273. Ibid., p. 77. Reference in Atkins, op. cit., p. 285.

274. Trans. Philip M. Pope, quoted in Atkins, p. 302.

275. Ibid., p. 291. Cf. Vatsyayana, *Kama Sutra* (New York: Castle Books, 1963), p. 34 ff.

276. According to McLaurin Meredith, a biblical translator from Austin, Texas—as well as my brother. At 76, he is also a senior regional Olympics tennis and table tennis champion—and has wonderful teeth. See *Time*, February 15, 1993, pp.

47-53. See Dr. Thomas Bianchi [meta-molar Stockton dentist].

277. One thinks of James Joyce's *Portrait of an Artist as a Young Man.* While an actual priest would lift up the bread to "heaven" and then place it in the mouth of the believer, the whore (as an earthly priestess) puts her tongue in Steven's mouth. A highly charged communion this—and, as Lawrence would say, "drinking life directly from the source."

278. Martin and Jacobus, *The Humanities through the Arts* (New York: McGraw-Hill, 1975), p. 4.

279. Ibid., p. 177.

280. Edward T. Hall, *The Hidden Dimension* (New York: Doubleday, 1966), p. 74.

281. Ibid., pp. 80-81. See "Gay Canterbury" [*San Francisco Chronicle,* A1, April 28, 1999].

282. See Philip Rawson and Laszlo Legeza, *Tao: Eastern Philosophy of Time and Change* (New York: Avon Books, 1973); Al Chung-liang Huang, *Embrace Tiger, Return to Mountain* (Moab, Utah: Real People Press, 1973). The pictures facing pp. 1, 11, 33, 55, 73, 95, 103, 125, 149, 163, and 175, animate the full force of "gathering in space."

283. See Elisofon and Watts, *Erotic Spirituality: The Vision of Konarak* (New York: Collier Macmillan Publishers, 1971). Particularly pp. 21-29, 49-53; p. 116 also shows that there is nothing new under the sexual sun.

284. Alexander Dorner, *The Way Beyond "Art"* (New York: New York University Press, 1958), pp. 136-137. See Marshall McLuhan and Harley Parker, *Through the Vanishing Point* (New York: Harper and Row, 1968); Gaston Bachelard, *The Poetics of Space,* trans. Maria Jolas (Boston: Beacon Press, 1969); Lincoln F. Johnson, *Film: Space, Time, Light, and Sound* (New York: Holt, Rinehart, and Winston, 1974); Emile Male, *The Gothic Image* (New York Harper and Row. 1958); Peter Brook, *The Empty Space* (New York: Avon Books, 1968); Victor Zuckerkandl, *Sound and Symbol: Music and the External World* (New York, Pantheon Books, 1956); Al Chung-liang Huang, *Embrace Tiger, Return to Mountain* (Moab, Utah: Real People Press, 1973); Jean-Paul Sartre, *What Is Literature?* trans. Bernard Frechtman (New York: Washington Square Press, 1966); M.C. Richards, *Centering in Pottery, Poetry, and the Person* (Middletown, Conn.: Wesleyan University Press, 1967); Maxine Sheets, *The Phenomenology of Dance* (Madison and Milwaukee: The University of Wisconsin Press, 1966); Jean Anthelme Brillat-Savarin, *The Physiology of Taste* (New York: Dover, 1960).

285. Richard Lewis, ed., *In Praise of Music* (New York: Orion Press, 1963), p. 15.

286. Ibid., p. 21.

287. George Leonard, *The Silent Pulse,* pp. 8-9. This is a penetrating, sensuous study, one in which he thought he had solved the "mind-body" problem. If one reads with "soft-eyes," he has. [see p. 188.]

288. Ibid.

289. Ibid., pp. 9-10.

290. William Sadler, *Existence in Love* (New York: Charles Scribner, 1969). p.

150.

291. Ibid.

292. Terry Ellingson, "The Tibetan Chordal Singing in the Tibetan Style," *American Anthropologist* 72, no. 4 (August, 1970): 826-31. See Joseph Campbell and Bill Moyers, *The Power of Myth* series on PBS. Moyers has now (1996) given Smith a new audience and renewed respect with his five hour series entitled *The Wisdom of Faith.*

293. Ibid.

294. Ibid., p. 237.

295. Ibid., p. 110.

296. Judith Jackson, *The Magic of Well-Being* (London: Dorling Kindersley, 1997), pp. 6-7. See *Scentual Touch: A Personal Guide to Aromatherapy* (New York: Henry Holt Company, 1986), pp. 1-4, for more on her introduction to this therapy. Judy has always resisted the idea that bodies need to disintegrate. At the age of ten she was trying to revive dead animals with whiffs of her father's scotch. A whiff of Judy has revived a variety of male animals.

297. Philip Rawson and Laszlo Legeza, op. cit., p. 26.

298. Kazuko Okakura , *The Book of Tea* (Rutland, Vermont: Charles E. Tuttle, 1973), p. 7.

299. Ibid., p. 24.

300. Tom Robbins, *Even Cowgirls Get the Blues* (New York: Bantam, 1976), pp. 415-16.

301. He was not alone. Ted Koppel of ABC TV *Nightline* was there, and so was Michael Jackson [before his own world was attacked by virulent assault on his character]. *The New York Times* carried the story, and ran Bhante's picture.

302. *I Am That: Talks with Sri Nisagadatta Maharaj,* trans. by Maurice Frydman, rev. and ed. Sudhakar S. Dikshit (Durham, North Carolina: The Acorn Press, 1988), p. 5. A favorite book, by the Asian way, of Milo Shepard, literary executor of Jack London's estate in Glen Ellen, California. He gave me Jack London wine and communion with greatness, including time with Captain Archetype: Dr. Earle Labor.

303. On June 26, 1999, Bhante (Samdech Preah Dhammavara Mahathera Bel Long) died. On July 10, I attended his funeral at Wat Dhammavaram in Stockton, along with hundreds from around the world, including Steven Seagal (the aikido instructor who taught Callison/Pacific students in Japan—now a Hollywood star of non-aikido adventures). Just as the service was to begin, we witnessed an adventure in Buddhist metaphysics. A young Cambodian woman, helping arrange the symbols surrounding the elevated body lying in state, brushed against a huge portrait of Bhante (three feet by four—protected by glass and resting on an easel just to the side of the death shrine). We watched the frame topple and crash exactly in front of the body, shattering and splintering on the place where the monks were about to enter and bow to the memory of their revered leader. In relative tranquility, the officials picked up the glass, swept and vacuumed, and propped up the glassless picture as best they could. A funereal parable, I thought. Life is transient, the Buddhists teach, and all efforts to fix the present will be shattered. Let the cremation begin.

304. Kazantzakis, *Zorba the Greek,* pp. 232- 233.

Chapter 5

305. Paul Weiss, *Sport. A Philosophic Inquiry.* (Carbondale and Edwardsville: Southern Illinois University Press, 1969), p.6.

306. *Evergreen,* November, 1969, p. 39.

307. *Sports Illustrated,* November 2, 1970, p. 13.

308. Eleanor Metheny, *Connotations of Movement in Sport and Dance* (Dubuque: William C. Brown Co., 1965), p. 40.

309. Günter Grass, *The Tin Drum* (Greenwich, Conn.: A Fawcett Crest Book, 1962), p. 131. The irony of identifying Jesus as an athlete has been modified by the canonization of Michael Jordan on the occasion of his retirement in January, 1999. As Jayson Williams of the New Jersey Nets put it, Jordan is "Jesus in tennis shoes." MJ might actually be a better candidate than the Nazarene for an ascension.

310. Isaiah 6: 1-7. Smoked tongue purgation: sufficient for a little forgiveness in the cave at Thaipusam. But Hindus are not seeking to overcome separation from the Holy. Pain is ecstasy.

311. Miller, *The Body in Question,* "Natural Shocks," pp.14-53

312. Ibid., p. 14.

313. Ibid., pp. 21-22.

314. Ibid., p. 20.

315. An anthropologist researching "body image" and internal organs might report the "correspondence" somewhat differently.

316. See *Newsweek,* August 5, 1996, p. 42. Kerri's teammates had given her the ageless advice: "Shake it off." Ratified by Bela Karolyi ("I encouraged her") and the lure of gold, she leaped into history—and Karolyi's arms. "It hurts," she told him. "Kerri," Bela bubbled. "You're an Olympic champion now. Enjoy it!" Gold medals must be the ultimate drug.

317. Elaine Scarry, *The Body In Pain: The Making and Unmaking of the World* (New York, Oxford: Oxford University Press, 1985), Chapter 3 "Pain and Imagining."

318. Ibid., p. 27.

319. See Adelson, *Making Bodies,* p. 20; Scarry, ibid., p. 47.

320. Scarry, op. cit. p. 162.

321. Scarry, ibid., p. 192.

322. (New York: Oxford University Press, 1979, p. 45. See pp. 45-48.

323. See Frank McConnell, ed., *The Bible and the Narrative Tradition* (New York, Oxford: Oxford University Press, 1986), pp. 3-18. Note the reference to *Alice in Wonderland* as a "sacred text" [p. 13]. Dr. McConnell was a long distance companion on this odyssey, having read the original draft, and stimulated my imagination by his writings, lectures, conversations, and instant powers of association. Frank taught English, Bible, and Film at UC Santa Barbara, wrote a column for *Commonweal* on Popular Culture, published on literary and film criticism—as well as detective novels, read everything and had an outrageously intelligent opinion on everything he read. His neurons set a world record for firing speed. They vanished into the surrounding silence in January, 1999. "Life is trouble, Boss, only death is not."

324. An alternative reason for God's "impotence" might be that, like the torturer, he needs us to "sin" so that he can alienate us from our body/selves and impose his absolute Power as dictator, and therefore our absolute submission.

325. "Jesus, thou son of the eternal God" wasn't orthodox enough. He required theological exactitude: "Jesus, Thou eternal Son of God!" As the flames ever so slowly roasted theological incorrectness, Calvin must have been overheard saying: "I expected something better from you."

326. See Calvin, op. cit., p. 419-422, on the relationship between pain and consciousness. The problem in human beings is the delayed tenderness and prolonged holding up instinct that are the problems—much more than initial pain, which is apparently designed to prevent further injury. Scientists are just now beginning to look at pain from a biological perspective [ibid., p. 421].

327. The whimsical phrase is William O. Johnson's in *Super Spectator and the Electric Lilliputians* (Boston: Little, Brown, and Company, 1971).

328. Small wonder, though, that the players struck for a larger share of a very juicy pie. After Denver dug into the Colorado gold supply for an untried Stanford alum [five million for Elway should have bought a slab of kryptonite—and it did!], Super Alchemy was inevitable.

329. *Sport* (Carbondale and Edwardsville: Southern Illinois University Press, 1969).

330. See Thompson, *Darkness and Scattered Light*, p. 122.

331. Eleanor Metheny, "The Symbolic Power of Sport," in Ellen W. Gerber,ed., *Sport and the Body,* (Philadelphia: Lea and Febiger, 1972), p. 222.

332. At the Pythian games at Delphi, the crown was made of laurels—Apollo's tree—hence the name Laurence/Lawrence. I was born to win.

333. Rex Warner, *The Stories of the Greeks* (New York: Farrar, Straus and Giroux, Inc., 1967), cited in Nestor Kraly, *Nestor Kraly's Amazing Sports Records and Other Oddities* (Greenwich, Connecticut: Fawcett Publications, Inc., 1975), p. 76.

334. See Paul Hoch, *Rip Off the Big Game* (Garden City, New York: Doubleday and Co., Inc., 1972), pp. 22-24.

335. Ibid., p. 93. See Tom Dowling, *Coach: A Season With Lombardi* (New York: Popular Library, 1970).

336. Frank Deford, "I've Won. I've Beat Them," *Sports Illustrated,* August 8, 1983, p. 78.

337. Ibid., p. 82.

338. *The Total Woman* (Old Tappan, New Jersey: Fleming H. Revell Co., 1973), p. 188.

On July 10, 1999, Pasadena became a different kind of symbol for the "total woman." The year of the "soccer babes" climaxed with the USA women's team beating China for the World Cup. Ninety thousand in the Rose Bowl and forty million Americans on television watched Brandi Chastain blast in the winning penalty goal, landing her ecstatic expression, sinuous muscles, and black sport bra on the cover of *Newsweek*—with a gigantic manifesto transecting her torso: GIRL'S RULE! [see July 19, 1999, and feature article by Mark Starr and Martha Brant, pp. 46-54]. Ellen Goodman, as usual, puts hype in perspective: "But have our daughters arrived? This moment was as much about changing lives of girls off the field as the women on the field. If there's a competition going on, it's between old and new images. For every Mia Hamm [another press darling among the 'Babes of Summer'] there are still dozens of supermodels." [*San Francisco Chronicle*, A 27, July 15, 1999]. And, I would guess, millions of Partial People.

339. *The Myth of Sisyphus and Other Essays,* trans. Justin O'Brien (New York: Vintage Books,1955), pp. 88-89.

340. See Skip Bayless, *God's Coach: The Hymns, Hype, and Hypocrisy of Tom Landry's Cowboys* (New York: Simon and Schuster, 1990), especially p. 150. "On Sunday, November 18, the Cowboys lost 34-20 at Washington. The Redskins even rubbed it in with a last-second field goal. Afterwords, Drew Pearson told me, 'Man, all this America's Team shit is killing us. That's all we heard all day from the Redskins: Whose team are you now, motherfuckers?'"

341. At the Atlanta Olympics, in the summer of 1996, Johnson ran the second hundred meters (in the 200) in 9. 32 seconds—by superhuman far the fastest time in history.

342. April 22, 1974, pp. 38-42, Edwin Shrake; cf. Howard Cosell, *Like It Is* (Chicago: The Playboy Press,1974), "So Long, 'Dandy,'" pp. 3-13.

343. Don has lived in Santa Fe for nearly twenty years now, interested more in family, friends, and sunsets than the repetitive ravages of pro football.

344. Albert Camus, *Notebooks 1942-1951,* trans. Justin O'Brien (New York: Harcourt Brace Jovanovich, 1978).

345. *The Ultimate Athlete* (New York: The Viking Press, 1975), p. 188.

346. Ibid., pp. 188-89.

347. Revelation 16:13-16.

348. Cf. John Bowman's article, "Armageddon," *The Interpreter's Dictionary of the Bible,* A-D (New York: The Abingdon Press, 1962), pp. 226-7.

349. Revelation 16: 17-18. See Part Three.

350. And President Clinton took his chances in playing the Grand Jury Game: "Thou shalt not admit adultery."

351. Dan Jenkins, *Semi-Tough* (New York: Atheneum, 1972), pp. 191-192.

352. John Simon, *Movies Into Film* (New York: Dial Press, 1971), p. 3.

353. David L. Miller, *Gods and Games: Toward a Theory of Play* (New York: World Publishing Company,1970), pp. 139-140. See Tom Jones, *The Fantasticks* (New York: Drama Book Shop, 1964), p. 28.

354. (New York: Vintage, 1986).

355. Wilson, ibid., p. 7.

356. Ibid., p. 8-9.

357. Ibid., p. 10.

358. Ibid. See Wilson's description of actually playing the piano [pp. 43-54]— how the brain processes information into action. Note the reference to *Alice peering through the door to wonderland,* prompted by the innocent question: how does our daughter make her fingers go so fast on the piano? [p. 11.]

359. (Bowling Green, Ohio: Bowling Green University Popular Press, 1977).

See pp. 31-49.

360. When the Yokozuna weighs almost 600 pounds, one shudders to think what fertility might mean if we're not talking about a rice field.

361. Schroeder, op. cit., pp. 40-41.

362. Maya Angelou, *I Know Why the Caged Bird Sings* (New York: Bantam, 1971), p.111-112.

363. Ibid., p. 113. The match described here is between Louis and Carnera.

364. Ibid.

365. Gerardus van der Leeuw, *Sacred and Profane Beauty: The Holy in Art,* trans. David E. Green (London:Weidenfeld & Nicholson, 1963), p. 74.

366. *The Republic of Plato,* trans. F. M. Cornford (New York: Oxford University Press, 1966), Chapter IX, p. 90. See Chester Pennington, ed., *Are We Set In Slippery Places?: A Christian Inquiry into Our Secular Society* (St. Paul, Minnesota: Hamline University Publisher, 1987), "Examining the Good Life," by Joseph N. Uemura, pp. 139-155. See also Joseph Uemura's article on *The Republic:* "An Antidote to Any Future Utopia." Plato, it seems, was *no* utopian!

367. Samuel Beckett, *Waiting for Godot* (New York: Grove Press, 1954), pp. 28-29.

368. The complete chromae: 1-orange/ 2-pink/3-red/4-mauve/5-purple/6-blue/7-green/8-turquoise/9-brown/10-cream/11-sand/12-yellow. I owe this reference to Elisabeth Schnitzer, a graduate student at Universität Graz, who monitors the colors of *kairos* between cultures. And she shares the *chronos* of August.

Chapter 6

369. I assume this spectrum speculation played no part in Japan's fiscal troubles in the late nineties.

370. Allan Wade, ed., *The Letters of W. B. Yeats* (London: Rupert-Hart-Davis, 1954), p. 922. [quoted in Thompson, *Darkness and Scattered Light*, p. 120].

371. Albert Camus, *Notebooks: 1935-1942*, trans. Philip Thody (New York and London: Harcourt Brace Jovanovich, 1969), p. 77.

372. Norman Maclean, *A River Runs Through It* (New York: Pocketbook, 1992), p. 1.

373. Ibid., p. 2.

374. Ibid., p. 104.

375. Ibid., p. 108.

376. Ibid., p. 113.

377. *A Brief History of Time* (New York: Bantam Books, 1990), p. 8.

378. Ibid.

379. Woody Allen, *Death* (A Play), in *Without Feathers* (New York: Warner Books, 1976), p. 106.

380. January-February, 1964. See Elisabeth Kübler-Ross, *On Death and Dying* (New York: The Macmillan Company, 1969).

381. Life has changed in America. See editorial by Jerry Roberts [April 23,

1994, *San Francisco Chronicle*] entitled: "How to Survive the Third Grade." (A 22) The "mysterious grade"—whatever it was in 1937—is now a military training ground, where in grammar schools like San Francisco's Potrero Hill children are being instructed in duck and cover maneuvers in case of shootings. Roberts comments: "the national shame of little children attending classes in fear is one symptom of a new kind of violence, an epidemic of Clockwork Orange brutality." Now the horror of Littleton, Colorado, makes Potrero Hill seem prophetic of survival in any grade.

382. See Sri Aurobindo, *The Life Divine* (New York: India Library Society, 1965), Chapter XX "Death, Desire and Incapacity," pp. 174-182.

383. Ibid., p. 180.

384. Perhaps Decca [as all her friends called her] will now be able to write an illuminating gloss on her best-selling text. She experienced whatever death is on July 22, 1996. See the *San Francisco Chronicle*, July 25, 1996, E-1 (Patricia Holt's appreciative column, "Jessica Mitford Was a Down-to-Earth Grande Dame"), and the *San Francisco Examiner*, July 28, 1996,B-9 (Joan Smith's tribute, "Model to a Generation of Journalists"). Herb Caen, Cecil Williams, and I agree: this literate, witty woman lived before she died.

385. Cf. Milton McC. Gatch, *Death: Meaning and Mortality in Christian Thought and Contemporary Culture* (New York: The Seabury Press, 1969), pp. 7-9.

386. Kazantzakis, *Zorba the Greek,* p. 144.

387. *Between Tedium and Terror*, p. 132-34.

388. Ibid., p. 134.

389. *Applause*, The Playbill of the Stockton Civic Theater, Volume XXVI Number 6, April 2, 1993, p. 9.

390. Edward Abbey, *Desert Solitaire* (New York: Ballantine Books, 1968), p. 242.

391. Ibid.

392. *The Works of John Wesley,* (Grand Rapids, Michigan: Zondervan Publishing House, 1872 reprint), Vol. XI, pp. 1-13, p. 1.

393. Ibid.

394. Ibid., p. 8.

395. Ibid., p. 5. He is talking here about earthquakes in England—but the message is occasioned by Lisbon.

396. Matthew 5: 43-48.

397. *I'm Alive* (New York: Harper and Row, 1980). *No Hiding Place* (San Francisco: HarperSanFrancisco, 1992).

398. Williams, *No Hiding Place,* p. 1.

399. Williams, ibid., p. 9.

400. Ibid., p. 10.

401. Ibid., p. 11.

402. August, 1997, pp. 42-55 [article by Kenneth Miller].

403. Nov. 15, 1989, p. 1089.

404. *The Works of John Wesley*, Vol. XI, "Advice to a Soldier," p. 201.

405. See Chapter One.

406. Cf. *Good Grief: The Story of Charles Schulz* (New York: Pharos Books, 1989), "Blessed Assurance," pp. 123-137.

407. Schulz in a vastly different way, of course, made the same journey—and jotted down a few observations.

408. See Ronald DiSanto and Thomas Steele, *Guidebook to Zen and the Art of Motorcycle Maintenance* (New York: William Morrow and Company, 1990).

409. Robert M. Pirsig, "An Author and Father Looks Ahead at the Past," *The New York Times Book Review,* LXXXIX (March 4, 1984), pp. 7-8.

410. Ibid., pp. 3-4. James Heffernan, Philosophy Chair at Pacific, provided this Pirsig reflection.

411. *Zen and the Art of Motorcycle Maintenance*, p. 406.

412. Pirsig, *New York Times Book Review*, p. 6.

413. Ibid., p. 7. When the ashes of John F. Kennedy, Jr. were scattered over the waters near Martha's Vineyard in July, 1999, was the requiem for American royalty, begun in November, 1963, finally complete? The dead son now salutes the father on the magazine called *Life.*

414. I was told by evangelists in Texas that it was sung by the faithful as the *Titanic* went down. James Cameron presents it as played by a sophisticated, restrained string quartet. In either case it is mournful music and bad theology.

415. (New York: Ivy Books, 1991).

416. (New York: Ivy Books, 1992). cf. Raymond A. Moody, *Life After Life* (New York: Bantam, 1988). In 1999, another light seems to have dawned on Dr. Moody—who reveals in his latest book, *Last Laugh*, that he has no scientific evidence—and never did have—to support his intimations of immortality. Testimony, as anyone with active brain cells should know, is not proof—and some "testimony" is deliberately faked. [See *Publisher's Weekly*, July 26, 1999.] Time to sing the Moody blues: it is the finality of death that illumines life. Beware, I say, of anyone claiming to be a tour guide for that "undiscovered country."

417. See Morse, *Closer to the Light,* pp. vii - xii. Don't miss the story of the car dealer who got hit by lightning on a golf course and felt himself getting sucked into an opening of radiance. Try not to think of a hole-in-one, I dare you.

418. See "20/20," with Hugh Downs and Barbara Walters for May 13, 1994. [Produced by Steve Brand, edited by Mark Stone and Robert J. Brandt.]

419. See Michael Shermer, *Why People Believe Weird Things: Pseudoscience, Superstition, and Other Confusions of Our Time*, (New York: W. H. Freeman and Company, 1997), Chapter 5, "*Through the Invisible*, Near-Death Experiences and the Quest for Immortality," pp. 73-87. The references to Susan Blackmore are on pp. 80-82. Shermer offers several naturalistic explanations, including Stanislav Grof (an imprinted memory at birth—the sensation of floating, the passage down a tunnel, and the emergence into a bright light—triggered by the trauma of death), and Goodman and Gilman (biochemical and neurophysiological causes triggered by such substances as belladonna alkaloids and ketamines). Those "doors of perception" are swung open in the brain through a variety of artificial substances (e.g. LSD, mescaline), and *natural* chemicals released by extreme traumae—the wild "trip" of dying certainly qualifying.

What follows at this point in my text is the answer to the last question (of the thirteen) asked in the preface. The questions are not idle inventions of mine—although I delight in such inventions. They are, in fact, questions asked by the Lake to Yudhishthira, eldest brother of the Pandavas (the founding family of Indian civilization), in the *Mahabharata* (the founding epic of Hindu culture). [See Peter Brook's film, *The Mahabharata*, and Garry O'Connor's book of the same name (San Francisco: Mercury House, 1989).] All the brothers had been exiled to the forest in a power struggle with the Kauravas (arch rival cousins), and four of them had drunk from the waters of the Lake, without answering these questions, and had died. Yudhishthira heeds the mysterious interrogator, responds correctly to each query, and is rewarded by life for him and all his brothers. I would hope that you are still alive as you have moved through the wilderness of this intellectual/spiritual odyssey.

420. See Joseph Campbell, *The Power of Myth*, PBS series with Bill Moyers.

421. At Pacific we felt especially close to the "new day" of which she wrote, remembering her many visits to Stockton. In the second volume of her autobiography, *Gather Together in My Name,* she comments on her first trip to the Central Valley: "A friend of Mother's who had a restaurant in Stockton needed a fry cook. I packed the clothes I thought we might need and set out for the eighty mile journey.... I refused to cry all the way in the back seat of a Greyhound bus." [Maya Angelou, *Gather Together in My Name* (New York: Bantam, 1974, p. 117.] "Stockton," she wrote, "had an unusual atmosphere....When I arrived, there was Wild West rhythm in the streets." In 1999, Stockton was chosen by the National Civic League for the All-America Award.

422. See *Encyclopedia Britannica*, article on "Mozart."

423. *Film Comment*, October, 1984, p. 55.

424. See David Thompson, "Salieri, Psycho," *Film Comment*, February, 1985, pp. 70-75. In somewhat the same way, Forman is not presenting Larry Flynt in *The People vs. Larry Flynt*. He is composing a love letter to the Supreme Court.

425. Ibid., p. 70.

426. Ibid., p. 71.

427. William J. Palmer, *The Films of the Eighties* (Carbondale and Edwardsville: Southern Illinois University Press, 1993), p. 274.

428. Barth, "The Freedom of Mozart," in Walter Leibrecht, ed., *Religion and Culture: Essays in Honor of Paul Tillich* (New York: Harper and Brothers, 1959), pp. 76-77.

429. See Barth, "Wolfgang Amadeus Mozart," p. 68.

430. Barth, "Letter of Thanks to Mozart," in Leibrecht, pp. 63-64.

431. My guess is that if you catch God in an unguarded moment, She will tell you She likes Rogers and Hammerstein better than Bach, but is embarrassed to say it around conservatory types.

432. Howard Mumford Jones and Ernest E. Leisy, eds., *Major American Writers* (New York: Harcourt, Brace and Company, 1945), p. 1617. Frost published "Fire and Ice" in *Harper's Magazine* in 1920.

Conclusion

433. Johann Wolfgang von Goethe, quoted in David Schiller, *The Little Zen Companion* (New York: Workman Publishing, 1994), p. 150. For other epigrammatic marvels, see James H. Austin, M.D., *Zen and the Brain* (Massachusetts Institute of Technology, 1998).

434. January 6, probably not incidentally, is also the day of the Triple Goddess in Celtic celebration: Maid, Mother, and Crone. As we all know, December 25 was chosen by Constantine as the birth of the Christ child, since it was already celebrated throughout the Greco-Roman world as the birthday of Mithra [which made astronomical sense for the sun god].

435. Halford Luccock, *Like a Mighty Army: Selected Letters of Simeon Stylites* (New York: The Oxford Press, 1954), p. 17. Dr. Luccock was always a surprise—especially as old Simeon.

436. Quoted by Luccock, ibid., p. 18. The original lines by George MacDonald [in slightly different form] can be found *The Oxford Book of Verse (1250-1918)* (Oxford: Oxford University Press, 1939), p. 944. The old Chinese story which follows was told to me by a former student at Callison College, Carl Dean. Carl thought, even then, that I looked fuzzy. Woody Allen, no stranger to fading himself, uses a similar idea in *Zelig.*

INDEX

Notations in brackets refer to the end-notes [by number] from pp. 185-209

ABOUT THE AUTHOR

Lawrence Meredith, Ph.D., Harvard University (History and Philosophy of Religion), has taught religious studies and film at the University of the Pacific (Stockton, California) for thirty-three years. He has held Senior Fulbright Lectureships in Austria and Indonesia, was an Affiliate at the East-West Center in Hawaii, and Resident Faculty for Callison College in Kyoto, Japan. He has received Distinguished Teaching Awards (National Association of United Methodist Colleges, and Pacific), and honorary doctorates from Hawaii Loa College and Southwestern University, his alma mater. In the spring of 1998, he taught world religions on the global voyage Semester-at-Sea program (South America, Africa, Asia) for the University of Pittsburgh, and in the summer of 1999 was an official observer at the Cannes International Film Festival. He has published over thirty articles and reviews, and a book, *The Sensuous Christian: A Celebration of Freedom and Love.*

Printed in the United States
4754